ANARCHY AND THE ART OF LISTENING

ANARCHY AND THE ART OF LISTENING

The Politics and Pragmatics of
Reception in Papua New Guinea

James Slotta

CORNELL UNIVERSITY PRESS   ITHACA AND LONDON

First published 2023 by Cornell University Press

Library of Congress Cataloging-in-Publication Data

Names: Slotta, James, 1979– author.
Title: Anarchy and the art of listening : the politics and pragmatics of reception in Papua New Guinea / James Slotta.
Description: Ithaca [New York] : Cornell University Press, 2023. | Includes bibliographical references and index.
Identifiers: LCCN 2022054935 | ISBN 9781501770005 (hardcover) | ISBN 9781501770012 (paperback) | ISBN 9781501770029 (pdf) | ISBN 9781501770036 (epub)
Subjects: LCSH: Listening—Political aspects—Papua New Guinea. | Listening—Social aspects—Papua New Guinea. | Anarchism— Papua New Guinea.
Classification: LCC P95.46 .S56 2023 | DDC 302.2/242—dc23/eng/20230207
LC record available at https://lccn.loc.gov/2022054935

Contents

Acknowledgments

This book would not exist were it not for the support of many people over the past two decades. First and foremost, this book exists because people living in the Yopno Valley opened their homes and their lives to me. In 2007 I traveled to Nian village to ask permission to live there for a year or more. I was taken to a large community house that would later become my home and I explained to a room full of people I had just met why I wanted to live with them. For what felt like an hour, I nervously waited as those gathered in the house discussed the matter with each other. In each of the villages I visited and lived in—Ganggalut, Weskokop, Gua, Wurap, and Wandabung—I had a similar experience, and each welcomed me with more generosity than I could have hoped for. My debt to the people I lived and worked with in the Yopno Valley is immense.

Unfortunately, there is not space here to thank everyone by name who supported me during visits in 2007–9, 2013, 2014, and 2015. But I want to single out those who hosted me and who were involved on a daily basis in my research: in Nian village, James, Damlap, and Martin Qaqa, Baiaŋgen, Sasa, Joshua and Yufori, and Katumoŋ, Roŋgum and Maŋgau all cared for me in every possible way during the year I lived there. Koki, Droŋo, Sawkepe, and Monaks in Weskokop; Yarekine, Kɨmake, and Willie in Gua; and Paul, Kembon, and Immanuel in Ganggalut did the same during my stays in those villages. Not only did these people provide food and warmth but they were also some of my closest interlocutors and dearest friends. I also want to thank Ginson Saonu, who first directed my attention to the Yopno Valley as a potential research site, and Bomi, who made my initial visit to the area possible. To the many, many people, too many to name here, who supplied me with gifts, tangible and intangible, without which this book could not have been written: bɨt kwak toksi, ya yaŋsi daisat.

Many others in Papua New Guinea were essential to the completion of this project. Georgia Kaipu and James Robbins at the National Research Institute of Papua New Guinea not only paved the bureaucratic way for this research to happen but also were interested and engaged onlookers. Leanne Ererepe at the National Archives of Papua New Guinea provided much assistance in locating patrol reports. The staff of the Tree Kangaroo Conservation Program in Lae—especially Ruby Yamuna, Karau Kuna Jr., Gabriel Porolak, Danny Samandingke, Sue Tallarico, and Toby Ross—provided much entertainment and assistance on my trips to Lae. A short stay at the SIL-New Guinea branch center at Ukarumpa offered me the chance to work with some consultants intensively in relative quiet. I must thank Andy Grosh and Rene van den Berg for their help arranging my visit and their hospitality during my stay. I especially thank David Troolin for giving me the opportunity to present some preliminary results of my research while at Ukarumpa and for the questions and comments of those in attendance. Many thanks to Wesley and LeeAnn Reed for their many helpful insights into Yopno language and social life during this stay.

In Australia, Nicholas Evans, Alexandra Aikhenvald, RMW Dixon, Nick Enfield, I Wayan Arka, Mark Donohue, and Andrew Pawley all provided valuable comments and support over the years. In North America, this book has benefited from conversations with and comments from many people: Shunsuke Nozawa, Aaron Ansell, Gretchen Pfeil, Alejandro Paz, Christopher Ball, Erin Debenport, Rob Blunt, Alex Golub, Anne Ch'ien, Jerrold Sadock, Danilyn Rutherford, Costas Nakassis, Paul Manning, Jordan Haug, Kathy Creely, Elizabeth Keating, Anthony Webster, Jason Cons, Kamran Ali, Craig Campbell, Paola Canova, Celina de Sá, John Hartigan, Ward Keeler, Rebecca J. Lewis, Sofian Merabet, Marina Peterson, Aaron Sandel, Pauline Strong, Jürgen Streeck, Maria Sidorkina, Deina Rabie, John Haviland, Kit Woolard, Judith Irvine, Barbra Meek, Charles Zuckerman, Ilana Gershon, Jack Sidnell, Laurie Graham, Greg Urban, Paige West, Niko Besnier, Norma Mendoza-Denton, Elinor Ochs, Alesandro Duranti, Marjorie Goodwin, Paul Kroskrity, Jessica Cattelino, Jason Throop, Paul Silverstein, Robert Brightman, Thushara Hewage, China Scherz, Eve Danziger, Ira Bashkow, Mark Sicoli, Ida Hoequist, Rachel Apone, and Misty Bastian. Jim Lance and Susan Specter at Cornell University Press along with Michelle Scott and Gail Chalew helped to transform my manuscript into this book and improved it significantly in the process.

Lise Dobrin, Don Kulick, Francesca Merlan, Joel Robbins, Alan Rumsey, Bambi Schieffelin, and Rupert Stasch not only provided valuable input at important moments along the way but their research and writings on Melanesia inspired much that is in this book. As ethnographers who have had a much longer relationship with people in the Yopno Valley than I have had, and whose research has laid the foundations for my own, I am grateful to Jürg Wassmann and Verena Keck for their supportive suggestions and comments over the years. Kensy Cooperrider and Raphael Núñez generously asked me to participate in research they were conducting in the Yopno Valley, and my experience working with them was profoundly eye-opening. The same is true for conversations with Hannah Sarvasy, whose linguistic research in the Huon-Finisterre region helped me understand so much about the Yopno language.

Portions of several chapters were published previously, and I want to thank the reviewers and editors for the care and attention they gave to these materials.

Part of chapter 5 appears in "Revelations of the World: Transnationalism and the Politics of Perception in Papua New Guinea," *American Anthropologist* 116, no. 3: 626–42. Chapter 4 includes sections of "Can the Subaltern Listen? Self-Determination and the Provisioning of Expertise in Papua New Guinea," published in *American Ethnologist* 44, no. 2: 328–40. And portions of chapter 1 incorporate materials from "The Perlocutionary is Political: Listening as Self-determination in a Papua New Guinean Polity," *Language in Society* 44, no. 4: 525–52, which are reprinted with permission.

My research would not have been possible without generous financial support in the form of a Wenner-Gren Dissertation Fieldwork Grant, a Fulbright-Hays Doctoral Dissertation Research Abroad Fellowship, a Committee for Research and Education Grant from the National Geographic Society, and a postdoctoral fellowship from the Endangered Languages Documentation Programme.

Michael Silverstein, Susan Gal, Amy Dahlstrom and Salikoko Mufwene have provided invaluable support over the years. Their influence can be found on every page here. So too can that of Manuela Carneiro da Cunha and Robert Moore, whose impact extends well beyond the pages of this book. Luke Fleming has been my constant intellectual companion for two decades, and I simply cannot imagine thinking, let alone having so much fun doing it, without him.

Courtney Handman has, more than anyone, made this book what it is. Questioning every thought of mine and supporting me in every attempt to answer her questions, she has made my life—scholarship and all—better every day that I have known her. I also owe a deep debt of gratitude to the youngest of my teachers, my daughter Adele, who reminds me every day how much I have left to learn. And to my first teachers, my mother and father, Karen and Peter Slotta, who along with my sister Katy, gave me the gifts of curiosity and empathy that drove me to anthropology and the research for this book.

I am fortunate in many ways, but none more so than in having had such caring, supportive, and inspiring people to learn from throughout my life. This book is for all of you.

Note on Languages, Orthography, Maps, and Names

In the Yopno language, *yopno* means "let's leave them" or "let's throw them away." Originally, the name belonged to a river that carves its way through the Finisterre mountains. I was told that the name commemorates the destruction of sacred ancestral objects at the behest of Lutheran missionaries, who instructed people living in the vicinity to toss these powerful objects into the river. Since then, the name of the river has come to name the valley formed by that river (the Yopno Valley), the name of the people living there (the Yopno people), and the language they speak (the Yopno language) in administrative documents, maps, and the work of researchers. These usages have also been increasingly adopted by people living in the Yopno Valley. Variations in the spelling of the name—Yupna, Yupno, Yopno—reflect the dialectal diversity of the Yopno language. I follow the pronunciation of people living in Nian village, where I spent most of my time.

The Yopno language is a Papuan language of the Huon-Finisterre family spoken by virtually all the eight thousand or so people living in the Yopno Valley. In addition, most men and most women under age fifty in the valley also speak Tok Pisin, the English-based creole spoken in much of Papua New Guinea. The language of schooling in the country is primarily English. But outside the school context, except for a few phrases, English is not generally used.

For ease of exposition, I present most of the verbal interactions discussed in this book only in English translation. These translations were a collective endeavor, incorporating the insights of participants and others who worked closely with me in the Yopno Valley. For readers interested in exploring these materials in their original languages, most can be found in Slotta (2015), in the supplementary materials that accompany Slotta (2014, 2017a), and in the recordings and transcripts collected in Slotta (2017b).

Where I do include words and expressions in Yopno in the following pages, they appear in italics. Tok Pisin words are underlined. The Yopno orthography used here was developed by SIL Bible translators and is widely adopted in Yopno communities. Most letters in Yopno and all those in Tok Pisin have about the same pronunciation as they would in Spanish or Italian. The barred-i (ɨ) in Yopno is a mid-central vowel like the one in the English word *sun*. Engma (ŋ) is pronounced like the combination *ng* in English *sing*; (j) is a postalveolar affricate like the one in English *judge* and (r) is an alveolar tap like the *t* in *butter*.

Maps of the Yopno Valley and environs can be found online at https://maps
.jamesslotta.com. Except in a few cases, I use pseudonyms to conceal people's
identities throughout the book. One exception is a well-known public figure. The
others are people who asked that their actual names be tied to the stories they
shared with me.

ANARCHY AND THE ART OF LISTENING

THE POLITICS AND PRAGMATICS OF LISTENING

From the heights of the Finisterre mountains on the north coast of Papua New Guinea—the "ends of the earth," as the French explorer Jules Dumont d'Urville dubbed them—the Yopno River cuts a deep gorge on its route to the Bismarck Sea. Perched on the steep mountainsides above it and in the small side valleys along its course are twenty-five or so villages, home to roughly eight thousand people. At the center of virtually every one of those villages are two buildings: a church and a school. Over the past century, since the arrival of the first Lutheran missionaries in 1928, these villages and the lives of people in them have been re-fashioned around these two institutions. The men's houses, which had been the ritual and educational centers of life, were disbanded, and the sacred, powerful objects they housed were buried, burned, or tossed into the Yopno River. Families who had lived in scattered fenced homesteads surrounded by their fields gathered into centralized settlements built around mission schools and churches that took the place (often literally) of the men's houses. There, people were taught a new language, Kâte, the language of the Lutheran church in the region. They learned how to read, children attended school, and an entirely new cosmology with a new set of ritual practices became part of their lives.

Not only do churches and schools stand at the physical center of villages today, they also stand at the center of village life (see figure 1). People devote a signifi-cant amount of their time, energy, and resources to these institutions: building and maintaining them, hosting celebrations and fundraisers for them, giving of-ferings to the church and paying school fees for children. But more than any-thing, what people do in these institutions is listen. They listen to sermons and

FIGURE 1.   Students at Nokopo Primary School line up for announcements at the end of the day, with the Nokopo Lutheran church in the background.

Photograph by author.

English lessons, histories and Bible stories; they are taught rules, presented with knowledge, and offered advice. As in many parts of the global south, a significant part of people's participation in colonial, national, and transnational networks involves listening—listening to the words of missionaries, educators, development experts, NGO workers, and colonial officials.

Words, as we know, have power. They have the power to influence the way people think about themselves and the world around them, to shape their actions and stir their bodies. But this is not a book about the power of speech to refashion the lives of people living on the rural margins of the world system. This is a book about what goes on on the other side of the word, in the act of listening. This is a book about the agency of listeners and the power of listening.

The World-Changing Power of Listening

In November 2009 hundreds of people gathered in the village of Nian to celebrate the tenth anniversary of its church building. Constructed of sawn timber, with concrete piers and a tin roof, it is by far the largest structure in this village of roughly 350 people. There are no roads into the Yopno Valley, and so the building materials had to be delivered by boat to a village on the coast fifteen miles away. From there, people from Nian carried them up to their village, 7,000 feet above sea level. It was indeed a structure worthy of celebration.

The anniversary celebration itself was a multiday affair, the kind of event that always seems to be happening in one of the villages in the valley. People from throughout the region came to socialize and meander around the temporary market set up in the village plaza. A number of Nian villagers now living in towns around the country returned to celebrate and visit with family. Two other villages sent delegations to lead church services during the day and perform ceremonial dances at night. Pigs were bestowed on honored guests, and visitors were plied with pork.

One of the highlights of the celebration was a skit (Yopno: *wurop*, Tok Pisin: <u>drama</u>) performed by residents of Nokopo, the neighboring village just a fifteen-minute walk down the hill.[1] In the central plaza of Nian, the visitors reenacted perhaps the most significant event to happen in the village in the last century: the villagers' acceptance of Christianity. The first missionaries in the region, mostly converts from the valleys to the east, spread the Word of God village by village. As people in one village converted, they leveraged their kinship and other ties to help coax people from neighboring villages to convert. By the 1960s, all twenty-five villages in the valley, including Nian, had converted. It was the village of Nokopo, their long-standing enemy just a short way down the hill, that had played an instrumental role in their acceptance of Christianity. And so, of course, on Nian's big day, people from Nokopo paraded up to Nian to publicly reenact the story.

As the audience wrapped itself around the central plaza, two groups formed in the center. On one side was a group portraying the leading men of Nokopo, dressed in the clothing people now wear every day—t-shirts, shorts, pants, and the like. On the other side of the plaza, the actors portraying Nian villagers were clad in traditional clothing—bark cloth capes and loin cloths—the usual sign of the material and spiritual "primitivity" of the characters in performances of this sort.

As the skit begins, a missionary urges a man from Nokopo to go up to Nian and bring the people there back with him so that they can learn about the new religion. This man walks across the plaza to the group gathered on the other side, who listen with hyperactive nervousness, falling over each other with fear. This is a trick, they warn each other; they are trying to lure us to their village where they will kill us! At this, the audience bursts into laughter. The exaggerated expressions and the foolishness of the ancestors draw a dependable laugh in skits of this sort. And here was a truly laughable misunderstanding. Afraid of Christianity! Living in the Christianized present, the audience knew better than to fear this call to convert.[2]

As they watched and laughed, people in the audience busied themselves working out whom the actors in the skit were portraying, calling out the names of their parents, grandparents, and other fixtures of the community when they figured out who was who. As the skit proceeds, the first emissary from Nokopo returns to his village, his efforts for naught. The Lutheran missionary stationed in Nokopo sends another person, who is also rebuffed. And then a third. Each time a new character from Nokopo walks over to the people of Nian, and each time Nian rejects the call (*kaliŋ*; singaut).

But then, things go differently. A man in Nian welcomes the emissaries from Nokopo, and he listens to what they have to say. "You are speaking the truth," he responds. "All right, I will heed what you are saying." Finding that what he has been told is true, he agrees to follow them back to their village. That is the turning point: one man in Nian hears things differently, and as everyone in the audience knew, life in Nian would be completely transformed.

As this story has it, what is perhaps the most consequential event in the past century in Nian village turns on an act of listening. Again and again, emissaries from Nokopo summon the people of Nian, and again and again their call is rejected. The words spoken never really change over the course of the skit. What does change—what makes all the difference—is how the people in Nian listen: one man takes the Word of God not as a trick to be ignored but as a truth to be followed, and with that, life in the village is set on a radically new course.

As we will see in the chapters to come, people in the Yopno Valley are alive to the consequentiality of listening. At times, listening is held up as a matter of potentially world-changing importance, as in the story of Nian's conversion. But it is also a routine concern in the daily affairs of village life. In both big and small ways, there is a sense that listening matters—that how people listen will affect their future. But as the story of Nian suggests, listening is also complicated. How should people listen to the emissaries from Nokopo? Is the summons a trap set by a long-time enemy? Or are their enemies from Nokopo opening the way to something new and beneficial? Although the particulars vary, these are the kind of questions that routinely confront listeners in the Yopno Valley. Whom does one listen to? How does one interpret what is said?

The questions that surround the act of listening have only grown with the arrival of a host of new interlocutors over the last century: missionaries and the Christian God, the Australian colonial administration and now the government of Papua New Guinea, teachers, pastors, a US-based conservation NGO that works to preserve tree-kangaroos in the valley, and, of course, anthropologists, among others. Listening to neighbors and little-known foreigners alike requires care, because it poses serious risks. There is the danger to the listener's life, of course, dramatized in the skit of Nian's conversion. But listening to others' words puts in jeopardy many other things people value as well. By listening carelessly—at times lending an ear too willingly, at other times not willingly enough—people worry that they will lose the land they depend on for their livelihood, that they will wind up another's "servant" (*oman amɨn*, <u>wok boi</u>), losing their independence and what control over their future they have.

At the same time, listening carefully holds out the possibility of gaining wealth, enhancing one's power, and creating valuable connections with the wider world, just as their ancestors appear to have done when they accepted the Word of God. In the face of predatory neighbors and mining companies who would steal their land; of expanding government and NGO involvement in the valley; of educational and religious institutions pushing new knowledges; and more generally, of people's sense that they lack the ability to bring about the futures they desire, the act of listening is both potentially fruitful and fundamentally risky.

This, then, is an ethnography of listening as a form of communicative action—as a way that people in the Yopno Valley are working to shape their collective futures. In these efforts, listening plays not only an important part but an essential one. In the chapters to come we look at the different practices of listening people use to try to control their destiny. We consider the complexities and challenges that they face as they try to "listen well." We see how people's efforts to listen well shape the ways they engage with one another and with the wider world. And ultimately, I hope, we gain an appreciation for the significance of listening in the lives of people in the valley and, more generally, as an activity of political importance in its own right.

Powerful Speakers, Passive Listeners

Listening may appear to be an unlikely means to fashion the future. In matters of power and politics, there is a long-standing bias toward the other side of the communicative equation. From the earliest texts of the Western rhetorical tradition, speech has been regarded as a vital tool for influencing others and shaping the social world. Rhetoricians have sought to lay bare the secrets of persuasive speech as a means of wielding power in political and legal domains.[3] In today's global politics of voice, "speaking up," "speaking back," and "giving voice" are *the* privileged means of exercising political agency.[4] Theorists of politics emphasize the central importance of public sphere discourse as a form of democratic political participation.[5] And across the humanities and social sciences, speech and speaking are held up as important means through which people perform their identities, build and transform their social worlds, and even construct reality itself.[6]

There is simply nothing comparable on the listening side of the communicative equation. As Susan Bickford (1996) remarks in her pioneering work on political listening, the topic has been neglected by political theorists going back to Plato. The same point has been made by scholars of rhetoric and media studies.[7] This is not to say that the politics and power of listening have been completely neglected; in the next section I draw on Bickford's work along with that of others to make a case for more sustained attention to the political work involved in listening.

But before turning to the politics of listening, it is worth dwelling a bit first on speaking and speech, because the ways they have been theorized significantly color our visions of listening. Indeed, a prime reason for the lack of attention to the political work of listening is the widespread perception that listening is a passive or submissive activity—a view that has much to do with the way speech and speaking have often been privileged as *the* powerful and politically significant elements of communication.

In this section, I draw attention to two prominent visions of the power of speech and speaking that crop up again and again in fields across the humanities and social sciences. The first is a vision of political communication that centers on what might be called "sovereign speech." The second focuses on what I call the "rhetorical word." In spotlighting these two figures here, my aim is to indicate just how ubiquitous the emphasis on the power of speech and speaking is and how this emphasis marginalizes the political significance of listening.

Sovereign Speech

The first figure I want to draw attention to—sovereign speech—is grounded in the close and highly visible connection between the act of speaking and sovereign power. Commands, laws, judgments, decrees, executive orders, policy documents, and other sorts of verbal directives: these kinds of speech are the everyday form that sovereign power takes.[8] As the anthropologist and ethnographer of anarchic societies Pierre Clastres (1987, 151) notes, speaking and sovereign power go hand in hand: "Whether prince, despot, or commander-in-chief, the man of power is always not only the man who speaks, but the sole source of legitimate speech: an impoverished speech, a poor speech to be sure, but one rich in efficiency, for it goes by the name of *command* and wants nothing save the *obedience* of the executant."

As Clastres points out, the speech of the sovereign is notable for its power and effectiveness: it is backed by the threat of violence and other coercive measures the state can impose. When the commander-in-chief issues an order, the jury a verdict, the judge a sentence—when agents of the state make declarations and issue commands—these words are vested with power by the robust coercive forces that the state can bring to bear on people. As Judith Butler (1997) notes, many of the classic examples of performative utterances—words that seem to *do* something through the mere utterance of them—are taken from this sort of sovereign speech. "I sentence you to ten years," "I find you guilty," "I now declare you man and wife"—these are utterances that have transformative effects on the world.[9] But their efficacy does not derive from the words themselves; there is no force lurking in the sounds. They draw their efficacy from the state and other institutions that can back up these words with effective means of coercion. For the sovereign speaker, the act of speaking is indeed an exercise of agency.

To a significant degree, it is this power of sovereign speech that renders speaking a matter of such political importance. This is nowhere clearer than in the focus on speaking in democratic political theory and the politics of voice. There, the sovereign speaker is the proverbial "voice of the people"; citizens in a democracy govern themselves by formulating their own laws and policies.[10] Of course, the interests, perspectives, and wills of citizens diverge, such that it is typically impossible for them to speak unanimously with a single, sovereign voice. As a result, public sphere discourse and other modes of expressing views and preferences such as voting must mediate between the voices of many citizens and the single voice of the sovereign. In political theorist James Tully's words, the fundamental democratic freedom of citizens is "having an effective say in a dialogue over the norms through which they are governed" (2004, 99). In effect, through speech in the public sphere and in other modes of expressing their voice, citizens gain the opportunity to take on the role of sovereign speaker—to have their voice *speak* through the laws and the policies of the state.

The role of the sovereign speaker thus stands at the pinnacle of a wider field of democratic political communications. Through speaking in the public sphere, citizens work to shape public opinion and ultimately the actions of the state as they, in effect, vie to assume the voice of the sovereign speaker themselves. In this way, the connection between power and speaking embodied in the sovereign speaker comes to shape an entire field of political communication, linking acts of speaking in the public sphere ultimately to sovereign power.

Operating according to this vision of democratic communication, it makes a good deal of sense that political theory and the politics of voice both give so much attention to the act of speaking. Speaking in the public sphere appears to be *the* means through which citizens are able to exercise sovereign power. It is also understandable why significantly less attention is paid to the act of listening: listening is not a means of exercising political power—of acting as a self-governing citizen—in this communicative framework.

Where attention does turn to the other side of the word, normative accounts of democratic listening tend to stress its pliant, docile, and even submissive character. The listener backgrounds their self—their views, their experiences, their interests, their desires—allowing the words of others the opportunity to reshape the listener's self. For instance, Benjamin Barber (1984, 175) argues that strong democracy nourishes the "mutualistic practice of listening" in which "the empathetic listener becomes more like his interlocutor as the two bridge the differences between them by conversation and mutual understanding." Susan Bickford (1996, 147) emphasizes that listening is "a passage to another's experience" that creates the possibility for radical self-transformation. And Andrew Dobson (2014, 68) advocates "apophatic listening" as a model of good democratic listening, which in the words of Michel and Wortham (2007, 89) involves "opening the self to the other and holding one's own categories in abeyance."

It is hard not to see the central role of *speaking* in public sphere discourse in these images of the empathetic and impressionable democratic listener. Without this kind of openness and willingness to be transformed, voice is unable to work its magic, and the democratic model of self-sovereignty proves ultimately unworkable. For "the people" to take on the role of sovereign speaker—and for everyone to have an equal opportunity to do so—it is necessary that listeners remain open to the words of others. And indeed, a failure to listen in these open and empathetic ways is often derided as deeply undemocratic. This is especially true when those in positions of power are accused of failing to listen to the marginalized and disempowered.[11] When the powerful are urged to heed the words of others for a change, the submissiveness of democratic listening emerges with notable clarity: speaking is held up as an act of empowerment, listening an act of submission.[12]

The centrality of voice in democratic political communication thus has the effect of eclipsing the act of listening. In a liberal democratic context where political agency is exercised largely through the act of speaking, listening is rendered ancillary to the sovereign voice of the people.

The Rhetorical Word

But what of contexts where speech is not backed by sovereign power? As Judith Butler (1997) reminds us, much speech that is in a broad sense political is not buttressed by the coercive force of state power. The speech that takes place in the public sphere, for instance, is not backed by the force of the state, at least ideally.

Even as we turn our attention outside the domain of sovereign speech, however, the act of speaking has a way of once again eclipsing the political significance of listening. In this, an important part is played by a second figure, one that has long attracted the attention of students of politics: the rhetorical word. Unlike sovereign speech, the rhetorical word does not depend on the coercive force of the state or other powerful institutions to give it power; it alone is sufficient to exercise power over even the most powerful figures in society. There is thus a kind of magic to it. Power seemingly inheres in the rhetorical word itself, generated, quite literally, out of thin air.[13] The *rhetor* Gorgias, in his dialogue with Socrates, gives a good sense of the magical quality of this power, which manages to enslave even the most powerful:

> What is there greater than the word which persuades the judges in the courts, or the senators in the council, or the citizens in the assembly, or at any other political meeting?—if you have the power of uttering this word, you will have the physician your slave, and the trainer your slave, and the money-maker of whom you talk will be found to gather treasures, not for himself, but for you who are able to speak and to persuade the multitude. (Plato 1892, sec. 452)

Although the rhetorical word differs in some ways from the power of sovereign speech, it shares with it a vision of the listener as a powerless participant, at the mercy of the speaker and their speech. Note that in Gorgias's account, it is listeners who are effectively rendered slaves in the face of the powerful, rhetorical word. Literary critic Kenneth Burke's (1969, 41) definition of rhetoric explicitly lays out the relative balance of power in the communicative encounter with the rhetorical word: rhetoric is "the use of words by human agents to form attitudes or induce actions in other human agents." In this definition, the speaker is the first human agent, the one who wields the power of the rhetorical word to "form attitudes or induce actions." The second human agent is the listener, who really is not an agent at all. As with sovereign speech, the power of the rhetorical word comes at the expense of the agency of the listener.

This vision of the rhetorical word is hardly confined to the field of rhetoric: it is widespread in the humanities, the social sciences, and in the field of communications.[14] It is found in the way anthropologists and others have sought to understand the power of oratory "as speech to a listening collectivity that is understood to have potentially powerful consequences by dint of the speech's own qualities" (Stasch 2011a, 160). It is found in communications scholars' efforts to understand the workings of propaganda, disinformation, and advertising.[15] And it is found in political theorists' discussions of public sphere discourse, in which citizens seek to influence each other and ultimately public opinion by discussing and debating the issues of the day. Even so-called rational and logical argumentation in the public sphere is rhetorical insofar as it is "used to form attitudes or induce actions in other human agents" (Burke 1969, 41). When it exerts some force on the listener, it is rhetorical in my (and Burke's) sense of the term—even if that force is "the unforced force of the better argument," as Jürgen Habermas puts it (1996, 306).[16]

But perhaps the most far-reaching accounts of the rhetorical word are found in explorations of what Pierre Bourdieu (1991) calls "symbolic power": the power of words and other symbols to shape people's vision of the world, and thereby to shape the world itself. This is a view with a very old philosophical legacy, rightly identified as a kind of nominalism that emphasizes the role of names in organizing the way humans perceive reality (Hacking 1999). But the focus in its contemporary, constructivist iteration is less on the metaphysical implications of nominalism and more on the sociopolitical and pragmatic ones. Who wields the power of representations to shape people's visions of the world, and what effects do these representations have? Those are the questions at the heart of the post-Nietzschean interest in the world-making power of symbols (Srinivasan 2019).

It is hard to overstate the attention given to this world-making power of symbols in the humanities and in social theory over the past half-century. As Karen Barad (2003, 801) laments, "Language has been granted too much power. The linguistic turn, the semiotic turn, the interpretive turn, the cultural turn: it seems that at every turn lately every 'thing'—even materiality—is turned into a matter of language or some other form of cultural representation." As part of these turns, language, discourses, master narratives, cultural representations, texts, images, and other symbolic forms assume an immense power over people. They offer up visions of reality that lead people to misrecognize their true interests and desires.[17] They naturalize relations of domination and exploitation by making them appear to be intrinsic to human social, political, and economic life.[18] They establish norms, ideals, and models of reality that shape the ways people see the world, engage with others, and understand and work to transform themselves.[19] The words and other symbols that people absorb in the course of their socialization, their education, and their daily routines come to form the basis for their very sense of reality and how they act within that reality. In short, symbols constitute people as subjects—their ways of thinking and feeling, their desires, and their reality.[20]

This then is another instance of the rhetorical word (or, more generally, the rhetorical symbol) that "forms attitudes and induces actions" in listeners. But it is a version of the rhetorical word that cuts much deeper than the one found in the classical rhetorical tradition. This kind of symbolic power is not a matter of exerting influence on listeners on a particular occasion or on a particular issue;

instead, it is the elemental power to mold subjects. It is a modality of exercising an immense power that operates in the seemingly innocuous words of educational and religious institutions; of the mass media and culture industry; and of experts, humanitarian agencies, and civil society organizations. As social theorists have sought to move beyond a sovereign model of power—to understand how power operates in a more dispersed fashion throughout public and private spheres—it is precisely the rhetorical word, and its ability to colonize consciousness, that has become a focal point in analyses of the workings of domination. Heteropatriarchy, white supremacy, capitalist exploitation, European imperialism, and other modes of subjection and domination are all underpinned in important respects by the power of the rhetorical word.[21]

And again, in its various forms—from the symbolic constitution of the subject to the power of persuasive oratory—the rhetorical word imposes itself on the *listener*, the receiver of symbols. It not only locates communicative power out of reach of the listener but it also renders the listener a target of this power. Listening is rendered a non-action; it is a state of susceptibility or vulnerability to the influence of symbols and those who wield them. Just as we saw with sovereign speech, it is clear here why listening is not regarded as an important political activity: it really is not a form of action at all.

This is not to say that these figures of sovereign speech and the rhetorical word provide fundamentally flawed visions of the politics of communication. Quite the opposite: they offer rich and important insights into the ways language and communication, power and politics intersect. But they also impart a particular vision of listening, one in which it figures as a state of passivity, submissiveness, pliability, or vulnerability—a condition of disempowerment lacking in agency. They thus offer some insight into why listening has not figured as a matter of much importance when it comes to the study of politics and power. In neither case does the business end of politics—the exercise of power and influence—lie on the listening side of the communicative equation.

The Politics of Listening

Over the past two decades there has been a burgeoning of scholarship about the senses, listening among them. As the history and anthropology of the senses have extensively illustrated, proponents of an "enlightened" modernity privileged vision and the written word as modes of experience that were seen as enabling a dispassionate objectivity and rationality that were valued epistemologically and politically.[22] The sensory experience of listening, by contrast, was viewed as dangerously embodied, sensuous, and affective—associations that served to degrade listening as a mode of sensory experience and to (wrongly) diminish a sense of listening's importance in so-called modern life. Pushing back against this invidious set of associations, a growing body of work in sound studies and the sensory humanities places auditory experiences of sounds and soundscapes front and center. Attending to everything from music and noise to the sound of machines and the human body, this work shines a light on the rich and vital role that the sense of listening plays in diverse times and traditions, including in European modernity.[23]

In some respects, the focus of this book is quite different. Here, it is not listening as a sensory modality nor sounds and soundscapes that are at issue in Yopno efforts to steer their future. Listening, as I use the term, is primarily meant to designate not a sensory experience but a communicative activity, the reception of meaningful speech.[24] Whose words people listen to, what kinds of speech they listen for, and how they process what they hear—these are the consequential forms of listening that are the focus here. (In places I use the term "listening" in a broad sense to mean simply the reception of speech, regardless of medium—not only hearing the words of others but also reading them.)

But like the turn to listening in the sensory and sonic humanities, my aim here is in part corrective. As we saw in the previous section, listening as a communicative activity has a way of being devalued; it is commonly seen as an activity associated with disempowerment and a lack of agency. There are, of course, exceptions. A few types of listeners, in particular, have inspired important discussions of the power and agency of listening: judges, psychologists, asylum officers, priests, and even sociolinguists all listen in ways that can be hugely consequential. Typically sanctioned by expertise and institutionally empowered, these figures listen "diagnostically." They analyze what they hear, classifying what and whom they have listened to in ways that can dramatically shape the course of people's lives. How these figures listen matters, and thanks to the careful analysis of scholars across several disciplines, we have detailed portraits of how they do so.[25]

It is one of the overarching aims of this book to suggest that this same sort of close attention to listening practices is needed more broadly. Even in rural communities in Papua New Guinea—where listeners are typically neither experts nor institutionally empowered—it matters how people listen. But so long as the study of political communication centers on the way *speech* functions in political life—on the workings of sovereign speech, the rhetorical word, and the like—the work of listening tends to be obscured. To appreciate the pervasive significance of listening in political life then, it will be helpful to turn our attention to moments when speech *fails* to function, to moments when speech does not achieve its intended or anticipated effects, to the routine moments where speaking proves ineffective and insignificant. There we can begin to glimpse more clearly the political work of listening.

Anarchy and Listening

Failures of speech were an important spur to my own growing interest in the politics of listening. I first traveled to the Yopno Valley in late 2007 to study political oratory, a topic of long-standing interest in a region where oratorical skill and persuasive ability are widely regarded as important qualifications for leadership. But in my first few months there, what I found striking was not the ability of community leaders to wield the rhetorical word effectively as a tool of influence. Rather, I was struck by how inconsequential the speech of community leaders often was.

One of the daily routines of village life was a particularly visible showcase for the ineffectiveness of speech. A few times each week, community leaders in the central plaza of the village call out (*kaliŋ yaŋ*; <u>singaut</u>) announcements about the day's events: a community meeting, for instance, or a collective task like cleaning the church grounds or repairing a school classroom. Newly arrived in the village of Nian and hoping to meet people, I eagerly heeded these calls. I would show up at the appointed time and place, almost invariably to find only a few people there. We would wait for an hour or two, and when few others showed up, we would go our separate ways. A few days later there would be more calls and more waiting.

As I now appreciate, these aborted community activities echo in their own mundane way the story of Nian's conversion with which I began this chapter. A call is issued, and those on the receiving end heed it—or, often, they do not. In those moments, the speech of the so-called leaders seemed so insignificant. Community leaders themselves even remarked on the futility of their efforts as they implored people to heed their words.

The routine ineffectiveness of community leaders' speech serves as a daily reminder of the broadly anarchic character of social life in the villages of the valley. Though the term anarchy is often used as a synonym for disorder, here I use it in its etymological sense: it is a political environment without rulers, without governments or state institutions that have the power to issue commands, adjudicate disputes, and enforce laws. To a significant extent, there are no authorities in the Yopno Valley with the power to compel people to act. Local village leaders have little power to force people to pursue a course of action if they do not want to. And the Papua New Guinean state, as Robert Foster (2002, 4) notes, "hardly qualifies as a 'strong state,' capable of coercing its citizen-subjects through persuasion and/or violence" (see also Douglas 2000). This is especially true in rural regions like the Yopno Valley that are not home to the sort of resource extraction projects that draw the attention of state actors. Although only sixty miles from the city of Lae, Papua New Guinea's industrial hub, the region has remained largely peripheral to the projects of the Australian colonial administration and, since 1975, the government of Papua New Guinea.

The relatively anarchic character of social life in the valley will likely be familiar to anyone who has some knowledge of the ethnography of Melanesia. The scholarship on the societies of the region has often emphasized their egalitarian character and the lack of centralized and institutionalized political authority.[26] As critics have rightly pointed out, there are often significant inequalities in these "egalitarian" societies; for instance, gender-based inequalities are common and often quite pronounced.[27] Nor are these societies truly anarchic, if that is taken to mean there are absolutely no distinctions of status or power. An extensive literature has explored how people acquire leadership in these "anarchic" polities through wealth exchange, skill at warfare, the accumulation of powerful knowledge, and other means.[28]

Still, people who do achieve positions of leadership in these ways typically have only a limited ability to impose their will on others. That is certainly true in the Yopno Valley. People there—especially adult men—value their self-determination and are wary of efforts to control them. And leaders do not speak with what I call the sovereign word, backed by a coercive apparatus that gives that speech force. What verbal power leaders are able to muster derives from their persuasive abilities and their oratorical prowess, often noted components of leadership in Melanesia.[29] But even for those well known for their rhetorical abilities, speech frequently proves ineffective. "No leader can be sure that his opinion will be respected, that his orders will be obeyed, that he will be helped in avenging his wrongs, that his suggestion to hold a ceremony will be taken up, or that the points he makes in a bragging speech to another tribe will be supported by his fellow-tribesmen," as Paula Brown (1963, 6) writes of the "anarchic" Chimbu of the Central Highlands.

Statements like this are a running theme in the literature on leadership and politics in Papua New Guinea and, more broadly, in the scholarship on political communication in small-scale anarchic societies.[30] In such contexts, speakers are often enjoined to show deference to the communicative agency of listeners, speaking in ways that do not impinge on "the right of hearers to build freely and creatively on the speaker's own depictions," as Keith Basso (1988, 109) describes the Western Apache sense of the communicative rights of listeners. Or, as it is commonly expressed among the Navajo, speakers should not be too "bossy" (Webster 2019). The importance of allowing listeners a degree of interpretative and interactive autonomy is also, of course, a central feature of politeness forms, which frequently signal a situation of relative equality by shows of respect for the agency of addressees (Brown and Levinson 1987).[31]

In the Yopno Valley and elsewhere, then, those who would influence others must do so with verbal delicacy and due respect for the agency and autonomy of their listeners. Even then, speech often proves ineffective. Under such anarchic conditions, speech does not appear to be a particularly privileged mode of exercising political agency, as it does in settings where the sovereign exercises power through speech. That is not to say that speech is unimportant; the oft-noted connection between leadership and rhetorical skill in these egalitarian societies testifies otherwise.

But the routine failure of speakers to achieve their aims and the routine failure of speech to have its anticipated effect point to other loci of communicative power—particularly to the consequential role that the listener plays in communicative encounters. There is an unpredictability to the outcome of communicative events that lends itself to what Joel Robbins (2001a, 906) has nicely characterized as a "run-it-up-the-flagpole-and-see-who-salutes view of semiotic function," which appears to be prevalent in Melanesia. In this view, speakers do not fully control what happens in communicative events. They "run-it-up-the-flagpole" and wait to see who, if anyone among their audience, will "salute."[32]

Here, in a political environment where "none can offend, command, or give orders, and speakers must negotiate the agreement and understanding of their opposites," the agency of listeners and the significance of listening stand out (Rosaldo 1973, 221). In these sorts of anarchic contexts, the listener is a conspicuous locus of power in the communicative event. And as a result, how people listen is a matter of considerable political importance.

Democratic and Critical Listening

As a growing literature on democratic listening makes clear, the political importance of listening is hardly confined to anarchic political contexts. Even in the democratic public sphere, where voice is such a central element of politics, practices of listening—and not listening—play a vital part as well. As this literature reminds us, for people to have a voice it is not enough merely to speak: others must listen. "Listening is necessarily constitutive of debate, discussion, deliberation and other hallmarks of democratic activity. To *be* speech, sound-making needs an audience" (Calder 2011, 129–30).

And as Gayatri Spivak (1988) has influentially pointed out, even when voices are in a sense heard, that does not mean that they are truly understood. Listeners often assimilate what they hear into their own conceptual frameworks, distorting the speaker's message in a way that prevents their voice from being truly heard. Democratic political theorists promote the kinds of open and empathetic listening described in the previous section as a way to ensure the voices of others are not only heard but understood. As these theorists argue, the hermeneutic efforts of listeners are integral to democratic politics.

It turns out, then, that listening—as much as speaking—is constitutive of voice in the democratic public sphere. Once we shift our focus from how speech and speaking (should) function in the public sphere to the routine failure of voices to be heard, it becomes clear that there is nothing automatic about the power of voice: the ways audiences listen also matter. And even more, it becomes clear that democratic listening is a particular kind of listening that requires skill and attention of its own. As Kate Lacey (2013) argues, democratic listening requires that people "listen out"—to keep their ears open to the voices of others, especially those that might easily go unheard. Others, as we saw in the previous section, emphasize the need for an empathetic, open effort on the part of listeners to step out of their own shoes and to try to adopt the outlook of others through listening (as ultimately impossible as that might be).

My concern here is not with the details of what makes for good democratic listening. Indeed, the kinds of listening promoted in this literature are quite different from the anarchic listening in the Yopno Valley described in this book. But this literature has made clear that even where voice is politically essential, listening too matters. In fact, listening matters precisely *because* voice is so important. The capacity of listeners to listen in different ways—and in the process to facilitate or disrupt the intentions and expectations of speakers—makes listening as important in democratic politics as is speaking.

The ability of listeners to interpret texts in different ways also serves as an important counterweight to the power of the rhetorical word, as literary and communications scholars have argued.[33] In a world where media texts and cultural artifacts enshrine the views of the dominant, "resisting readers," as Judith Fetterley dubs them, have the power to deconstruct and critique what they read, hear, and see.[34] By unmasking the symbolic power latent in texts—pointing out that the visions of reality these texts present are often false or arbitrary in character and oppressive in effect—these accounts work to induce a more critical stance toward the representations we are presented with. They push us to ask, "What practices and forms of life do [our representations] help sustain, what sort of person do they help construct, and whose power do they help entrench?" (Srinivasan 2019, 142). By making us more attentive to the power of representations, they enable us to break the hold that symbolic power has on us.

In a similar vein, we find efforts to counter the powerful effects of propaganda and disinformation through media literacy, which aims to train people to listen, read, and view texts in more careful and critical ways.[35] Even speech as vis-cerally powerful as hate speech, Judith Butler (1997, 39) insists, can be countered by how people listen and respond to them.

It should be noted that these efforts at resistance do not look much like the kind of hermeneutic listening argued for by theorists of the democratic public sphere. Indeed, the anti-hegemonic, decolonial, resisting, or critical listener is something of the opposite of the empathetic listener of democratic political theory. What joins the two is a shared sense that how people listen, read, or otherwise receive messages matters politically. As the varied literatures discussed here all illustrate in their own ways, (1) there are multiple different ways of listening, and (2) these different ways of listening have different political effects. The result is a recognition that listening is an activity with the power to shape the future. For democratic political theorists, careful empathetic, hermeneutic listening plays an essential role in sustaining the public sphere and democratic values of equality and self-governance. Alternatively, uncritically absorbing the words of dominant others has the potential to reinscribe heteropatriarchal hierarchies or political orders sustained by propaganda and dis-information. There are real stakes involved in how people listen, which makes listeners agents in sustaining and disrupting these sociopolitical orders.

The Pragmatics of Reception

I draw together these accounts of listening—the anarchic, the democratic, the critical—to highlight a concern they all share. In different ways, all are concerned with the *pragmatics of listening* or, more broadly, the *pragmatics of reception*. Under the heading of pragmatics, linguists and others consider the ways language is linked to the contexts in which it is used; that is, how different ways of speaking are appropriate to and effective in different contexts.[36] The discussions of listening I highlight here bring that pragmatic perspective to bear on the listening side of the communicative equation, considering how different ways of receiving messages are appropriate to and effective in diverse contexts. What is the appropriate way to listen in the democratic public sphere? How should one listen to propaganda? What effects do hermeneutic listening or resistant reading have in these different contexts?

As we will see in the chapters to come, people in the Yopno Valley too have sensibilities about the pragmatics of listening. They too seek to understand and marshal the power of listening to achieve social and political ends of their own. Who to listen to, what to listen for, how to interpret what is heard, why one needs to listen—these pragmatic issues are not only subject to scholarly analysis but are also the subject of reflection by listeners in the Yopno Valley and, I would venture, of listeners everywhere.

In a much-cited remark, Franz Boas claimed that language was one domain of culture that people do not think much about.[37] People reflect on religion, manners, social arrangements, and politics but not much on the languages they use, which seemed to Boas a matter of unconscious habit. For the past four decades, linguistic anthropologists have shown that this is simply not the case. Everywhere, people have ideas about what language is and how it is used. Indeed, linguistic anthropologists have shown that these "language ideologies" are key to understanding how language is used in different contexts, how its uses and structures change, and how it is linked to all manner of political, economic, and social projects and processes.[38]

Listening too, we might say, has its ideologies. The ways people conceive of the power and pragmatics of listening influence the ways that they listen: who and what they listen to, how and why they listen. And like language ideologies, these ideologies of listening link practices of listening to religious, political, and social projects; for instance, to democracy or the decolonization of consciousness.

This book focuses on a set of ideologies and practices of listening that are closely linked to the anarchic ethos prominent in Yopno politics. It is an ethnography of a kind of *anarchic listening* that serves to advance listeners' self-determination and their equality with others in the face of those who try to control or dominate them. In different contexts, anarchic listening takes different forms.[39] At times, it involves listening critically and resisting the words of others. But it also involves listening carefully and holding onto others' words. What kind of listening is appropriate on certain occasions is a nuanced matter and one that is not always clear even to those doing the listening. In the chapters to come, I explore the ins and outs of some of the most important considerations that factor in people's efforts to listen anarchically.

These considerations, I argue, lead right to the doorstep of the churches and schools that stand at the center of Yopno villages. For many people in the valley, these two institutions are essential venues for the kind of anarchic listening detailed here: they are places where people listen in an effort to safeguard their self-determination and to gain a measure of equality with others. These are, of course, institutions that scholars and activists have often found to be anything but anarchic. Thoroughly hierarchical in their organization, they have been described as loci of domination and subjection; they are institutions where people become socialized to colonial and state governance, as well as to the class divisions of a capitalist economy.[40] In the Yopno Valley, schools and churches *do* enmesh people in hierarchical organizations with a national and even global reach, and they introduce new forms of inequality to the villages of the valley, including incipient class divisions. In that respect, they indeed seem anything but anarchic.

But as I hope to show, much of the appeal of schools and churches for people in the valley lies in the kind of anarchic listening they are seen to facilitate. If we hope to understand the place of these institutions in the lives of people in the Yopno Valley, we need to grasp the pragmatics and the politics of listening as people in the valley see them. One may disagree with their views about the effectiveness of listening in various contexts. I certainly have my doubts at times (and though I make an effort not to give voice to these doubts, they will undoubtedly show through). Still, Yopno ideologies of listening have a major impact on life in the valley today, which is nowhere more evident than in the schools and churches that stand at the center of almost every village. To understand contemporary life in the valley, one must understand how and why people listen.

Methods and Context of Research

After decrying the attention that speech and speaking receive in the study of political communication, it may seem peculiar that this book dwells at length on people's speech: snippets of conversations, public announcements, debates in community meetings, sermons, historical tales, comments in interviews, and the like. But as largely intangible matters, practices and ideologies of listening must be studied through their outward manifestations—and speech is one of the most illuminating manifestations there is.

For this reason, speech plays a central part in most ethnographies of listening. Even in ethnographies that center on hearing nonlinguistic sounds, discourses *about* listening provide an important resource for the ethnographer. Sometimes these "meta-discourses" are relatively well codified in written or verbalized teachings about listening, as Charles Hirschkind (2001) has observed in the Islamic tradition.[41] Sometimes these meta-discourses only emerge during people's reflections in interviews or in informal conversation. The portrait of anarchic listening I present here draws heavily on the routine ways people talk about listening while engaging in a variety of activities: meetings, announcements, sermons, interviews. The vocabulary and the expressions people use to talk about listening, the advice they give to one another about how to listen, the explanations they offer about why listening is significant—all provide important evidence about the pragmatics of anarchic listening as people in the valley see it.

But the role of speech in this ethnography goes beyond talk *about* listening. Central to my account is the talk (and other nonlinguistic activities) that surround acts of listening. As the Russian semiotician V. N. Voloshinov notes (1973, esp. 115–24), one of the best indications of how listeners actively receive others' speech is the way they adopt and use others' speech themselves (in reported speech, for instance). The world of intertextual references to others' speech—quotations, citations, and the like—provides valuable evidence of how listeners listen and process the speech of others.[42] My citation of Voloshinov here, for instance, offers evidence of how I read and interpreted that work. Even the way people respond to a previous turn at talk, as Erving Goffman (1976) so richly pointed out, can offer an indication of how they listen to what has been said. In much the same way, nonverbal reactions and sequelae to the words of others offer an indication of how and why people listen. And so, I look closely at how people adopt, adapt, and respond to others' speech.

I also look closely at the speech itself that people listen to. As scholars of media and political persuasion alike have highlighted, speakers often shape their utterances with the needs, interests, perspectives, and desires of their audience in mind.[43] Speech itself thus provides a potentially valuable indication of how and why people listen. As we will see, community leaders in the Yopno Valley spend a fair amount of time trying to tailor their speech to cultivate most effectively the involvement of listeners. Such speech, oriented to listeners' interests and desires, gives us a glimpse of what it is people are looking for when they listen to the words of others and what they are looking to accomplish by listening.

In these different ways, speech plays a central role in this ethnography but always with an eye to what it can tell us about what goes on on the other side of the word. It was speech—my own speech, in fact—that first forced me to reckon with the value my interlocutors in the valley placed on listening. From my first weeks in the valley, I was asked to speak: to give speeches and sermons, to host workshops, to run classes, to help with homework, and in other ways to speak publicly and authoritatively. Having gone to the Yopno Valley to study political oratory, I found that people wanted *me* to give speeches. And having gone to learn about people's lives there, again and again I found myself cast in the role of an expert, with people asking me for insight into Christianity and environmental conservation, homework problems and government policy—even into their own genealogies, migration histories, and forest spirits.

At first, I found this quite disconcerting; as an ethnographer, I felt my primary task in the valley was to *listen* to people there. These requests, however, pushed me to recognize that listening was a matter of importance to my interlocutors as well. They also pushed me to consider more carefully my own position within the communicative ecology of the valley. For the past century, people in the Yopno Valley have been on the receiving end of discourses hailing from the global north—Christianity, Western-style education, economic development, environmental conservation, and so on. That history forms an important context for how people view me: an educated, white, male student—now teacher—

from the United States. It made me someone whom it might be worth listening to, someone with insight and expertise.

This positioning shaped my experience in the field, and it fundamentally shapes this ethnography.[44] Men, who have long monopolized specialized expertise in the men's houses of the region, sought to monopolize my time, and they succeeded fairly well. This was especially true of those men—community leaders, teachers, church workers, government officials, and recent school leavers—who are today the leading "knowledgeable people" (*nandak nandak amɨn*; saveman) in Yopno villages. These men trade in knowledge, and a number of them adopted me as their student even as they were also interested in what I might be able to teach them on a variety of subjects: schooling and Christianity, the government of Papua New Guinea and the US-based NGO operating in the valley, how to apply for grants, and how to speak English. Although I made efforts to spend time with everyone in the communities where I lived—especially in Nian village, where I lived for a year in 2008—this ethnography is deeply shaped by how people perceived and managed me in the villages where I lived. That context should be kept in mind in reading this book, and I reflect more on it in the epilogue.

Like all ethnographies, then, this is a partial account of life in Yopno villages. But the importance of listening in the valley goes well beyond the part I played in people's lives, as I discovered once I started to look more closely at the issue. Listening plays an important role in day-to-day politics in Yopno villages—in community meetings, behind-the-scenes confabs, public oratory, and the like—as people in these largely anarchic villages try to formulate collective plans and make joint decisions. And listening plays an important part in people's engagements with the wider world beyond their villages as they integrate themselves into global flows of discourse, much of the time as listeners on the receiving end of rules, dictates, advice, and knowledge that circulate through churches and schools, through the mass media, and through NGOs. To understand the ways in which people in the Yopno Valley engage with each other and the wider world, it is vital to understand how and why they listen. And so, in the chapters to come, we explore in some detail the pragmatics of anarchic listening as people in the valley understand and practice it.

In chapter 1, I introduce readers to life in the rural villages of the Yopno Valley, both the subsistence-based economy of the region and the predominantly anarchic character of village politics that this underpins. In this region, people value their self-determination, and they have the economic and social means to exercise it much of the time. In daily life, anarchic values and practices manifest themselves prominently in a place too often overlooked in the study of political communication: in the ways people listen. As I highlight in chapter 1, listening is a means of undercutting the authority of others, demanding respect for oneself, and expressing one's independence. I focus on three practices of listening—"disregarding," "evaluating," and "holding onto" the words of others—that play a vital role in people's efforts to constitute themselves as self-determining agents and their villages as anarchic polities. The art of anarchic listening is knowing when to employ each of these practices.

Chapter 2 focuses on one of the main factors that makes listening both essential to anarchic politics in the valley and yet a difficult art to perfect. Unlike the "ontologically secure" subjects that so often feature in ethnographies—subjects with seemingly well-established beliefs and ontologies—people in the Yopno Valley are prone to doubt and uncertainty. Reality is regarded as deeply enigmatic, and humans are liable to misunderstand the nature of the world around them. Where ignorance and confusion can lead people to act against their own will and desires, one of the most serious threats to their self-determination is, in essence, their own selves. This chapter explores how the sense of uncertainty cultivated in daily life provides a motive for a particular practice of anarchic listening, one in which listeners seek out better, more accurate understandings of the world. By "holding onto" the insights and advice of others, people work to become more self-determining actors.

Chapter 3 builds on the context of uncertainty introduced in the previous chapter, showing how it underpins the power of experts and expertise in the anarchic villages of the valley. As much of the scholarship on the subject has emphasized, expertise often serves as a technique of power, a potent means of shaping the behavior of others. That is certainly how it is used in the Yopno Valley, where community leaders routinely offer up their purported expertise in an effort to steer the actions of often recalcitrant community members. But we also look at the politics of expertise from a less familiar perspective in this chapter—that of listeners. From the perspective of the uncertain listener, expertise offers a way of getting a grip on reality and of taking greater control of their future. Expertise thus serves two seemingly contradictory political aims simultaneously: it is a technique of power used by speakers to control and influence their audience, and at the same time it plays an essential role in the anarchic politics of Yopno villages, supporting listeners in their pursuit of self-determination. As a medium of politics, expertise reconciles domination and self-determination, leadership and anarchy in a way that enables experts to assume the peculiar role of anarchic leaders in the villages of the valley.

Though listening holds out the possibility of empowerment, it is an activity laden with risk. Chapter 4 centers on one of the major concerns people have about listening: their worries that community leaders, NGO workers, and government officials are deceiving them. Deception and dissimulation are indeed common-place in the valley, regarded as a necessary means of keeping the peace in Yopno villages. And listeners are alert to the ever-present possibility that they are be-ing tricked into acting against their own will. But the danger that deception poses to listeners often leads people to listen even more. Listeners seek out people who can help them listen better by evaluating others' words for them, sorting out good advice from bad, truth from deception. In effect, listening becomes a collec-tive endeavor as people turn to family, friends, and new sources of insight—missionaries, teachers, anthropologists—who might prove helpful and trust-worthy aids to listening.

In chapter 5, we turn to two institutions that have had a profound impact on life in the valley over the past century: churches and schools. Their appeal, I ar-gue here, has much to do with their role as venues for the kind of anarchic lis-tening I sketched in the preceding chapters. People in the valley see these institutions as a source of powerful knowledge, knowledge that has enabled others in Papua New Guinea and especially the global north to achieve power and wealth far beyond their own. Viewed in this way, as local outposts within a worldwide circulation of power-giving knowledge, these institutions—and the listening that occurs in them—are rendered means of empowerment and of achieving greater equality with the rest of the world. At the same time, however, schools and churches are thoroughly hierarchical institutions, responsible for generating new forms of inequality in the valley. In the end, we see how the global contexts in which people in the valley situate their listening practices legitimize present-day subordination and inequality among people who value the very op-posite. And we see how anarchic listening is enmeshing people in national and global institutions that are anything but anarchic.

THE ART OF ANARCHIC LISTENING

In September 2008 I joined a group of people in Nian village for a community meeting. These meetings are a regular part of life in the Yopno Valley, where people gather to discuss and coordinate their activities: hosting soccer matches, church gatherings, and school fundraisers; building and maintaining schools and churches; preparing ceremonial dances and gifts to give to other villages on special occasions; and so on. That September day, we gathered in a house to discuss the anniversary celebration for the Lutheran church in Nian discussed in the introduction. The village of Nian was marking the tenth anniversary of its church building and had secured the participation of speakers and ceremonial dancers from two other villages in the region. Visitors from throughout the valley and beyond were anticipated, and as the hosts, the people of Nian needed to provide food, housing, and gifts for the participants, all of which required a great deal of planning. The celebration was to be held in two months, and discussions and preparations had been going on for several months already. But in the days before that meeting a new concern had arisen: it had become clear that the church was short of pigs to give to the invited guests. If visitors came and provided entertainment, support, and gifts, and Nian could not offer them hospitality and gifts in return, this would be a tremendous embarrassment.

So, a meeting was called to figure out how to procure pigs for the event. The bell that sits in the central plaza of the village rang out, summoning people to the meeting. And as often happened, those of us who showed up sat around waiting to see whether others in the community would come. Meetings of this sort are called on a regular basis, about every week or two, but whether people will attend is always a question. As we waited, the conversation turned, as it usually did, to why people were not showing up. Raipe, a leading woman in the community, intimated that the husband and sons of another woman in attendance, Soŋgum, would not attend because pigs were on the agenda.

Soŋgum herself was an older woman, originally from the neighboring Domung region, who had married into Nian village, learned the Yopno language, and became a reliable fixture at community events. She was seemingly always there to support others with food, labor, and whatever was needed. Her husband, in contrast, was not. A member of one of the smaller clans in the village, he chafed at the power of the larger clans, and he and his brothers sought to assume some of the leadership roles dominated by members of these clans; for example, as members of the school board or as church leaders. Yet he spent much of his time in the village closer to the seacoast where his wife was from, seeking an escape from the tensions and frustrations in his own village.

Raipe's remark about people avoiding the meeting because pigs were on the agenda found its target. Soŋgum's husband had indeed borrowed pigs from the church and failed to repay them.[1] Soŋgum responded to Raipe's comment:

> SOŋGUM: We ask my husband's family about the pigs all the time, but we get no response. They sap the strength of you leaders. When will they listen to what you are saying? Yesterday we started to talk about the pigs, and when they heard this, they went down to the coast.
> PETER: [joking] Your husband's a warm weather kind of guy!
> PASU: He's sleeping in a cave somewhere.
> RAIPE: With that kind of behavior, they have sapped our strength. Our strength has completely collapsed, so what can we say?
> SOŋGUM: My husband and his family will explain what's going on later. I mentioned to them that there is a debt in our clan, asking, "What is to be done about that?" When they heard me ask that, they became afraid and ran away.
> RAIPE: [to Pasu] Old man, no one is here. Let's go. . . .

"When will they listen?" In meetings like this—and in public speeches, sermons, school lessons, and the like—talk often turns to the topic of listening: why people should listen, how they should listen, and especially how they do not listen. It is a truism that people do not listen; and it is often true. People ignore the words of others, disregarding things they were urged to do, advice they were given, and lessons they were taught. Like Soŋgum's husband, when people hear announcements about meetings or about community work, they often disregard them, disappearing to their gardens or houses in the forest, fleeing to extended family in neighboring and distant villages, or simply avoiding community activities and going about their business.

As we sat waiting for people to arrive at this meeting, talk turned to some of the other activities that community members were failing to do. Teachers at the school requested that sand be brought from a stream a good distance away to mix concrete for a new school classroom, but few showed up to do that. Discussing all the work on the school that was not getting done, Raipe identified the character flaw that is often held to be the reason why things do not get done in Yopno villages: "We really disregard talk (*gen kɨrɨŋɨt*; "to disregard talk; lit., to 'cut' talk"). We have no respect."

In this chapter, I explore the connection that Raipe draws here between practices of listening (e.g., disregarding talk) and the anarchic politics of Yopno villages. In a context in which "listening" can be used as a synonym for "obeying," not listening is a prime mode in which people push back against the efforts of would-be leaders to exert control over others. In a classic account of political communications in "anti-state" societies in South America, Pierre Clastres (1987, 154) notes in passing the part played by listening—or rather, not listening—in the anarchic politics of the region: "In societies without a State, power is not found on the side of the chief: it follows that his word cannot be the word of power, authority, or command. An order? Now there is something the chief would be unable to give. . . . A chief forgetful of his duty who attempted such a thing as an order would be met by a sure refusal of obedience, and a denial of recognition would not be far behind."[2] In his discussion of anarchic political communication, Clastres's attention remains firmly focused on the political significance of speaking; the chapter is in fact called "The Duty to Speak." But here, in passing, he captures something of the potential power of listeners and the political importance of listening in an anarchic political environment. The power to refuse obedience and even recognition is a way of reminding forgetful chiefs that they really have no authority over others.

In the Yopno Valley, we find much the same thing; disregarding or not listening to the words of others is a routine practice of anarchic listening, one that foils the efforts of community leaders to impose their will on others. I elaborate on this point later in the chapter. But there is a good deal more to anarchic listening than this sort of disregard. In the following sections, I introduce several other practices of listening, which we will return to over and over in the chapters to come: in addition to the practice of disregarding, ignoring, or not listening to the words of others, there is the practice of "evaluating" others' speech (*gen sɨlɨp aŋ*) and the practice of "holding onto" it (*gen abɨdaŋ*). Taken together, these three practices of anarchic listening serve as a way for people to assert and enhance their self-determination while constraining the power of others. But before turning to these, let me spell out in more detail what I mean when I speak of the anarchic character of politics in Yopno villages.

Anarchic Villages

I first arrived in the village of Nian in December, just as things were gearing up for Christmas (see figure 2). In some ways it was an ideal time of year to arrive. The village was swollen with people. Normally home to more than 350 people, it often did not seem that way. Much of the time, people are off in their fields or the forest tending to gardens or pigs, or merely escaping from village life. Most families have multiple houses, one in the main village settlement and one near their gardens or their hunting grounds, to which they decamp for anything from a few hours to weeks.

But during the Christmas season, people left their gardens and their other responsibilities behind and converged on the main village settlement. There they spent their days in the central plaza, playing soccer, socializing, and marketing garden produce and store-bought goods. Church services were held in people's homes in the evenings and in the main church building a few times each week.

FIGURE 2.   The central plaza of Nian village with the Lutheran church and many houses in the background.

Photograph by author.

Adding to the excitement, family and friends who had moved to other parts of the country to attend school, work, or sell goods at markets had returned to Nian for the holiday.

Life in the Yopno Valley, I would discover, has an ebb and flow to it. Christmas was a period of flow in Nian. But just a ten-minute walk away, in the neighboring village of Nokopo, things could not have been more different. As the Christmas and New Year's festivities were wrapping up in Nian, a small group of us traveled down to Nokopo on January 2 to attend the funeral of an older woman, a relative of one of the men who had taken charge of me on my arrival in the valley.

We arrived in Nokopo to find the village almost completely deserted, with only a small group tending to the body of the deceased. Yopno funerals are typically huge affairs lasting multiple days and drawing relatives from long distances, who crowd into houses to mourn and sing and pass time in the vicinity of the body of the deceased. This was nothing like that. Those who were there explained that people had been coming from their forest houses to sit for a while, but they all had returned to their forest and garden houses.

As I learned later, the village had been empty throughout the entire Christmas season. The Lutheran church worker who was based in Nian had led the Christmas Day service at the church in Nokopo, and he reported that virtually no one had shown up. People in Nian were scandalized; except for Easter Sunday, no day is more important than Christmas in the local Christian calendar.

As it turns out, a rumor was circulating that someone had been murdered in the community, and everyone had fled to their forest and garden houses in fear. At the time, people were reluctant to talk to me about any of this. But I later learned that the murder was merely one of a number of deaths that had occurred around the Christmas season, including the death of the woman whose funeral I attended. These deaths were all attributed to occult violence—sorcery or witchcraft (*sot mawom*; poisen sanguma)—perpetrated by members of the community. Fearful for their own lives, the people of Nokopo had fled the village settlement en masse.

If Christmas in Nian was the flow of social life in the Yopno Valley, then Christmas in Nokopo was its ebb. Shortly after the Christmas season ended, Nian experienced its own ebb, when much of the community decamped to their forest houses to harvest pandanus nuts, which fruit every year or two and are gathered and smoked over the course of a month or longer. Many of the people I had met during the Christmas season did not return to the main settlement for months, except for an occasional visit. Less extreme than the desertion of Nokopo and occurring for very different reasons, this exodus changed the tenor of Nian's social life in a striking way.

In addition to pandanus gathering season, people routinely live for periods of time in relatively small family groups away from the main village settlements.

There, they escape the difficulties and frustrations of village life, where petty theft is a constant complaint; malicious gossip can leave people feeling constantly monitored and subject to criticism; and there is a constant stream of demands for support from relatives and friends, community, church, and school leaders. People say their ancestors did not live in large settlements as they do today. In the past, they lived scattered in homesteads built on their clan land, surrounded by their own gardens of sweet potato, taro, and other staples, which were fenced in with the kind of elaborate fences made of wild sugar cane still found in the region. The past is spoken of as a time of greater danger, where occult violence was common and neighboring villages conducted murderous raids on each other regularly. Seclusion with clanmates and extended family offered a measure of protection.

Multiple clans (*jalap*), often six or more, make up what I am calling a village (*kukup*), with clan size varying widely from roughly a dozen people to close to a hundred. People inherit their clan identity, along with their rights to use clan land, from their fathers. Fathers designate portions of their garden and forest land, and the trees and bamboo that they planted, for their children to use.[3] Clans control their land independently of other clans, and within each clan the same is true, for the most part, of lineages and sibling groups.[4] Clans and extended families were—and remain—central to people's sense of identity; they are key social units for economic production, social reproduction, and personal protection.

In the past, the clans that made up a village would gather for educational and ritual activities on occasion in the men's ceremonial houses (*bema yut*). There, men from different clans would conduct rituals to harness the power of spirits, ensure abundant harvests, and bless each other's activities. The men's houses were also institutions where young boys were educated in the arts of ritual and warfare and in the knowledge they would need to act morally and succeed as adults. The clans that make up a village also united in overt warfare against other neighboring villages. But from the way people talk about it now, village-level groupings were only an occasional occurrence. Much of life was spent in extended family groups and among clan mates on land belonging to the clan.[5]

With the arrival of Lutheran missionaries in the 1930s, however, that pattern of living began to change. Missionaries gathered people together into village settlements to facilitate missionization and education. These village settlements were anchored by a church and a mission school, which remain the central institutions of Yopno villages, often built on the very locations of the former men's ceremonial houses. As people tell it now, their ancestors were generally quite willing to adopt the new religion after some initial concerns, such as those dramatized in the skit discussed in the introduction. Christianity is now widely seen to have created an era of relative peace and freedom in the valley. People no longer have to live scattered on the land, they often note, constantly fearful of attacks of occult and physical violence. As the deaths in Nokopo illustrate, such concerns have not entirely vanished; village settlements are hardly free of tension. But people say they are much freer than their ancestors ever were to come and go as they please, traveling not only from village to village within the valley but also to the coast and beyond to urban areas for markets and schools. As the head teacher of the Nokopo school put it during the Independence Day celebrations in 2008, "Lutheran missionaries brought us independence first. Papua New Guinea's independence came later."

Today, villages are the collectives responsible for many of the activities and institutions that most engage people's interest. They support and maintain what are now the prime institutions in Yopno life—schools and churches—with each village having its own or working with a neighboring village to support them together. And villages are responsible for organizing most of the major events that happen in the valley—the soccer tournaments, gift exchanges, and dance festivals that punctuate the daily grind of tending to gardens and pigs, collecting firewood, and cooking.

To get a sense of all that village life both offers residents and demands of them, these are some of the events the people of Nian village collectively participated in in the two months of September and October 2014: an exchange of gifts with people from a distant coastal school; a soccer tournament at the government center Teptep; the launch of the five-year plan for a US-based conservation NGO in the village of Isan; a grant proposal writing course that I organized; the ceremony marking the start of the fourth term at the local schools; a coffee-planting workshop sponsored by the conservation NGO in the village of Nian; a three-day fundraising celebration for the local elementary school in Ganggalut, with all-night ceremonial dances and a market; the eighth-grade exams for students trying to get into high school; and preparations for a ceremonial dance performance at the opening of the church in the village of Nombo at Christmas. Not everyone in the village participated in all these events, and there are times that are less busy than this two-month stretch. But this list gives a good sense of the time and effort that people put into events organized by their own and neighboring villages. These events are typically the source of much excitement and anticipation, and they play an important part in promoting the good name of a village and its leaders.

But mounting these events poses a constant challenge. Planning and preparations for these events—not to mention the events themselves—require significant outlays of time, energy, and resources from people who are often busy with other activities that demand their attention and resources. Virtually everyone in the valley is a subsistence agriculturalist, living off the food they grow in the fields around the villages and building their houses from materials harvested from the forest and grasslands.[6] Every day, villagers must tend to their gardens and gather food for the day's meals, work that is most often done by women. There are pigs to take care of and firewood to gather for cooking and heating houses on the cold nights. Then there are larger projects—building fences and houses, for instance, or preparing bridewealth payments for a son's marriage. These activities can take weeks if not months of effort and require considerable resources and the support of extended family and friends.

There is also the need to make money to pay children's school fees: at K50 (US$20) per child for primary school, that was the largest recurring monetary expense for most families at the time of my research.[7] Villagers also need money for bridewealth payments, death compensation payments, and luxuries like rice, oil, or, more extravagantly, solar panels for light. Money, however, is hard to come by. Over the years, economic development projects promoting cash crops and the sale of "European vegetables" (peas, cabbage, carrots, and the like) all collapsed due to the expense of air freight and the difficulty of carrying forty-kilogram bags of coffee two days over the mountainous terrain for a pittance. Despite decades of promises from politicians, there are still no roads into the valley. To make money, people raise and sell pigs, which can fetch up to US$150, a significant sum. They carry produce and tobacco for two days to the buses (to the south) or boats (to the north) that take them on to urban markets. And they go to the coast and buy betelnut, which they sell in village markets in the upper reaches of the Yopno Valley, where the sought-after stimulant does not grow. To afford the school fees of those children who have been accepted into high school (US$180–350 per child per year), parents often go and live in urban areas where they buy goods at wholesale stores and sell them in roadside markets.

It is hardly surprising, then, that when community leaders ask people to provide their time, energy, and resources for village activities and institutions, these requests are often met with a tepid response. Every village in the Yopno Valley has a set of older men who are recognized as leaders—the heads of clans, school board members, and people who hold positions in the Lutheran church—who are responsible for organizing community work and public events like the church celebration. They make announcements (*but pɨsok*) about the work that needs to be done or the meetings that are to be held. But there is little that these leaders can do to make people show up for meetings or do community work.

Lines of authority within families and clans are more developed, although even there the capacity to get others to do something that they do not want to do is limited. A wife is expected to follow her husband's lead, and biblical injunctions to that effect are often noted; in practice, however, the dynamic varied quite a bit from family to family. Some women lived largely independently of their husbands, coming and going as they thought fit, though with an eye toward the needs of their husband and children. Others were subject to routine requests and demands. Women do push back when they feel they are being over-burdened or mistreated, publicizing the unfair demands made on them with a wisecrack—"What am I, your donkey?"—or fleeing to their family's village when their husbands try to violently enforce their dictates. But women are at a disadvantage in the battle of wills with their husbands. They generally move to the husband's village after marriage, and so their family is often not around to lend them support. Even more, the families of married women have received bride-wealth payments from the husband and his family, making them reluctant to interfere in and jeopardize the marriage.

Children too are expected to heed their parents and are disciplined regularly for failing to do to so. Many of my interlocutors recalled the beatings they got from their parents when they were young for skipping school and other infractions. But children are also generally given a fair amount of latitude to do as they please—and they often do as they please, as testified by the many beatings they recall. Memorably, a mother with whom I was having lunch told her young son of about six years to go take a shower at the tap outside the house. He did not want to and returned wielding a large shovel—one quite a bit larger than himself—trying ineffectively to hit his mother with it. She laughingly fended off his feeble blows until he gave up. When I went to leave, we discovered that the young boy had used the shovel to bar the door from the outside, locking us in. His mother once again laughed and commented on how crazy children are, before screaming at him to open the door.

Other than in families and clans, though, institutionalized inequalities and relatively well-defined lines of authority are largely absent. Village leaders do try to direct the collective efforts of the community to build schools, host church celebrations, and the like. But they have no authority to order others about nor the means to enforce their dictates. They are the relatively impotent leaders of anarchic villages, a fact they are continually reminded of as community members ignore their advice and their directives. And that makes listening—or not listening, in this case—one of the more conspicuous expressions of the anarchic ethos and the anarchic politics of Yopno villages.

Anarchy and Subversion: Disregarding Talk

My first months in the Yopno Valley provided an object lesson in the relative impotence of community leaders. As the beginning of the 2008 school year approached, the leaders of Nian village were trying to get the local primary school up and running. People throughout rural communities in Papua New Guinea are responsible for much of the work of building and maintaining school buildings, providing labor and materials from their fields and forests. In Nian, a new classroom and a new house for one of the teachers assigned to the school needed to be built. And so school board members from Nian and its neighbor Nokopo—which shared responsibility for the Nokopo Lutheran Primary School—were busy trying to get people to do this work.

The efforts kicked off on January 6 with a large event in which regional education leaders and teachers spoke to the community about the importance of education. The event was attended by a large number of people from both villages, who heard about the value of education and the need to prepare the school for the year ahead (see figure 3). But the day after the inspirational speeches—the day of the week designated for community work projects—virtually no one showed up at the school to do the work. I spoke later in the week with the vice chairman of the school board—a man from Nian village—who explained that no one showed up because he had not brought about consensus (*but esal aŋ*; kamapim wanbel) about the work that needed to be done. He said he was plan-

FIGURE 3.   Listening at an education awareness rally, with the unfinished classroom in the background.

Photograph by author.

ning to hold a meeting to consult with community members before the next week's community workday. But when the next week rolled around, few showed up to work once again.

The preparations for the start of the school year had coincided with the annual harvest of pandanus nuts and much of the community left the village settlement to spend a month or more living in their forest houses harvesting and smoking nuts. Calls for the community to come together and work on the school continued whenever people gathered—at village markets, church services, and another education awareness event held February 3 to coincide with the start of the school year. But still nothing happened. By early March, about a month after the school year was supposed to start, the work remained incomplete.

This sort of situation exemplifies what I mean when I speak of Yopno villages as anarchic. Villages do not have centralized authorities with the power to issue commands, adjudicate disputes, or enforce laws.[8] Even more, people value this political arrangement. They do not appreciate being bossed around, which only adds to the challenge of organizing village activities. As part of the ongoing efforts of villages to build and maintain churches and schools, host events, and attend those in other villages, people are subject to a stream of demands—to provide labor and resources, to prepare pigs, to give money, and, of course, to participate in constant meetings. These demands often lead to complaints from community members that the village leaders are treating them as their "laborers" (*oman amɨn*; wok boi), an insult that highlights a person's subordination and submissiveness in a context where equality and self-determination are prized.[9] As one man I overheard put it while the school board vice chairman was announcing work to be done at school, "Who does he think we are, his slaves?" using the term slev ("slave") familiar from the Tok Pisin Bible.

When people feel community leaders are being overbearing, asking too much, or dictating a course of action that community members disagree with—or when people would just rather be doing something else—they simply disregard these announcements and go about their business. Few show up to a meeting, the work on the school does not get completed, the pigs needed for a celebration do not materialize, and there is little that can be done: none of the leaders have the power to enforce their dictates.[10]

After months of encouraging people to complete the work on the school, all to no avail, Topa—who was the owner of the one small store in the village and whose son attended the school—summed up the situation in a frustrated plea at the market one day: "Those of us speaking out about the work that needs to be done at the school are not many. When we talk about this, I can see that you don't respect us. Sorry, I am finding it really hard to speak. There are a lot of you, and I'm just one person talking, so you won't listen to me."

Here, we return to the topic of listening—or rather, not listening—as a manifestation of the anarchic character of Yopno politics. The routine way in which people disregard the words of the community leaders is a constant reminder of these "leaders" lack of power. Community leaders recognize this and routinely comment on it. In Yopno, one of the meanings of the verb "listen" is "to obey" or "to heed." This is true of other languages of the region (Robbins 2001b; Stasch 2014), as well as in English and many other languages as well (Sweetser 1990; Evans and Wilkins 2000). To speak of people as "not listening" serves as a way of talking about a lack of obedience, an anarchic condition where people do not respect the dictates of would-be leaders—where they "follow their hearts" (*butni yol*) as it is often put, instead of "following instructions" (*gen yol*).

Yopno villages are fragile collectives.[11] As in the anarchic communities of upland Southeast Asia described by James Scott (2010), people at times flee village life to escape the efforts of would-be leaders to control them. The land that people control as members of clans and patrilines provides something of a refuge from the difficulties and demands of village life. When people feel burdened by the demands on them in the village or when tensions arise there, they flee to their own land or to other villages where they do not have to deal with the gossip, the requests of others, and the occult violence that can plague life in a village (see figure 4).

But such full-scale flights are often unnecessary. Much of the time, people simply disregard what village leaders tell them to do and go about their own business. As Audra Simpson (2014) has forcefully argued, acts of refusal can be important modes of exercising sovereignty. Though less dramatic than the examples she describes, the routine refusal to listen in Yopno villages is a way in which people assert their self-determination and subvert the power of would-be leaders. It too is an "art of not being governed" (Scott 2010).

But there is more to anarchic listening than refusing to listen. Indeed, a willingness to listen—and to listen a lot—is often a vital element of anarchic politics; as David Graeber (2010) writes, "Listening to what everyone has to say rather than letting one person decide for everyone else" is a very anarchic approach to decision making. This sort of willingness to listen carefully also has a part to play in the anarchic politics of Yopno villages. Anarchic listening does not consist of a single practice of listening. Rather, there are several practices, which taken together help sustain the anarchic character of Yopno politics, constraining the power of would-be leaders while promoting people's self-determination. Listening to what everyone has to say plays an important part in this, although we need to consider more carefully the nature of this listening and how it achieves its pragmatic—anarchic—effects.

FIGURE 4.   A forest house away from the main village settlement. Residents often go to these solitary encampments when they want to have a break from the intense sociality of village life.

Photograph by author.

Anarchy and Collective Action: Evaluating Talk

Faced with listeners who routinely subvert their authority by disregarding their words, community leaders devote a good deal of time to talking about listening. Recognizing that the effectiveness of their words hinges on what listeners do with them they regularly exhort their audience to listen up, urging them to "hold onto" the valuable talk they are hearing (*gen abɨdaŋ*), to "look after" the important advice and information they are being given (*gen kudaŋ*: "to care for, protect, look after talk" using the verb *kudaŋ*, which is used to describe the act of caring for a dear person or looking after a prized possession). In a context where people readily disregard the words of others and "follow their hearts," it is listeners who quite conspicuously shape the outcome of communicative events. How they listen clearly matters, and so naturally, community leaders talk a great deal about listening.

In addition to exhorting their audiences to listen, community leaders speak a good deal among themselves about how to "hold the hearts" (*but abɨdaŋ*) of their audience, how to move the audience's feelings and thoughts with their words. The form of persuasion that is propounded in these discussions involves several characteristic ways of describing the act of listening. In some of these, the listener is treated less as an agent than the affected party in communicative interaction, and it is the speaker or their speech that is the agent. So, for instance, people talk about "inspiring" their listener, which in Yopno is literally "to cause their heart to go up" (*butni awo*). Or, the speaker may affect their listener by "reaching inside their heart with their talk" (*gen yek but kai pɨkɨ*).[12]

But often when it comes to the task of persuasion, it is the agency of the listener that is the nub of the issue: What will listeners do with the talk they hear? Will they disregard it or hold onto it? On this point, there is an expression that conveys a key facet of anarchic listening in Yopno political life. To illustrate, let me return to the discussions about the church anniversary celebration in Nian and the search for pigs.

In November 2008, exactly two months after the meeting discussed in the opening section of this chapter, pigs were still needed for the celebration, then only a week away.[13] The organizing committee for the event called an emergency meeting to figure out how the pigs would be procured. Often, community leaders meet in this way, working together to fashion a persuasive appeal before presenting it to the community at large. As in other meetings of this sort, much of the discussion centered on how the community leaders would present the need for pigs to the community, considering in detail how the audience would listen, process, and respond to what they would say. Numerous speakers offered ideas; one church leader suggested that they explain to community members that giving pigs as offerings for church events is a way to secure blessings for themselves:

> In the meeting with the community and outside as well we should mention to our friends who have various sorts of problems that giving pigs for the celebration is a way to secure blessings from God. Let's go speak out about it to them.
> "I see this is good talk they've made, so it would be good that I do this [i.e., give pigs]. Afterward my life will improve."
> Community members themselves will evaluate (*sɨlɨp aŋ*) it like that and they will bring pigs. That would be good.

The way in which the church leader presented his proposal has a three-part structure that one often finds in discussions of listening and its effects:

The first part of this structure is the announcement itself that the church leader is proposing the leaders should make: "we should mention that giving pigs is a way to secure blessings." The idea here is that if people give pigs for the anniversary celebration, God will help them with their problems.

The third part of this structure is the effect that will be produced by this message: "community members will bring pigs." That is the result that the community leaders gathered there were hoping to achieve: securing pigs from the community to give to the invited guests.

And, interposed between the announcement and its effect is an act of listening, in which the audience evaluates (*sɨlɨp aŋ*; skelim) what has been said and agrees with it. The church leader spells out how the listener will evaluate this speech, verbalizing it: "'I see this is good talk they've made, so it would be good that I do this [i.e., give pigs]. Afterward my life will improve.'"

This three-part structure of (1) speech, (2) evaluative listening, and (3) outcome is a common way people talk about the relationship between talk and its effects.[14] In this structure, the listener plays a central, decisive role in determining the outcome of communicative events. As this model of speech and its effects implicitly recognizes, if listeners do *not* think "this is good talk they've made"—if they disagree with it—then the announcement will not produce the desired effect. The audience will simply disregard the words of community leaders as they so often do.

Given the decisive role played by listeners in this view of communicative action, much of the discussion that evening concerned how exactly the audience would evaluate various possible proposals. How, for instance, would the audience view a request for money donations in lieu of pigs? What would they think if community leaders demanded the return of pigs that people had borrowed from the church? What if they asked for pigs as offerings that would be rewarded with God's blessing?

The verb most often used to describe this evaluative activity is *sɨlɨp aŋ* ("group, sort, distribute, organize").[15] *Sɨlɨp aŋ* can also be used to describe how a woman distributes food from a pot to individual plates, how a person arranges items for sale at market, or how gifts are organized and distributed at an exchange ceremony. When I asked people about the meaning of the expression *gen sɨlɨp aŋ* ("sort out, weigh, evaluate talk"), they would often say something like, "You sort out talk, this part of the talk is good, this isn't" or "This part is true, this isn't." This explanation was often accompanied by gestures that mimicked distributing food from a pot onto plates—taking talk from the pot and putting it on one plate ("good talk") and then taking other talk and putting it on another plate ("bad talk").

The meaning of this expression can be further clarified by considering another expression it is often paired with: the description of listeners as "breaking up" the talk that they hear (*pudaŋ*; brukim; "break up, split"; for a more idiomatic English translation, one might use "dissect"). In the same way one speaks of breaking up firewood, talk can be "split": "we will break up (*pudaŋ*) this talk and evaluate it (*silip aŋ*)." Thus, "breaking up" (*pudaŋ*) talk is the first step in "sorting it out" (*silip aŋ*); dissected into its various parts, listeners then determine which parts are good and which bad, which true and which false, and what meanings and implications are hidden inside it.

In talking of listening as an act of breaking and sorting out talk, listeners are the agents in the process of political communication. They do not mindlessly follow instructions, nor do they mindlessly disregard them.[16] They weigh proposals and advice to gauge their truth and their utility—to see, ultimately, whether what they hear is something that they agree with and want to support. In the act of evaluation, listeners are presented as self-determining subjects: "I see this is good talk they've made, so it would be good that I do this [i.e., give pigs]. Afterward my life will improve." Listeners who evaluate in this way give pigs not because community leaders dictate that they must but because they think it is a good idea.

People not only talk about this kind of evaluative listening in the course of political life but they also routinely perform it in the seemingly endless discussions that are a centerpiece of the anarchic politics of Yopno villages. (What I am calling "discussion" here is a translation of the Yopno term *yaŋ nandaŋ*, which is composed of the verbs "speak" and "listen"; it might be literally translated as "speaking and listening" or, more idiomatically, "back-and-forth"). Most weeks at least one discussion takes place in a Yopno village involving some segment of the community, with each one part of a long series of discussions on an issue like the need for pigs for the church celebration or the work that needs to be done on the local school. In most discussions, nearly all the participants are adult men, although women take the lead when it is an event organized by the village women (e.g., a church women's group).

The basic discursive activity of Yopno discussions consists of participants offering up their suggestions and concerns about community issues and then evaluating the suggestions and concerns of others. The following example is drawn from the same meeting we have been looking at, in which community leaders were scrambling at the last minute to find pigs for the church celebration. One suggestion, offered up by the community's church worker (known as an *evangelist*), was that the church ask community members for money that could be used to buy the pigs they needed.

> EVANGELIST: Another possibility is those congregants who don't feel able to give a pig, they can get together and gather money and we buy another pig. Tomorrow at a meeting of the wider community, let's speak out about all of this.
> [This is followed by another man's speech, which is omitted here]

TIM: O Chairman! You can't go right to the option of money; forget it. We must gather the congregation and let them speak out from their heart about the pig situation. We can go with the money option but if we talk right away about money then the Congregation will go stand apart from us and say: "You yourselves do it with money!" Forget about the money option and inspire the Congregation. Afterward, either you'll see them bring what they've taken that belongs to the community or you can go with the money option. You go with money, you prevent them from returning the pigs. They'll say: "They will do something for me with money" and will take the pig that belongs to the community and put it in their area. This is just what I have to say, so you all evaluate (*sɨlɨp aŋ*) it.

Throughout his speech, Tim does two things that characterize discussion as a speech genre. First, he verbally evaluates the talk of the evangelist, identifying its problems. Second, he offers up his own suggestions that, as he says, are to be evaluated by others in turn.[17] Discussion thus comprises a great deal of talk about others' talk. It is common at the beginning of a turn at talk in discussion to explicitly link one's contribution to earlier talk, emphasizing that one is performing a variety of actions on another's talk: "Good, I want to add to something that he said . . ."; "Chairman, this thing you say just now, it's . . ."; "What you have said about putting money, it's . . ."

Following these opening phrases, participants break up (*pudaŋ*), evaluate (*sɨlɨp aŋ*), add to (*saŋpɨŋ*), strengthen (*aŋteban aŋ*), and otherwise work on the talk preceding their own. In other words, they do exactly what listeners are said to do with the words of others. In effect, they play the role of agentive listeners, breaking up and evaluating the talk of others in a verbal and public way.

The agency of the listener—the "active reception of other speakers' speech" (Voloshinov 1973, 117)—becomes palpable in discussion, and it is an essential part of the political significance of this activity. In asserting themselves as agentive listeners in this process, participants assert their self-determination: their capacity to work on the talk of others and not simply be passive recipients of another's dictates. It is when people do not feel they have been consulted in this way that complaints arise about being treated as the laborers or slaves of community leaders.

At the same time as participants assert their self-determination by evaluating the speech of others, they display their respect for others' self-determination in offering up suggestions for them to evaluate and discuss. The point is brought home in a standard formula used to wrap up a turn of talk in these meetings:

"This is just what I have to say, so you all evaluate (*sɨlɨp aŋ*) it." This formula describes the very activity that characterizes discussion: the speaker is putting talk out there for listeners to publicly evaluate.

Discussions of this sort take place on a wide variety of issues: planning for events like the church anniversary celebration, organizing community work on the school, hosting soccer tournaments, preparing to attend fundraisers in other villages, and the like. Any event that involves the coordinated effort of the village is potentially ripe for discussion, and so there are generally discussions on one or more topics going on every week. If agreement cannot be reached in one meeting, the discussion is typically taken up again later, or if reaching consensus seems unlikely, it is dropped. Individual meetings like the one discussed here are usually embedded within a wider web of discussions—a series of meetings occurring over weeks or even months—that (ideally), over their course, come to include most of the adult men of the community.

After community leaders have discussed a matter and reached a consensus about how to proceed, they communicate that to other members of the community for them to discuss, evaluate, and make suggestions of their own. After telling community members of the consensus reached by the village's leading men, one leader put it this way:

> I am telling you what the leaders have said and it is clear to you.
> You think this over and talk about it.
> The talk we leaders are putting forward, you see if it is good or not.
> You all evaluate (*sɨlɨp aŋ*) it and talk.

The leading men of the community formulate a plan through discussion, bring it to the community for further discussion, after which the leaders may meet again to revise the talk and perhaps each hold meetings with their own clans, and so and on and so forth.

Discussion ideally concludes when, after much examination, a plan of action is collectively approved by all the men in the community, who respond *o* ("yes") when asked if they are "of one mind, of one will" (*but esal aŋ*; <u>wanbel</u>). In effect, this agreed-on course of action is the collective "talk" (*gen*) or will of all. From self-determining participants who each speak and evaluate the speech of others there emerges a consensus, a common word, and a common will. Through the work of discussion—evaluating and suggesting, listening and speaking—participants work to constitute a collective in which all participate as self-determining agents.

But discussions frequently fail to realize this ideal. Even after rounds and rounds of discussion, some members of the community remain dissatisfied and aloof from community affairs.[18] They avoid going to meetings if they feel excluded, chastised, or pressed to do things they would rather not do. Recall Soŋgum's husband, who fled for the coast when talk of pigs was broached. When the process of discussion breaks down or when people disregard the announced plans of community leaders, the typical solution is more discussion. When people did not show up to work on the school at the start of the 2008 school year, the school board vice chairman explained to me that it was because he had failed to gain the agreement (*but esal aŋ*; <u>kamapim wanbel</u>) of community members. Follow-up discussions were held during which people could make suggestions and offer up their evaluations, all in an effort to formulate agreement. They too failed to produce results, and so discussions continued. "Dialogue, rather than closure," as Laurence Goldman (2003, 4) says of dispute among the Huli, is "the processual essence of this system."[19] Through these ongoing discussions, villagers work to forge an always unstable, partial, and temporary union of the wills of self-determining men—an anarchic collective.

Eventually, after much discussion the 2008 school year began without all the work being completed; the headmaster and teachers agreed to allow more time for people to finish the work, which they did by that August. As for the church anniversary celebration, community leaders ultimately found the pigs they needed a week before the event. They asked people to offer pigs as a way to secure god's blessings—as Tim among others had suggested—and several stepped forward. In my experience the collective projects of villagers generally did come off, but only after weeks and more often months of back-and-forth talking and listening—and then, there were seemingly always some like Soŋgum's husband who did not participate, asserting their self-determination by not listening. Listening plays a central role not only in the efforts of adult men to forge an anarchic collective but also when that collective fragments into a set of fractious, willful, self-determining factions.

Self-Determination and Mutual Aid: Holding Onto Talk

In the past, I was often told, the plans and projects currently organized through discussions were formulated in the men's houses (*bema yut*; <u>haus man</u>), where adult men would gather, share a meal, and come to agreement about joining forces in various endeavors. This was the true source of the power associated with the men's house, according to a few of my interlocutors.

Today too, many of the most important activities in people's lives only succeed with the support of others. Without pigs provided by others for bridewealth and gifts, without labor provided for building houses and schools, without the blessings of the Christian God and other spirits, people cannot realize the futures they desire. The point is implicit in a threat often made by community leaders: if people do not participate in community affairs, they will have to fend for themselves. As the headmaster of the school put it in a speech he gave in Nian, if parents do not complete the work on the school and pay the school fees for their children, "You'll be on your own" (yu yet nau).

In speaking of the value that people in the Yopno Valley place on self-determination, I do not mean to suggest that they desire autonomy or freedom, two terms often used synonymously with self-determination.[20] Not only is autonomy not a precondition for self-determination, often it is a threat to people's ability to effectively take control of their future. A major theme of the ethnography of Melanesia over the past several decades is what has been termed the relational or composite sense of personhood prominent in the region. In this relational view persons are not regarded as intrinsically autonomous beings, the kinds of individuals who populate much philosophy and social science in the European tradition. Rather, this Melanesian sensibility regards persons as intrinsically the product of others, embedded in a web of social relations that create and sustain them.[21] The self is seen to be constituted by others, it is dependent on others, and as a result it has obligations to others.

In line with this relational sensibility, the efforts of residents in the Yopno Valley to control their futures often involve sustaining and cultivating relationships with others: people in other clans, villages, and around the world. Of course, as we have seen, people do withdraw from community affairs and ignore the words of community leaders when they feel overburdened or simply do not want to participate. Sometimes a degree of autonomy is just what people are looking for when they escape to their forest houses or go live in nearby towns for a while. Children ignore their parents' dictates because they would rather be doing something else. Women return to their home villages at times because they want to end a marriage.[22]

But often, the point of withdrawing and disregarding the words of others is not necessarily to cut oneself off from others. It is often a form of protest that is meant to encourage others to modify their plans and demeanor. Withdrawal is not an end but a means: a way to get a husband to change his behavior or to get community leaders to take a different course of action. One of the few English words I regularly encountered in the Yopno Valley was "strike," which was frequently on the lips of a particular young man in Nian who was known as something of a hot-head. He would often threaten to go on strike from his position as the one and only preschool teacher in the village when others did something that upset him. On one occasion, for instance, a group of young men broke into his house late one night. The community leaders had not resolved the issue to his satisfaction, and so he told them they could find someone else to teach preschool: he was quitting. His aim in striking was not to enhance his autonomy by withdrawing from community life but to elicit a response from the community leaders, and it worked. They followed up on his complaint, resolving it to his satisfaction, and the young man continued in his job.

In contrast to what might be called an individualist view of self-determination—which holds up autonomy and self-sovereignty as ideals—a relational view of self-determination places emphasis on the support that people need and the added power they gain from working with others. It is self-determination through mutual aid, to use Pyotr Kropotkin's (1902) expression. As Kropotkin saw it, the support individuals provide to one another is an essential factor in both biological and social evolution. Sociality is a source of power that enables animal species, including humans, to survive and thrive in a harsh environment.

In much the same way, a relational view of self-determination stresses the role of others' aid and support as a source of power that enables people to realize the futures they desire. This relational sensibility is prominent in a number of areas of Yopno life. It is evident in the erstwhile functioning of the men's houses and the practice of discussion today, as I have noted—and as we see later, it is there in the ways people ritually engage with the Christian God and forest spirits, which provide much-needed support for people's endeavors.

One of the most striking ways this relational ethos is institutionalized is in the relationship of "partner clans," known as *gapma-gapma* in Yopno. Every patrilineal clan in the Yopno Valley is paired with another, which is termed its *gapma*.[23] These clans reciprocally serve as representatives of each other's clan spirits—they are each other's "gods" (*koŋ*; got), as people say. Before embarking on major endeavors, people seek their *gapma*'s approval. So, for instance, the first fruits of new gardens and pandanus harvests go to one's *gapma* to ensure the future fruitfulness of one's gardens and pandanus orchards.[24] One's partner clan is the "road of blessings" (*gɨsam dakwon kosit*): if it supports your endeavor—planting a new garden, for instance, or arranging a child's marriage—then that endeavor will be blessed; if it does not, the project will fail. In essence, people cannot control their future without the support of their *gapma*, and so they seek their *gapma*'s agreement before any major endeavor.

This relational sense of self-determination also permeates people's efforts to secure the support of actors and institutions hailing from outside the valley. Laments about the lack of state services are a routine part of speeches and discussions in the valley. As evidence of state neglect, people point to the shrinking number of poorly stocked health posts, the abandoned police outpost and jail, the lack of roads and electricity, and the decades-old, cracked, and unreliable pipes that deliver water to public spigots in the villages of the valley (most of which were installed by the development wing of the Lutheran church). In these complaints, the lack of involvement of the state and other powerful organizations in their lives is held to be a prime reason for the poverty and backwardness of the region.[25]

There is even some nostalgia for the colonial era and a sense that people in the Yopno Valley missed out on the opportunities for development that colonialism afforded other parts of Papua New Guinea. People in the region did not experience much of the domination and exploitation that were part of the colonial experience elsewhere in Papua New Guinea and the world. Since the first patrol through the region by colonial officials in the 1930s, the Australian administration largely neglected the area, doing little more than sending an officer on an annual patrol to collect demographic information, settle any court cases that came to his attention, and appoint village headmen, who had little authority. Some of the older people I spoke with spent time working on colonial-era copra plantations on the coast in their youth, but they returned home to their own land when they grew tired of that work. There is the occasional critical remark about Australians' sense of superiority, based on people's past experience with bosses and teachers outside the valley. But generally, complaints about the colonial and postcolonial era concern the region's neglect and the notable lack of state support.

And so, people in the valley look to cultivate relationships with other powerful actors and institutions from outside the valley to gain support for their own endeavors. At the time of my research, a US-based conservation NGO was a major actor in the Yopno and neighboring valleys, having worked for years to monitor an endangered species of tree-kangaroo in the region, establishing a conservation area in 2009 to protect it. In return for local communities' support for their conservation efforts, they provide funding to educate teachers and run medical aid posts; they established a pilot kindergarten program and in 2014 were working to train enforcement officers and establish courts to administer the conservation area.[26] The title of Paige West's book (2006), set in another region of Papua New Guinea, fits the situation well: *Conservation Is Our Government Now*, a sentiment people have expressed approvingly to me on a number of occasions.

Despite the quasi-state-like role that the conservation NGO has adopted, people I spoke with were largely unworried that the NGO would become a domineering presence in their lives. When I expressed my concerns about the establishment of courts and enforcement officers to a village leader in Nian, he told me not to worry: "We Papua New Guineans have ways to sabotage such things, if we want." People tend to be more concerned that the conservation NGO will steal valuable sources of power found in their forests than that it will rob them of their autonomy, a point I return to in chapter 3.

In placing so much importance on the aid of actors from outside the valley— the state, the conservation NGO, the Lutheran church—some might see inklings of a "dependency complex" among people in the valley (Fanon [1952] 2008), the very opposite of the ethos of self-determination I attribute to them.[27] But self-determination and the support of others are not necessarily opposed to one another. Many turned to the conservation NGO in an effort to realize their own goals—to ensure that there would be animals on their land to hunt in the future, to solidify their ownership of parcels of forest, or to obtain scholarships for their children to enroll in teachers' training college. In seeking to determine their own future, people look to outside actors and institutions that can provide support for their endeavors.

At the same time, these outside actors and institutions—the Lutheran church, government schools, and the US-based conservation NGO—rely heavily on the support of locals for their own activities in the valley. Community members supply the land, labor, and many of the resources used to build schools and aid posts, and they support their staff by giving them housing, food, firewood, and garden land. Churches are built by community members using their own resources on their own land; their workers are supported by gifts of food from the communities they serve, and they also use housing, garden and forest land provided by these communities. The conservation NGO requires permission from local landowners to traverse the forests, the help of locals to carry equipment, and the agreement of landowners to pledge the land that makes up the conservation area.

Much like collaborations among villagers in building schools and hosting celebrations, collaborations with outside organizations are managed through the sort of discussions introduced in the previous section. When I first arrived in Nian village, I participated in what I now assume was a discussion of this sort. I explained the research that I hoped to do in the village, people asked me a few questions, and mostly they talked among themselves before agreeing to allow me to live in the village. The conservation NGO operating in the valley, the Papua New Guinean state, and the Lutheran church are all regularly the subject of discussions too. When agents of these organizations solicit the support of villagers, people gather to discuss whether to put aside land for conservation, to support the building of new schools, or to accept church workers in their communities. Evaluative listening is a key mode in which people assert their self-determination, weighing the proposals of actors and organizations from outside the valley— agreeing to the ones they support, rejecting or ignoring the ones they do not.

But there is more to the act of evaluation than indicated by my description so far. It is not enough merely to evaluate the proposals of others: to assert control over their future, people need to evaluate these proposals *well*. Let me illustrate what that means with an example. One of the abiding hopes of many in the valley is that a resource extraction company will find something of value there, such as gold, natural gas, or oil. In rural parts of the country, mining and natural gas projects are among the few opportunities for the kinds of development and wealth that many desire. Of course, projects like this rarely live up to expectations for many local landholders, and the conservation NGO has sought to tamp down this interest by pointing to all the bad effects of resource extraction, using a nickel-cobalt refinery built by a Chinese corporation not far from the Yopno Valley as an example of the misery that mining-related development can bring.[28] At the site of the plant, locals were displaced from their land, had their gardens and fishery polluted, and were subject to the violence of workers.[29]

But the Yopno people with whom I talked about this refinery rarely criticize the corporation that runs it or the Papua New Guinean government, which pushed for the project. As the tale is told, responsibility for the misery of the locals lies in the hands of the locals themselves: they did not understand what their agreement to this project would entail, thinking only of the money and jobs they would receive. This is not an entirely accurate version of how the project came about; in fact, residents protested the refinery and undertook legal efforts to prevent it. But this version points up the importance that my interlocutors place on the work of listening and evaluating the proposals of others. It was the failure of those in surrounding communities to evaluate the mining-related proposals well—to fully understand what they entailed—that is the source of their misery.

At a conservation gathering in Nian village, one young conservation worker from the nearby village of Isan made this point to his audience: "We have to be clear about this. You want to agree to some big mining exploration, be careful. They'll give you a forty-page contract to read and sign. We're Papua New Guineans! We aren't going to finish those forty pages. . . . You'll thrill at the prospect of money and say, 'OK, I'll sign.'"

One of the greatest threats to people's self-determination, as the NGO worker pointed out, is their inability to evaluate the words of others well. Evaluation is an assertion of self-determination, as we saw in the previous section. By weighing the options and coming to agreement in the course of discussions, people take control of their future. But when done poorly—when people do not understand the options that they were given and their ramifications—listeners risk surrendering control of their future.

Here, in the words of the conservation worker, a third practice of anarchic listening comes into play. As the conservation worker put it at the conclusion of his speech, "I've raised a major bit of talk that we all need to hold onto." To listen well and carefully evaluate the proposals of others, people must hold onto (*abɨdaŋ*; holim pas) the good advice and instruction of others.[30] Warnings, explanations, and advice like that offered by the conservation worker are tools that can help listeners evaluate others' words more carefully in the future, enabling them to bring about the future that they desire.

In a way, holding onto the words of others is the opposite of disregarding them, the first practice of listening discussed in this chapter. One way that people shame those who have disregarded others' words is to use the expression, "You've taken what they've said and left it where?" (*yaŋ dainɨ pɨkɨ paga jipgwan yopmek ekwaŋ*). In this idiom, the listener is presented as quite literally not holding onto talk. Talk is "taken" (*paga*) as one takes a physical object, and it is "left" or "placed" (*yopmaŋ*) somewhere: it is mislaid or lost. The talk is not with the listener anymore, as it would be if he or she had held onto it. As two ways of talking about listening, "holding onto" and "leaving behind" speech form a pair that coalesce around the sense that listeners actively handle speech, either holding it in mind, as it were, or mishandling and losing it.

Although opposed to one another in this way, both holding onto and disregarding the talk of others play a central role in people's efforts to assert and defend their self-determination. Disregarding talk does so in a way that is relatively clear, in line with a prevailing view of anarchic politics that privileges the subversion of authority. By contrast, holding onto the talk of others is less obviously anarchic in spirit. Yet, it too plays a vital part in Yopno listeners efforts to sustain their self-determination. Just as material forms of mutual aid help people to realize the futures they want, so too do the verbal advice, guidance, and expertise provided by others—if listeners hold onto it.

As part of a relational view of self-determination, control over one's future requires holding onto the words of others as well as disregarding them. The trick—the art of anarchic listening—is knowing what to disregard and what to hold onto. Should one be wary of the offers of mining companies, as the NGO worker advises? Or should one be wary of the advice of the NGO worker, who might be steering people away from the wealth they could possess?

There is much at stake in the act of listening, as we have seen in this chapter; both the listener's future and their control over it hinge on listening well. But anarchic listening is not a straightforward activity. To secure one's self-determination in a world of powerful and ambitious others requires the use of diverse practices of listening: disregarding, evaluating, and holding onto the words of others especially. The art of anarchic listening is employing the right practice of listening for the context.

The Pragmatics of Anarchic Listening

The three practices of listening I introduced in this chapter are interconnected with one another, each playing a role in sustaining the anarchic character of politics in the Yopno Valley. None is sufficient on its own. Disregarding the words of others is an important way in which people cut would-be leaders down to size, but to merely ignore the words of others is to overlook proposals and advice that could help realize the future one desires. Evaluating the words of others is a way to see how the suggestions and proposals of others align (or do not align) with one's own interests, desires, and understandings, but there is the danger that one will evaluate others' words poorly, misunderstanding the implications of what they propose. Holding onto the words of others is a way to improve one's understanding and become a more effective evaluator and actor, but this too has its dangers: holding onto the words of community leaders and others can lead one, effectively, to become their slave, if one does not hold onto the good advice and ignore the bad.

Listening well and realizing the future one desires require the use of all these practices of listening in different contexts. This is the pragmatics of anarchic listening: using the right mode of listening in the proper context. Employing the appropriate mode of listening helps listeners ward off those who would take advantage of them, thereby maintaining and even enhancing their control over the future. In the chapters to come, we will explore in more detail this pragmatics of anarchic listening as people in the valley think and talk about it.

And talk about it they do. The anarchic politics of Yopno villages has a way of bringing into focus the power and political significance of listening. Where people readily disregard the words of others and "follow their hearts," it is listening—even more than speaking, at times—that stands out as a communicative activity freighted with power. Albert Hirschman (1970) draws a distinction that is useful for understanding the significance of listening here. He distinguishes between two possible ways that citizens, customers, and members of organizations can respond to a situation they are dissatisfied with. They can speak up and try to remedy the situation (i.e., use their voice). Or they can vote with their feet; that is, they can exit.

Voice is obviously an important and much-discussed facet of political communication in many parts of the world (see the introduction for a more detailed discussion of this point). And it is also important in the Yopno Valley. But exit is a notably conspicuous political strategy there as well, as we have seen. Withdrawing from collective activities or simply disregarding them is a routine way people assert their self-determination. And where exiting is an important mode of exercising political agency, listening comes conspicuously into view as a political activity of significance: under such conditions, people exercise political agency quite visibly through the way they listen to—or do not listen to—the proposals and dictates of others.

In a discussion of John Austin's (1962) account of speech acts—actions performed using speech and, seemingly, speech alone (e.g., making promises, giving orders)—Judith Butler (1997) makes the important point that many of the speech acts discussed by Austin derive their force from the backing of powerful institutions: "I now declare you man and wife," "I give and bequeath my watch to my brother," "I sentence you to ten years." Indeed, Austin's typology of different speech acts include a fair number that draw on the state and other powerful institutions to give force to their utterance, including verdicatives (e.g., acquit, convict), exercitives (e.g., appoint, excommunicate), and commissives (e.g., contract, consent). These acts are not only verbal but also are fundamentally institutional in nature. They are carried out by duly authorized agents of institutions (a point emphasized in Bourdieu 1991), and they concern statuses, obligations, and rights that are bestowed and secured by institutions.[31] As such, the agency of the utterer of many of Austin's speech acts is parasitic on an elaborate institutional apparatus that both speakers and addressees are bound up in. In short, the notion that "saying it can make it so" (see Austin 1962, 7) is a view of linguistic agency that owes a great deal to a decidedly non-anarchic political context.

In the absence of such institutions or in a context in which their power is limited, the focus in a discussion of speech acts needs to attend more closely to listeners and to how *they* do things with words. In the anarchic environment of Yopno village politics, how listeners' listen—how they evaluate, disregard and hold onto the words of others—is quite palpably a matter of political significance; it is a way in which people shape their collective futures. That makes the pragmatics of listening not only a matter of academic interest but also a vital concern of people in the Yopno Valley.

SELF-DETERMINATION IN A WORLD OF UNCERTAINTY

Repetition is a conspicuous feature of Yopno public discourse and one that is often remarked on. Community leaders repeat the same announcements day after day, encouraging people to participate in community work, to prepare pigs for upcoming events, and to show up for more community meetings where the same topics will be discussed again at length. Even as community leaders make the same announcements again and again, they publicly bemoan their own repetitiveness. "I've spoken to you about the construction work that needs to be done on the school so many times, I won't say it again," a school headmaster announced to people in the plaza of Nian village. And a week later he was back there, making the same announcement.

Repetitiveness is a part of the churchgoing experience as well. At the end of Sunday service, people exit the church and gather outside to smoke, chew betelnut, and listen to announcements from church and community leaders. More often than not, one of these leaders will start by rehashing the sermon that everyone has just heard. Or, perhaps I should say, they rehash the sermon that everyone should have heard but undoubtedly failed to pay attention to. These sermon reruns are typically peppered with comments about how the people who had just sat through the church service failed to hear what was going on in that service; or, having heard the sermon twenty minutes earlier, they had already forgotten what was said.

Here is how one sermon rerun began on Ascension Sunday in 2009, the day in the church calendar that marks Jesus's ascent into heaven. We had all just piled out of the church into the village plaza where there was to be a performance marking the holy day. But first, a lay leader from the church began to quiz us:

> We just heard about the time Jesus went to heaven. What did Jesus say to his disciples at that time? You come out of the church, and you've already forgotten what you heard inside? I see. . . . Have we just heard the gospel inside or not? We come outside and already we've forgotten. We don't want to come outside and forget, so let's hear again outside what we've just heard inside.

With that, he began to rehash the sermon.

The concern that drives the postchurch sermon rerun is the same concern that drives so much repetition in Yopno discourse: leaders worry that listeners are ignoring them. And as we saw in the last chapter, they are right to worry. The repetition that pervades community announcements is offered to get people to hold onto (*gen abɨdaŋ*) the words of others—to listen, remember, and act on what they have heard. Indeed, this is explicitly stated by church leaders in a mantra that often accompanies the reiteration of a sermon: "These are important words we've heard. Let's hold onto them!" (*Gen madep nandamaŋ. Un abɨdoneŋ*).

In the previous chapter, I claimed that holding onto the words of others plays a major role in the Yopno art of anarchic listening. But the efforts of church and community leaders to get people to hold onto their words can make the practice seem anything but anarchic. By holding onto others' words, listeners are influenced by them; their thoughts and actions are reshaped by them. To hold onto the words of community and church leaders is, in effect, to allow them to colonize one's consciousness, as Jean and John Comaroff (1991) described it. As the Comaroffs along with many other scholars of Christianity emphasize, missionization has played an important role in the European colonial endeavor, undermining traditional ontologies and knowledge practices while molding subjects fit for colonial and capitalist modernity by introducing new ones.[1]

And indeed, the efforts of Yopno church leaders to get listeners to hold onto the Christian message *is* explicitly aimed at transforming the subjectivity of listeners—to bring it into line with Christian doctrine. In that respect, holding onto the words of others seems to undermine rather than advance listeners' power and self-determination. By holding onto the Christian message, listeners surrender their "conceptual self-determination," to borrow Viveiros de Castro's (2015a, 41) apt expression.

But as I hope to show in this chapter, holding onto others' words is indeed an essential facet of anarchic listening in the valley, although one that is not without its dangers. To appreciate why, we need to turn to an epistemology that is pervasive in the Yopno Valley, which emphasizes the opacity of reality to untrained human perception. From an early age, people learn that reality is deeply enigmatic, and humans are liable to misunderstand the nature of the world around them. This epistemology and the sense of uncertainty it engenders have a formative impact on political life in Yopno villages. And they render the work of holding onto the words of others essential if listeners are to secure their self-determination.

A Culture of Uncertainty

I first began to appreciate the role of uncertainty in Yopno political life when I started to ask about men's houses (*bema yut*). In many Melanesian communities, men's houses historically were hubs of political and religious life.[2] In addition to being the prototypical space for discussion of everyday concerns, they were the sites in which young men were trained in ritual and mythological esoterica and where older men came into contact with sacred sources of power.

As the commonly used anthropological term indicates, "men's houses" typically divided communities along the lines of gender and age. Before Lutheran missionaries arrived in the 1920s, they were the prime educational institutions in the valley, where men trained young boys in the skills and knowledge that would make them successful gardeners, fathers, hunters, and warriors.[3] Women and young children were not permitted to participate in these activities and were not supposed to know the many power-giving secrets transmitted to male youth in the men's houses. They were also expressly forbidden from learning about the powerful spirits that lived around the *bema*, which were a source of men's power.

But my efforts to understand the cosmology that was formerly transmitted in the *bema* repeatedly hit a roadblock. The first story people typically shared with me when I started asking about the men's houses was not about spirits, magical power, or the ancestral founders of these institutions, but about deception. In the past, I would be told, the ancestors claimed that there was a spirit in the men's house, evidenced by its cries for food, which terrified the women and children. The men would tell them that the spirit was hungry and that they should bring pigs for it to eat. But in truth, the storyteller would mirthfully tell me, the cries of the spirit were made by men turning a bullroarer unseen by women and children, who were kept away from the men's houses by the tall fencing that surrounded them. The pig that was brought to appease the spirit was in fact destined for the men in the men's house to eat.

In a wonderful twist on my efforts at salvage anthropology, the erstwhile cultural practice I sought to dig into was revealed to me to be, in fact, a fraud. Traditional beliefs in spirits and magical power, as well as the institution that played a significant role in organizing social life, all turned out to be nothing more than a deception perpetrated by some men hungry for pork. The story certainly could be taken as an indication of the hold that Christianity has over present-day histori-cal consciousness, framing the heathen ancestors as practicing a "religion" that was nothing more than a fraud. Indeed, the Lutheran mission did expend great effort to undermine the men's houses, instructing the men to burn the sacra housed in them and to toss powerful relics into the Yopno River. The humorous story of the men's house thus sounds like what we might expect, given the effects of missionization and the later influence of Western-style education, which both deliberately sought to undermine local knowledge throughout the region.

But this story of the deception that lies at the heart of the men's house is not unique to the Yopno Valley, nor is it of particularly recent vintage. In an account of the Gahuku-Gama in the Highlands of Papua New Guinea, Kenneth Read tells of a flute that was used to deceive the women of the community. The women were told that the sounds it produced were the calls of the sacred *nama* birds, which in fact do not exist. "The secrecy surrounding the flutes, even the penalty of death extracted in the past, are thus designed to prevent women from learn-ing the truth. 'Should they know,' the men explained, 'they would laugh at us'" (Read 1952, 6). Secrecy and deception—and the powers they yield to men—are a recurring theme in discussions of Melanesian men's houses.[4] Perhaps, then, it is not Christianity that destroyed the cosmology transmitted in the men's house. Perhaps, the men's house was indeed founded on deception, having only one se-cret at its core: the secret that the spirits do not really exist.[5]

But my impression of the men's house shifted again after I started to have trou-ble sleeping. At the time, I was living in a house built on the site of a former *bema* in Nian. That the community housed a Lutheran church worker and his family, as well as me, in this space initially reinforced my sense that the spirits of the men's house were indeed a ruse. Why permit outsiders—especially Lutheran church workers—to live in an area if it was a hub of spiritual powers? But a few days after mentioning to a friend that I was not sleeping well, he showed up in my house with materials to ward off the spirit of the men's house (*koŋ*). It was that spirit, he explained to me, that was the likely cause of my sleeping troubles.

The easy dismissal of the men's house spirits I was initially presented with had suddenly given way to talk about the spirit of the *bema* as if it were present and af-fecting my sleep. Indeed, in the following months, people began telling me of mem-bers of the community who continue to feed these spirits in the hopes of gaining power from them to win card games, harm others, or succeed in school. I was told this is why members of the community had located churches and the houses of missionaries on these particular plots of land: the church and its leaders were the ones who could keep the spirits in check and keep people from feeding them.

The story of men deceiving women in the past was looking more and more like a story used to deceive me in the present. Yet, even if the original story I was told about the *bema*—in which it was part of an elaborate ruse to obtain pork—were not true, it did seem to have at least a nugget of truth in it: deception does in fact lie at the heart of the men's house. So, perhaps the initial dismissal of spirits I had encountered was merely a way of masking an underground but still vital indigenous ontology. Perhaps.

But, as I kept asking about the men's house, new answers emerged. A few months later, an older man who was widely respected in the community explained to me that the power of the men's house was really the power of a group of men sharing a single will or mind (*but esal*), an explanation I heard from several others in the years that followed. The "spirit" was indeed a deception—or, perhaps we might say, the spirit was the apotheosis of the power of men working together. Was this finally the true secret of the men's house, was this itself a deception, or was this just an idiosyncratic view?[6]

That is a question to which I do not have an answer. In the end, I did not discover what the real truth of the men's house was, if there is such a thing. Instead, I received a lesson in the way uncertainty is fostered in daily life in the valley. In part, the dizzying variety of accounts of the men's house I encountered are undoubtedly the consequence of a recent history in which people have been confronted with a variety of moral and ontological frameworks—Christian and ancestral, esoteric and exoteric—that raise new questions and provide new solutions. In this "postcultural" condition, as Ryan Schram (2018, 18) has termed it, where people "cannot orient themselves toward either a past horizon of tradition or a future horizon of modernity," uncertainty abounds.[7]

But there also seems to be nothing particularly new about this condition in Melanesia. Ethnographers have long been confronted by the fragmentary, incoherent, and even contradictory character of people's ontologies there. In the words of Roy Wagner (1984, 147), "The play of ambiguity (and often ambivalence), innovation, and nescience in Melanesian culture generally is established ethnographic fact." In a now distant debate over "misconstrued order in Melanesian religion," Ron Brunton (1980, 112) noted some of the challenges facing the ethnographer who seeks to uncover *the* indigenous religious system: "informants appear uninterested in topics about which they might have been expected to have very definite views; people contradict themselves and each other and appear unconcerned when this is pointed out; there may be a high rate of ritual obsolescence and innovation." The question at the heart of the debate was the way in which order could be found in this apparent disorder, the assumption being that there was some principle of coherence that just needed to be found.[8]

To this, Dan Jorgensen offered an alternative view that grew out of his research on the men's house at Telefolip. In the Telefol men's house, an initiate progresses through a series of initiation grades, learning in each one that what he was told previously was wrong or incomplete. At the end of the initiation process, in which again people learn that everything they had learned up to that point was wrong, Jorgensen (1981, 490) suggests that the lesson they walk away with is that "men cannot be certain of what they know except for the certainty that their knowledge will always be incomplete and perhaps mistaken."[9]

Thus, what initiates gain is not a coherent ontology or cosmology but a deep sense of uncertainty that such a thing exists and an awareness of their own lack of knowledge. This was very much my experience in trying to understand the truth of the Yopno men's house. As I hope to show in this chapter, a similar sense of uncertainty and feelings of incomprehension are vital elements of Yopno people's sense of self. Theirs is a self that senses its own epistemological limits, its ignorance, the possibility that its cosmologies and ontologies may be misguided: it is a self that continues to look—and listen—for better, truer, and more powerful insights.[10]

Today in the Yopno Valley, this sense of uncertainty and feelings of incomprehension are no longer generated in the men's house in the way Jorgensen describes for Telefolip, if they ever were. Rather, they are cultivated through a wide range of discursive activities: "myths," dream interpretations, sermons, and school lessons, to name a few. These are the sort of discursive materials that ethnographers have long looked to as sources for people's beliefs, concepts, or ontologies. Here, however, I show how these are sites where a deep-seated sense of uncertainty is produced—an uncertainty that, as Michael Cepek (2016) notes, complicates contemporary efforts to find order in the alternative ontologies (Kohn 2015), metaphysics (Viveiros de Castro 2015b), cosmologies (Cadena 2010), and concepts (Skafish 2011) found among peoples supposedly living outside the ambit of Western modernity. The ontological security (Giddens 1991) presumed in many accounts of indigenous ontologies too often sidesteps the role of doubt and uncertainty in cultural life. Certainly, discursive practices embody their practitioners' beliefs and ontologies. But as Nils Bubandt (2014) observes, these practices may also bring beliefs and ontologies into question, spotlighting doubt and uncertainty as matters of cultural significance.

Here, it is not a distinctive Yopno ontology or belief that is the focus of our attention. It is the way, just as in the Telefol men's house, that multiple, conflicting representations of reality routinely circulate together, producing the impression that reality is something hard to pin down—and in the process, producing a subjectivity that is uncertain, aware of its lack of understanding, and open to new and better ways of seeing the world.[11] It is within this culture of uncertainty that the insights and knowledge of others are rendered something worth holding onto.

The Opacity of Reality in a Multiplicity of Perspectives

For people in the Yopno Valley, reality is, in significant ways, difficult to grasp. Witchcraft and sorcery (*sot mawom*; <u>poisen sanguma</u>) are taken to be the cause of most illnesses and deaths, but who the perpetrators are or what the reasons for their attacks might be are rarely evident. Specialists must be brought in to try to divine the causes and provide remedies, but even then uncertainty often lingers. On returning to Nian in 2015, for example, I learned that a middle-aged friend of mine had died unexpectedly. His family hired a specialist who laid blame for the death on a bespelled betelnut given to him by a man in the village. The family demanded compensation from the man and burned down two of his forest houses when they did not receive it. The accused man sought out a specialist himself, ultimately finding one far off in a neighboring valley who could explain what really happened. According to this specialist, the death was the result of a curse from God for wrongdoings committed by the dead man himself. Of course, that second opinion did not resolve the matter. During the following month, I heard several other theories circulating in the community—some vague, some quite specific. But there was no consensus and little certainty.

Curses (*jobɨt*) too afflict people for a variety of often cryptic reasons, from the misdeeds of their ancestors to failing to care for a person's cat (the latter was supposedly the reason why one father bestowed a curse on his adult son). At times, curses are publicly announced in a way that is hard to miss, yet more often the source and reason for a curse lie unseen, with possibilities ranging from the actions of long-deceased ancestors to acts that upset co-villagers unbeknownst to the actor. The result is that a great deal of uncertainty surrounds the cause of most misfortunes. After the young son of the school headmaster in Nokopo died, some suggested his death was the result of an ancestral curse while others claimed it was the result of sorcery or witchcraft perpetrated by people in the village. Disagreements festered and the headmaster left the village, certain his son was the victim of witchcraft but unsure who was responsible.

Adding to the atmosphere of uncertainty is the fact that it is assumed that people hide their true thoughts and feelings about their neighbors, masking the anger and jealousy that drive occult and patent violence, and sickness as well.[12] Uncertainty also surrounds the histories that people tell today of their ancestors' long-ago migrations into the valley, which are central to clans' claims to ownership of land. Different clans often tell quite different histories, and people frequently expressed to me their uncertainty and their concerns that they do not have the knowledge they need to support their claims to land ownership. This is not to mention the colonial legacy that has increased the list of actors whose natures are inscrutable: the Christian God, missionaries, government representatives, a US-based conservation NGO, and, of course, anthropologists.

And then there are the spirits that fill the forests and haunt the men's houses. Like other obscure beings that are hard to perceive in everyday life, spirits are most often encountered in verbal representations, particularly so-called myths (which I call "historical narratives" because they are told as histories of events that actually occurred).[13] These verbal representations play an important role in generating the perception that these spirits—and reality more generally—are opaque to human perception. That is, the sense that reality is difficult to grasp is in large measure an effect of how these narratives are constructed and of how discourse is structured more generally.

Key to this effect is what I have elsewhere called a "play of perspectives" (Slotta 2014): the presentation of multiple perspectives on the same reality. Historical narratives commonly feature characters who take one perspective on reality, only to discover that it is fundamentally wrong before gaining a new understanding of the situation they find themselves in. Narrators tack back and forth between characters' perspectives and a more omniscient view of the situation, generating tensions that get worked out over the course of the narrative as the protagonist gains a better understanding of reality or deals with the consequences of his or her misunderstandings.

As an illustrative example, consider the widely known history of a demon baby who once terrorized the village of Ganggalut. This version of the narrative was told to me by Yaŋ, a friend in Nian who is related through his mother to people in the village of Ganggalut. The demon continues to terrorize people today, and Yaŋ explained to me that he was the appropriate person to tell me this history because his family connection to the village where the demon is from allows him to speak of it without endangering himself or me.[14]

> A long time ago, this ancestral spirit of Ganggalut (*kukup kɨdat*) existed as just a little baby. . . . Two women, his mother and her sister, looked after him. . . . but he never put on weight and grew. . . . Those who were born at the same time had grown up and gone out of the house. [Babies and their mothers traditionally remained in the birth house until the baby is a month or so old.] But this baby did not.
>
> Its mother and her sister looked after him, but they were getting frustrated. They wanted to go out and get food from the garden. So, they put him in a net bag and left the house. He watched them as they left. Quietly he got out of the bag and went up to the shelf where they kept bows and arrows. He held a bow and arrow [which are used for sorcery]. He put on a loincloth [the clothing of adult men]. He covered himself

with black earth [a decoration used by sorcerers]. He put on a bark-cloth cape, a necklace of pigs' teeth, all sorts of things. He came out, gently opening the door and closing it, and then opening and closing the door of the fence. He went quietly. He went to a house, attacked the people inside with sorcery, and quietly came back and went into his house, putting his implements back on the shelf. He got back into the bag, and he turned into a little baby. He defecated and dirtied himself with piss and poop, and he slept. He heard the two women come and open the gate, then the door, talking and making noise, so he started to cry hard. He cried hard, so they opened the door, came in and cleaned up his poop and fed him. One of them fed him, and one got firewood and made a fire. She cooked food, and the other ate and fed him. They put him back in his bag and he slept.

That's what they would do. When they wanted to go to the garden, they would feed him and put him back in his bag and leave him. After they left, he would watch them go far away, and he would go get his sorcery bow and arrow, put on his loincloth, come out and go do his sorcery. When he was done, he would go inside and go back in his bag and sleep. When he went and attacked people, they used magic to figure out who was doing this by following his footsteps. They came to his door and blamed the women there. The women would reply, "There are no men here [men would be the potential sorcerers]; this is a women's house we live in."

That's how things went. One time the two women hid a little girl in the entrance room of the house in the middle of a big bundle of firewood. They secretly covered her with kindling and left her standing in the entrance room. They played a trick and covered her like that and left her standing there and went inside. They took their bags, fed the baby, and left. They told the little girl and left to go to the garden. Quietly the young girl stood in the entranceway and watched. The young man in the bag was sleeping when he heard the people leave. Hearing that, he got out of his bag quietly and went again to the shelf. He went and put on his bark cape, put on his loincloth, he took his bow and arrow, came down and opened the door, came out, turned, and closed it. He went down, opened his gate, came out, turned, and closed it. He went to do his sorcery. He returned before it got light, went, and closed the gate again just like it had been. He went up, turned, and closed the house door just as it had been and went back into the bag.

The young girl stood in the veranda and watched. She watched him as he did that and went back into the bag. The two women came and opened the gate, and he started crying again. He was sitting there, dirtied with piss and poop. They went to the entryway, pretending to go put firewood away. The little girl who stood there came to the door: "That person is tricking us. He actually goes and attacks people, and then comes back and sleeps. Those who have tried to figure this out are led to our house, they accuse us, and what can we say? Just now, I saw what is going on. He tricks us and goes around doing sorcery and comes back and sleeps."

"He has done this while we care for him," his mother said, and she went up into the house and started a fire and sat down. The baby cried, and she left him and got the fire going. She went and got him out and held him. She held him and sat there. His mother said to him: "Sugar cane. *Kamdat* sugarcane." He thought to himself: "She's going to take off the skin of some sugar cane she brought from the garden and give it to me." She held out the *kamdat* sugarcane. "You pretend to be a little baby and sleep in the house, but then you go out and kill lots of people and come back and sleep. They try to figure out who is doing this, and they keep coming to our house. They follow the footsteps and ask us, and we don't know what to do. Just now we saw it was you." That's what she told him. With the sugarcane she hit him on his head and broke it open. He died. With his bones, they take the bones of this one who was killed and use them for sorcery. They still exist now.

We've reached the end of the story of my mother's ancestral spirit. My brothers and I, we do not tell the story of this spirit without a good reason. The spirit has good ears, so we don't tell this story lightly. Now, you want to record our story, so for that reason we have told it. The spirit of our mother, I have told its story. Just now someone died in Teptep who carried around a piece of the spirit's clothes. That's what killed him. He is a relative of Ganggalut. He is a relative of Teptep. The bones or whatever it was that he took around, he thought he was just using them to win at cards. He carried them around with him, and that's what killed him. It sought a victim, and when it did not find one, it killed its possessor instead.

A central organizing principle of many Yopno historical tales is the divergence between the characters' perspectives and that of the story's audience. This historical narrative does not mask who the baby is or what it is up to. Almost from the beginning, the audience is informed that the baby is in fact a sorcery-performing demon. But the story does require that audiences recognize that their knowledge of the baby is different from that of the characters in the story, particularly the women. For much of the story, the mother and her sister think they are living with an ordinary baby. It takes most of the rest of the story for these women to realize their misunderstanding and deal with the reality that confronts them.

But there are other divergent perspectives that form part of the structure of this narrative. The spirit thinks it is all alone in the house and goes off to practice sorcery in the fourth paragraph, but the audience and the women know that a little girl is hidden behind bundles of firewood. The spirit thinks it is going to get sugarcane in the second to last paragraph ("He thought to himself: 'She's going to take off the skin of some sugarcane she brought from the garden and give it to me.'"), but the mother has other plans for the "baby."

Turnabout is fair play in historical narratives. Like the two women, protagonists who are initially deceived by spirits often get their revenge or make their escape by deceiving the spirits in turn. A father in another historical tale has his eyes, thighs, and testicles eaten by a spirit after ignoring his son's warnings that a giant person who has visited their forest house is in fact a dangerous spirit. Seeing that he is next, the man's son manages to escape by tricking the forest spirit into letting him go out to the woods to defecate, at which point he runs away. Characters in these stories typically fail to understand the true nature of what is going on around them, but they also actively produce misunderstandings as part of their own plans. And the audience must track all the different perspectives on the unfolding action.

These narratives thus show little evidence of the "opacity of other minds" that has been described in other Oceanic communities.[15] In many other parts of Oceania, ethnographers have noted that there is little talk of others' thoughts or intentions, and people are reluctant to hazard guesses about them. When inquisitive ethnographers ask about the reasons behind a person's behavior, they are often given answers like "You'll have to ask them; I don't know what goes on in their mind." Others' minds are treated as opaque; their thoughts and perspectives are held to be inaccessible to outside examination. Rupert Stasch (2008, 446) describes a similar experience asking about characters' thoughts in Korowai myths:

> Very often when I interrupted someone's narration of a myth in order to ask why a character was doing something, the answer would be "He has his own thoughts" or "She has her own thoughts." Often, I would be told to "wait": the myth character's "thoughts" amount to a plan that the character knows will unfold, however odd the sequiturs of the elaborate narrated plot might be to me or other listeners. It is listeners' place to await the revelation of protagonists' intended logic. I also overheard narrators and listeners assert the opacity and autonomy of myth protagonists' thought in reply to interruptions from audience members other than myself.

The perspectives of characters in Korowai narrations are often opaque to the audience. In a kind of narrative "slow disclosure" (Ochs, Smith, and Taylor 1989), what is in the minds of the characters is gradually revealed to the audience over the course of the story.

Yopno historical tales, by contrast, require audiences to carefully track the perspectives of multiple characters—mothers, fathers, sons, spirits—and to share in the omniscient perspective provided by the narrator as well. The varied thoughts and perspectives of characters are essential to the architecture of these narratives; they are readily understood by audiences and often made explicit by narrators.

In a story a friend told me about his grandfather being deceived by a lake (again, a spirit), he spells out quite explicitly the state of mind of his grandfather. We are told that a lake is stalking my friend's grandfather because he was carrying a particular vine in his bag that one is not supposed to carry when near the lake. But though we as the audience know that this vine is in his bag, my friend's grandfather in the story does not realize it. And my friend makes sure to point this out to me—*udɨn yiknikwon soal kɨnda tawt un dɨma kek* ("He didn't realize that there was a vine in his bag"). It heightens the tension of the story: Will he or will he not realize in time that the vine is in his bag? The climax of the story occurs when he remembers just in the nick of time that he has the vine in his bag and then looks over toward where the lake normally is, only to discover it is not there because it is stalking him. He then throws the vine where the lake usually is and shouts, *"Nak dɨma kɨlɨt"* (Don't try to trick me!), at which point the lake returns to its usual place.

The mystery in a Yopno historical narrative is typically not about what a character is up to, but whether the character will realize in time the true nature of the situation they are in. The aforementioned father who had his body eaten by a spirit failed to do so and paid the price. His son pleads with him not to meet with the spirit, cries that they should run away, and is taunted by his father for it. The father seems to know something is up when the spirit, appearing in the form of a giant, shows up. The father at first tells the spirit to sit on his son's side of the fire, but he agrees to let the spirit sit next to him, in response to the spirit's request. The danger is obvious to the son and to the audience, and we watch to see whether the father will figure out what is going on. Unfortunately for him, he never does.

In these narratives, the sense that reality is opaque is produced by the audience's access to the characters' thoughts and perspectives. The audience sees that the characters do not see what it sees. The multiplicity of perspectives on reality both generates the narrative tension that drives many of these stories and cultivates a sense that there is more to reality than meets the eye.

But it is not simply the multiple perspectives on reality that produce a sense of reality's opacity. Viveiros de Castro (2015a, 2015b) highlights a "perspectivist" cosmology common in South America, which similarly involves a multiplicity of perspectives on the same reality. In this Amerindian "perspective on perspectives," different types of beings see reality differently because each has a different nature. What humans see as blood, a jaguar sees as manioc beer. What a human sees as a mud pit, a tapir sees as a grand ceremonial house. But this multiplicity of perspectives does not generate an "opacity effect"; reality does not seem hard to grasp within this perspectivist cosmology. Jaguars do not see reality any more or less clearly than do humans: rather, each being appears to inhabit its own reality (or an indeterminate reality; Nadasdy 2021). Much the same might be said of a kind of anthropological relativism that regards different perspectives on reality as equally valid: each culture has its own distinct view of the world, but no one of these views is more correct. Where different perspectives on reality are held to be equally valid, there may be multiple realities or multiple subjectivities—but there is no sense that reality itself is opaque.

In contrast, the multiple perspectives that permeate Yopno historical tales are not equally acceptable or appropriate to different characters: some prove to be more correct than others. The omniscient narrator generally provides a perspective to the audience early on in the telling that frames the other perspectives that appear later. Early on, we learn that the baby is a demon or that there is a vine in the grandfather's bag. The alternative perspectives of the characters that also appear in the narratives diverge from this omniscient perspective, and they prove to be incorrect or limited in one way or another, which becomes evident in the way the story unfolds. The baby is discovered to be a spirit; the vine is found in the bag. Often, characters' perspectives converge with that of the omniscient narrator as they figure out what is really going on. At times they do not, and then the characters suffer the consequences of their misunderstanding.

There is thus a moral and practical dimension to having the correct perspective that these stories emphasize. The wrong perspective inevitably gives rise to bad consequences (e.g., demons run free and eat people's eyeballs); in contrast, the correct perspective will save your own and others' lives. The value of a correct understanding of reality is gauged in these myths by the consequences that follow from having that knowledge. Better understanding leads to better outcomes.

The sense that reality is fundamentally opaque then emerges from these narratives as a result both of the multiplicity of perspectives contained within them and the presentation of one perspective as more correct than the others. The characters' difficulties in perceiving the *true* nature of their situations suggest to the audience that reality is hard to grasp, especially when it is filled with surreptitious spirits, deceptive actors, and intricate taboos. More than that, these narratives emphasize that having the right understanding matters: the characters' lack of understanding is a danger to themselves and others.

Although historical narratives emphasize the opacity of reality, they might also give the impression that this opacity is safely contained in the world of the narrative. After all, the dangers of opacity afflict characters in these historical narratives, but the audience remains secure in its omniscient grasp of reality. But as the end of Yaŋ's telling of the demon baby story makes clear, spirits are not confined to a separate mythical realm where things are fundamentally different from how they are in everyday life. These histories reveal important features of the world that the audience itself inhabits. The history of the demon baby is widely known and commonly referenced today because the spirit's bones and clothes continue to be used for sorcery. Narratives like this one are a prime source of the knowledge that people have about spirits that continue to have effects in the world; they reveal the hidden powers that lie inside ordinary seeming objects and landscapes encountered every day.

The stories thus not only depict a past world in which things are not as they seem but also reveal that the world inhabited by the audience is not what it seems. A bit of cloth, for instance, might actually be the diaper worn by the demon baby, which gets used for sorcery. A lake might contain a spirit, which will attack you if you carry vines near it. And like the characters in historical narratives, people continue to misunderstand the situations they are in. As Yaŋ notes at the end of the story, a person recently died because he used this spirit's relics ("He thought he was just using the relics to win at cards"). This person's failure to understand the true nature of the demon baby—its taste for blood—leads to his death.

These histories, then, are not idle or arcane tales set in another realm. They connect another unseen reality to the one familiar to the audience, and in the process the world of the audience is rendered opaque. As linguistic anthropologists have long insisted, historical tales should not be considered merely as narratives—"myths"—that reveal the "natives'" ways of thinking: they are vital instruments in social life.[16] In the Yopno Valley, they play an important role in acts of instruction, revelation, and reminding, conveying a hidden dimension of reality to listeners who do not know or have seemingly forgotten it. They are told so that the listener may hold onto them, gaining a better grasp on reality, avoiding danger and death, and taking greater control over their future—points we return to later in this chapter. But at the same time, they also make the opacity of reality a live issue for the audience itself.

An Education in Ignorance

Education is recognized as a lifelong process in the Yopno Valley. People enter the world as babies, wholly incapable of thought. They are idiomatically called *buruni mi* ("without a *but*," which designates the liver, the seat of thought and feeling).[17] As they mature, they develop the ability to listen and become subject to instruction through which their understanding is cultivated. But throughout life, people's mistakes and bad actions are chalked up to a lack of correct understanding; even adults are still in need of instruction. As the historical narratives suggest, a right understanding of reality is necessary to be an effective and an ethical actor.[18] Indeed, I was told many times that education in the workings of the world was important because it makes people into right-acting adults (*amɨn tai*; "good/proper people"). So, misdeeds, conflict, and imprudence—common elements of life in Yopno villages—are met with efforts to educate adults and children alike. The telling of historical tales like those in the previous section are one form that this education takes.

But if education is meant to help people better understand an obscure reality, it has an ironic side effect. The act of instruction itself is typically performed in a way that instills in listeners both a sense that reality is hard to grasp and an appreciation of their own deficient grasp of it. From an early age, people are exposed to instruction that distinguishes between two perspectives on reality: what "we think" is going on as opposed to what is actually going on. Such acts are explicitly thematized in a variety of domains of Yopno life but perhaps nowhere more regularly than in church services and school lessons, with their didactic objectives.

To get a sense of this structure, consider a typical school lesson offered to students in the preschool program in Nian village, which at the time of my research was part of the Tok Ples Pre-School (TPPS) program. These schools taught five- to seven-year-olds the basics of reading, math, and other subjects including Christianity before they started their formal education in primary school (grade 1). The curriculum was designed by a SIL Bible translator and his wife who had lived in the valley for decades and had produced an orthography, education materials, a New Testament translation, and other church texts, all in the Yopno language. The preschool teachers were local men and women of the community who had received limited pedagogical training. By the time I returned to the Yopno Valley in 2013, most of these preschools had been replaced by government-funded elementary schools, but even the government-run schools include lessons on Christian topics. It is safe to say that Christianity and school-based education are inextricably linked for people in the Yopno Valley.

To begin the lesson, the preschool teacher read the Bible verse chosen for that day, 1 Corinthians 3:16: "Don't you know that you yourselves are God's temple and that God's Spirit dwells in your midst?" He then offered an explanation of the text, using children in the class as examples:

> All the time, the Holy Spirit is inside us and it kneels and prays for us. It prays until it is tired. But we don't realize this. . . . Buse goes and tricks Samanda, who is upset and calls Buse a "dog."[19] The Holy Spirit inside of us is holding its stomach going "eeeeek" [noise of fear], "Samanda, Buse's name is not 'dog.'" His name is Buse." . . . Because Samanda has insulted Buse, the Holy Spirit is afraid and curls up in a ball. Because of Samanda's insult, it is deeply ashamed. Samanda has forgotten what he has done, and yet the Holy Spirit is kneeling and praying. It is still praying, and Samanda goes around and tricks Waindak. . . . And Waindak says, "Samanda, eat poop!" When he insults him, the Holy Spirit is watching and shaking with fear. Waindak forgets what he's done, and yet the Holy Spirit prays for Waindak. You all don't realize that you are the house of the Holy Spirit. Really, we don't recognize this. You forget this and do what you want. We insult each other. It says that you are the temple of God. God's Holy Spirit is inside of you. You don't realize it; that's what it says. It is true. When we do wrong, God's spirit is inside of us praying. We don't realize it, and so we continue to do wrong.

The explicit point of this lesson is that we should not call each other names because the Holy Spirit inside us is hurt by these things. But at the same time, children are also being taught that there is more to reality than meets the eye. The Holy Spirit lives inside of them, unbeknownst to them. Not realizing that it is there, they act in ways that upset it and put their own spiritual futures at risk.

This sort of instruction continues throughout people's lives. The same formulaic distinction between what "we see" or what "we realize" and what is really going on is a prime theme of Christian education directed at adults as well in weekly church services and occasional evening services held in people's houses. Indeed, we will see the same pattern of juxtaposed exoteric and esoteric perspectives recur in a host of other instructional and revelatory activities throughout the remainder of the book. Consider the following two examples, the first from a homily on 1 John 7–21 and the second from a homily on Matthew 14:22–33 (with the exoteric perspective in italics and the esoteric perspective in boldface):

> What can we do to make God appear in front of us? God is not going to come stand in front of us and say, "Look at me here!" Our friend next to us, who is that? That's our god. . . . We give them food, a flashlight,

fire, whatever they are looking for—who are we caring for? We are caring for God. *We think we're taking care of our friends*, but **we are taking care of God.** God will not come from up above and talk to us and
we worship God. God is with us.

> *We think about ourselves like this: "I do the job of the good news; I hear*
> *the gospel so I'm going to go to heaven. I act right so people praise me."*
> We think like that and put on airs like that. . . . But when Jesus comes,
> what will we do when he says, "Come!" **Can we walk on top of the**
> **water? No.** Why not? **What kind of people are we? We lack belief.**

The lessons of each homily differ. In the first, the lesson is that God is inside each
of us and that when we love each other we are also giving love and respect to God
(a regular theme of Christian instruction in the valley). In the second, the lesson is
that it is belief in God that leads to salvation, not how we act or what we do (a classic theme of Lutheranism). But there is a lesson common to both: what we think is
going on is not really what is going on. We think these are friends, but they are
really God. We think we will go to heaven due to our right actions, but we will not.

In the previous section, I noted that historical narratives often showcase a diversity of perspectives on reality, each held by different characters in the narrative. In the sort of instruction that we see in church services and school lessons,
in contrast, the diversity of perspectives on reality is highlighted in the very here
and now of communication. It is not the characters in the story who have different perspectives; it is the interactional participants themselves—speaker(s)
and listener(s)—whose perspectives are presented as differing.

More particularly, in acts of instruction, speakers' *esoteric* perspective is set
in contrast to their listeners' *exoteric* perspectives. In the common refrains, "We
don't see such and such" and "we don't understand such and such," the listener
learns that reality is opaque.[20] But more than that, they learn to doubt their own
understanding of it. In acts of instruction, people are recurrently told that things
are other than what they seem.

In some cases, listeners are not simply told they are confused; they are actively
made confused. Fostering confusion and uncertainty in audiences is a rhetorical
procedure that gives a valued sense of "depth" to public events. Beginning with a
puzzling object or verbal expression, a speaker goes on to reveal the metaphorical
or allegorical significance of this enigma. In one memorable event, the community of Nombo brought a small tree and placed it in the plaza of Ganggalut village, hanging gifts for a community fundraiser on it. Having never seen anything
like this, I asked what the tree was doing there. I got the response I received so
often when I asked for clarification of some particularly puzzling occurrence,
speech, or story: "Wait and we'll find out."[21]

Gift presentations, a frequent occurrence in Yopno villages, often involve this kind of rhetorical virtuosity. Audiences and recipients are enticed by the perplexity they generate. The initial confusion generated by an unlikely gift anticipates an explanation—a deeper significance (*mibɨlɨ*; "a basis, cause, or meaning") that lies below the surface, waiting to be disclosed. That was certainly the case with the gift-bedecked tree standing in the plaza, which generated a great deal of buzz as people gathered for the gift presentation. After a few minutes, the crowd quieted as a community leader from Nombo, Wandeyu, stepped forward to present the gifts and reveal to us the deeper significance suggested by the tree. Wandeyu explained that this particular kind of tree is known for bearing a fruit that attracts a large number of birds. In his speech, the tree served as a metaphor for education, which attracted the people of Ganggalut and led them to host the fundraiser to raise money to build an elementary school.

On another occasion, a visiting coffee buyer from the United States was presented with a pig's tusk necklace at the conclusion of a coffee-planting workshop, a gift the presenter identified with a bridewealth exchange. Enigmatically, the presenter handed the necklace not to the coffee buyer but to another man, telling him to place the necklace on the neck of the "young white woman" (*kwakŋɨ maŋat*)—even though the coffee buyer was obviously a young white *man*. The incongruous label clearly flummoxed the man who was translating these instructions from Yopno into Tok Pisin for the visiting dignitaries: "Take this and place it on the neck of . . . uh." Stumbling with the translation, another man then interjects, "*kwakŋɨ maŋat*" [the white woman], and the translator continued, "Place it on the neck of the white man. The gift presenter says, 'That's not a white man. That's a white woman.' You can put this on their neck." At this point, another man interjects, spelling out the metaphorical thrust of the presentation: "We are doing this to pay bridewealth for him/her." By "marrying" the American coffee importer, the community sets the stage for future gifts, wealth, and even "children" in return.

Initially puzzling and unexpected metaphorical relationships are clarified over the course of gift presentations like these. As a friend remarked to me afterward with evident satisfaction, the gifts given the coffee importer have "real meaning" (*mibɨlɨ toŋ*). The metaphorical links established in the way in which the gifts were presented generate a much-valued depth, playing on and reinforcing people's sense that the true significance of things lies below the surface.[22] Like historical narrations and the instruction that young people receive in school, these presentations carve reality into two planes. There is a surface that is obscure: a tree standing in the middle of the plaza, a man being called a woman. Then there are depths: a community flocking to education like birds to a fruiting tree, a coffee importer bound to the community like a bride to a husband's family that has paid bridewealth for her. The depths are what ultimately count. But they can only be appreciated with the guidance of others.

In gift presentations, it is the presenter's ingenuity at generating these depths that matters. The gift object they choose and the story they tell about it are both evaluated for their metaphorical meaningfulness. But a similar strategy of disorientation is also used in acts of instruction. On special occasions, a favorite device for instructing people in Christian knowledge is a skit (*wurop*; <u>drama</u>)—an allegorical tale with a didactic purpose enacted usually by young people (see figure 5). Although skits are meant to be instructive, they are often quite cryptic, requiring careful analysis to understand their import. Like the perplexing gift, the obscurity of these morality plays is a feature, not a bug. It gives audience members a palpable experience of uncertainty and of their own lack of knowledge, which sets them on the road to understanding. Acquiring knowledge, people emphasize, requires careful attention and analysis (*silip aŋ*), and the obscurity of these morality plays forces people to work at understanding what is going on.[23]

On Ascension Sunday in 2009, after listening to the sermon rerun that opened this chapter, the audience spread out around the village plaza of Wurap to wait

FIGURE 5.   Performers dressed in ancestral clothing for a skit.

Photograph by author.

for the skit that was the capstone of the day's celebration. Before the performance, six young girls entered the church grounds in three lines of two, with the girls in front dressed entirely in black and the girls behind dressed in white and carrying a bamboo torch. There were two other girls standing to the side, one dressed in black and the other in white, who were identified as "officers." As is typical in performances of this sort, before the play began the congregation chairman began priming the audience by asking questions about what they were going to see, reminding them that the activity they are expected to perform is *evaluation* (*sɨlɨp aŋ*; <u>skelim</u>): "What will these girls be wearing? We will see. What will they say? Let's evaluate it and see."

After all the girls were assembled, a titter worked its way through the audience, also a common feature in such performances; these were, after all, young girls known to all in the community who are dressed in a very unusual manner. The laughter was met with a stern rebuke. The congregation chairman reminded the audience again that their role was to analyze what was happening before them. But when the performance began, it was met with another roar of laughter, which elicited further criticism. The girls at the front of each of the three lines began marching, the first chanting "sin," the second "Satan," and the last "death." This continued for several minutes, at which point the officer dressed in white announced, "I am the light," and the three girls dressed in white standing behind the black-clad girls moved in front of them holding their torches. That was the extent of the skit.

After the girls' change of positions, the congregation chairman launched into a question-and-answer routine that guided the audience through an analysis of the tableau vivant they had just seen. The obscurity of skits often necessitates the intervention of a knowledgeable authority to help the audience make sense of what has just been seen. In this respect, plays of this sort and their public dissection stage a more general theme in Yopno Christianity: in a world that is opaque to untrained human perception, people need guidance from those who are more knowledgeable, who can break up (*pudaŋ*) and evaluate (*sɨlɨp aŋ*) what was just witnessed.

The authority of pastors, evangelists, congregation chairmen, and other church leaders is grounded in part in their ability to see and understand a reality that is hard to grasp and then to reveal this understanding to less knowledgeable congregants. Their analysis of skits of this kind can itself be seen as part of the moral of the play: it brings home to people their own lack of understanding, and their need for knowledgeable leaders to reveal the true meaning of what is going on around them.

In the confounding opacity of gifts, ritual sacra, and skits, people's uncertainty and sense of not knowing are cultivated and spotlighted. This is true of acts of instruction and revelation more generally. Listeners are shown that reality is more than meets the eye—that true meaning lies below the surface.

Many public events in Yopno villages have a pedagogical component, in which efforts are directed at helping people achieve a better understanding of reality through instruction. But part of learning to see the world more clearly is learning that your own way of seeing the world is wrong. Education involves cultivating people's sense of uncertainty and of their own ignorance.[24] And so, people learn that their way of seeing things is open to revision. That does not mean that they are always quick to cast aside their previous ways of understanding things. But this education in ignorance motivates a continuing effort on many people's part to get a better handle on reality by seeking out new and better knowledge.

Uncertain Selves and Open Minds

In the Yopno Valley, people are not generally understood to produce new knowledge themselves.[25] Of course, people learn things by observing the world around them. Yet these everyday observations do not typically penetrate the deeper reality that lies below the surface. To understand those depths, people need to listen to more knowledgeable sources: ancestors, spirits, local experts, knowledgeable foreigners, and others.[26] At times, the messages that people receive are themselves cryptic and must be decoded—evaluated in the way men evaluate each other's speech in community discussions. This is true of the gospel message in the Bible, which pastors and church leaders help interpret for community members. It is true of enigmatic gifts. And it is also true of dreams, in which spirits and ancestors appear and provide vital knowledge to people.

Dreams are often shared with others and their meanings discussed, with participants drawing on their own stores of esoteric knowledge to unravel their true meaning.[27] In the spring of 2009, I stumbled on a group of people in Ganggalut village who were discussing a man's dream from the night before about a large animal identified as the village's spirit (*kukup kɨdat*). These spirits were traditionally sources of money, and in the dream the dreamer sticks his hand out to receive money from the spirit, but to no avail. A deceased elder appearing in the dream chides the man, telling him he does not know how to interact with such spirits and so he will not get the money he wants. This ancestor offers him a bit of instruction: you are supposed to give money to the spirit, and it will put it in the bank for you. When you need help, the spirit will then provide for you.

After recounting the dream, a man named Po'o offered an interpretation supported by his younger brother, an elected official in the local-level government. At the time, people in Ganggalut and the other villages around the government station at Teptep were preparing to host a celebration marking the establishment of a conservation area in the Yopno and neighboring valleys. Spearheaded by the conservation NGO working in the region, this conservation area was the first of its kind in Papua New Guinea, and thousands were expected to descend on the host villages from throughout the region. Notably, national politicians, including the prime minister of Papua New Guinea, were also due to attend.

As a ritual expert, Po'o is sought out for his skill at making the adornments worn in ceremonial dances, and for the conservation celebration he had prepared a special gift for the honored attendees: a necklace bearing a traditional design on bark cloth (see figure 6). In his interpretation of the dream, Po'o referenced this gift and explained: "That is the paper money of ours that we will give [the politicians], and they will go put it in the bank. It will form a bridge and money will flow back to us." The recipient is not, as in the dream, the spirit animal but the visiting politicians, who will take this gift—a sacred object—to the capital Port Moresby and make money from it. Po'o supports his interpretation with an esoteric account of the nature of Papua New Guinean currency.

> Po'o: On the 2 Kina bill [the Kina is the currency of Papua New Guinea], there are all sorts of designs, pictures of people or other things, you see. They are the one who brought money into existence. They are the sacred objects and beings of different places, you see. So now we want to bring money into existence. We made our sacred object to give to them. The politicians will take it and make money in our name, and it will come back to us. We made our sacred object, all the Ganggalut children. You see the sacra on the 2 Kina note, they are the sacra of the Highlands [a region of Papua New Guinea]. You see the sacra on the 50 Kina note.
>
> Po'o's Brother: It's the Sepik's [another region of Papua New Guinea], their men's house.
>
> Tandeng: Those sacra of here [the Yopno Valley], only now will they make money with it. It will go to parliament and if they want to make some money with it, they will see it and make it?
>
> Po'o: You see the picture on the 10 Kina. You see the picture is of something of Madang's [a province of Papua New Guinea], there is a picture of a slit gong. That's Madang's. And on the 100 Kina the picture is of something of Morobe's [another province of Papua New Guinea]. We think that they just put the pictures, but there is a reason for those pictures. Now, YUS [Yopno-Uruwa-Som region], we want to put something of ours.

The basic idea here is that the sacred object that people in Ganggalut are going to give to the visiting politicians will be used to create money that bears the image of

FIGURE 6. A traditional design on a bark-cloth necklace given to dignitaries attending the conservation celebration.

Photograph by author.

this object and that will lead money to flow back into the Yopno Valley. This understanding mingles a traditional view of money as something supplied by village spirits with an understanding of the national government as the producer of the national currency. Together, these understandings are used to evaluate the dream in the context of the upcoming conservation celebration and produce an innovative conceptualization of money, one in which local sacra pictured on money are responsible for generating money and ultimately development in the communities from which they come (see figure 7). The relative wealth and level of development of other regions of Papua New Guinea compared to the Yopno Valley

FIGURE 7.   A 5 Kina bill bearing images of currencies traditionally used in three parts of Papua New Guinea.

Photograph by author.

are, in this analysis, explained by their already having their sacra incorporated into the money supply. Now, it is the turn of people in the Yopno Valley.

The groundwork of this revelatory account is the same uncertainty that we encountered in sermons and historical tales: the distinction between what "we think" and what really is. "We thought they just put pictures on the bills," as Po'o says, "but there is a reason (*mibɨlɨ*) for those pictures." The willingness to accept a new conceptualization of money here is premised on the possibility that people's current concept of money is flawed or incomplete.[28]

More generally, it reflects people's sense of uncertainty: the possibility that "we" do not understand how the world really works. This sense that "our" understanding might be deficient leads people to look outside themselves for insight. They look to dreams, in which spirits and ancestors provide people with messages—often quite cryptic ones—that shed light on the workings of the world. And they depend on others—often ritual experts and community leaders like Po'o and his brother—to help decipher what they find there.

The dream interpretation that day in Ganggalut ended with general agreement that the plans for the conservation celebration and the gift for the visiting politicians were matters of considerable importance. A few months later the gift was presented, along with a skit, to the dignitaries. To my knowledge, the hoped-for result did not come to pass: no Papua New Guinean currency bears the image of this sacred item, nor has wealth flowed into the valley as a result. I have not had the chance to ask how people view this gift in retrospect and whether their sense of the nature of money shifted as a result. It was perhaps, in the end, only a short-lived, relatively localized innovation in the way people thought about money and their ability to join more fully in the money economy. As Jorgensen (Jorgensen and Johnson 1981, 472) pointed out in that long-ago debate about order in Melanesian religion, where uncertainty and a sense of not knowing are well developed, we can expect to find not a settled ontology or cosmology but "a multiplicity of indigenous interpretations, often offered in a tentative vein."

That is certainly the case in the Yopno Valley. In ways both big and small, the sense that reality is obscure and hard to grasp—that people's understanding of the world around them and its workings is often limited and even mistaken—makes people willing to experiment with new ideas in the hope that they will provide a better grip on reality. Indeed, as people tell the story now, it was this sense of uncertainty that played a central part in their ancestors' acceptance of Christianity in the mid-twentieth century: their ancestors accepted the gospel message because it seemed to offer insight into unseen powers around them, a point we return to in chapter 5. Today, as we see in this section, people continue to be on the lookout for new sources of understanding. Where reality is regarded as opaque to untrained human perception, people are willing to listen to others— in dreams and dream interpretations, in church, and in school—where they hope they might find insight into the world that confronts them.

Self-Determination and the Uncertain Self

To appreciate the pragmatics of holding onto the words of others, this chapter has introduced an epistemology prominent in the Yopno Valley, one that accentuates people's lack of understanding and their need for help to gain a grip on reality. In a way, this epistemology is a manifestation of the relational sense of self I discussed in the previous chapter. This is a self formed through contributions of knowledge (*nandak nandak*) in much the same way as it depends on contributions of bride-wealth, food, and other material substances from a host of others.[29]

For this epistemologically relational self, listening to others is essential. People listen to others' dreams and their interpretation, to school lessons and sermons, to historical narratives and the exegesis of skits, all with an ear to enhancing their understanding of the world around them. This is not, for the most part, done out of an academic interest in truth for truth's sake. Instead, people seek a more accurate and more comprehensive understanding of reality so that they can act more effectively. When they are ignorant of the context they find themselves in, people invariably act against their own interests: they get eaten by spirits and almost killed by lakes. By contrast, when they understand the situation in which they act, they can take control of their future. A newfound conception of money offers hope of finally acquiring the money and development people want. The knowledge that the Holy Spirit lives inside them provides a way for schoolchildren to live correctly and save their souls. Understanding the true nature of the demon baby in Ganggalut will help people safeguard their own lives. For an uncertain self, listening and holding onto the words of others are necessary if one is to be a self-determining agent. In that respect, these acts are facets of the art of anarchic listening. Where people lack the understanding that they need to act effectively, holding onto the words of others is *essential* if they are to take control of their future.

In the wake of centuries of colonialism, missionization, and neoliberal globalization, there have been calls in recent years for anthropology to turn its attention (once again) to difference—to the alternative ontologies (Kohn 2015), concepts (Skafish 2011), metaphysics (Viveiros de Castro 2015b), and cosmologies (Cadena 2015) of "'extraordinary' or 'uncommon' peoples, those who live beyond our sphere of 'communication'" (Viveiros de Castro 2015a, 50)—people, I might note, who often turn out to live in the Amazon, the Andes, or Melanesia. For some proponents, this "ontological turn" is itself an important facet of a politics of self-determination: it supports the "conceptual self-determination of all the planet's minorities," as Viveiros de Castro (2015a, 41) has put it, in the face of the "colonization of consciousness" that has accompanied Western imperialism. It is a recent variant of a familiar anthropological effort to create space for different ways of knowing and living in the face of colonialism, missionization, and the spread of Western "reason."[30] By taking alternative ways of knowing "seriously" (Cadena 2010, 336; Kohn 2013, 21–22; Viveiros de Castro 2015a, 194; Holbraad and Petersen 2017)—by allowing them to stand on a par with the West's own philosophical systems and scientific worldview—these ontologies can be liberated from the confines of Western reason. They are not to be explained (away) by the anthropologist but treated as true equals that may even influence Western philosophy and "our" own conceptual systems.

But here we must ask, what does the politics of self-determination look like when people do not take their ontologies and concepts quite so "seriously"? What does conceptual self-determination mean when people are unsure of or dissatisfied with their concepts, their cosmology, or their ontology? The reflexive potential for dissatisfaction with one's own thought renders the political and ethical aims of the ontological turn—and many other strains of anthropology, for that matter—more complicated than they might at first appear. Are people in the Yopno Valley conceptually self-determining when they seek to hold onto the message of Christianity in order to transform their understanding? Or should Yopno people be encouraged to trust in "their" cosmology passed down in the men's house on the premise that it is fundamental to who they are? Can we even presume that there was a time when the Yopno had a stable cosmology in the past and try to salvage it; for instance, to go in search of the truth about the men's house? Or, given the conceptual instability reported in ethnographies from around the region, are epistemological uncertainty and a sense of not knowing in fact the characteristics that are most true to the Yopno self? What composes the true self: a person's concepts or their conceptualization of their own and others' concepts?

In a curious way, the sense of self I presented in this chapter is reminiscent of one figure found in the work of proponents of the ontological turn: the ontologically minded anthropologists themselves. Dissatisfaction with established ways of thinking in "the West" is a recurring rationale for the turn to ontology.[31] We anthropologists should seek out the ontologies of others to provide the conceptual material to transform "our" own thought: to generate new concepts, to liberate our thought from its conventional rigidity, and even to transform the deleterious ontology of the West. By taking alternative (typically, Indigenous) ways of knowing "seriously," it is not only these ontologies that are liberated from the confines of Western reason but also so are "we." In this respect, the ontological turn is itself a perfect example of the way a reflexive dissatisfaction with "one's own" concepts drives efforts to listen to others and seek out new understandings.[32]

As with the ontologically minded anthropologist, for people in the Yopno Valley—and presumably many others around the world—the notion of protecting and preserving "their" concepts is often not the point. They are at times doubtful of and dissatisfied with them. In this respect, people in the Yopno Valley do not seem to fit the ontological turn's model of an ontologically secure (Giddens 1991) Indigenous subject.[33] Self-determination is not a matter of preserving and defending their ontology but often of finding better understandings of a world that is not what it seems. And that makes listening "seriously" and "holding onto" the words of others essential to the politics of self-determination in the valley.

ANARCHY, POWER, AND THE POLITICS OF EXPERTISE

While waiting for community members to show up to a meeting one day, Raipe—whom we met in chapter 1 waiting around at another meeting—turned the conversation to how different things were in the past. She spoke of a former leader of the village, Bagwo, who could really get people to show up for meetings. He would tirelessly bang his drum and make announcements until people showed up and finished whatever work the community needed to do.

While waiting for people to show up to meetings or other events, talk often turns to the ineffectiveness of today's leaders and the lack of respect community members have for them. At times, talk also turns nostalgically to an earlier time when leaders were able to get community members together to do things. Through tireless efforts and often the use of powerful magic, men like Bagwo managed to bring people together and execute collective projects. The expression *tɨmɨt tɨmɨt amɨm* ("people who gather others together") is an appellation applied to successful leaders like Bagwo, who have a magical ability to bring people together.

But in stories of past leaders such admiration is often mingled with a strong measure of condemnation. In Raipe's recollection, she made a point of noting the "good manner" (*aŋpak tai*) in which Bagwo operated. He was tireless and pushy but not violent or terrifying. Many successful leaders, however, were not so gentle. In Weskokop village, my host, a community leader in his own right named Nanda, told me the history of the many daunting characters who led the community in the past. The first village leader, back when the village was centralizing at the behest of Lutheran missionaries, was Minibao. Nanda told of how he successfully brought dispersed and anxious community members together to build new houses for themselves alongside a church, forming the present-day settlement of Weskokop. But Minibao was also known for his harsh discipline. He would punish young troublemakers in the community by making them dig holes, fill them in, and then dig them out again. Sometimes he would even burn them with fire.

But Minibao is considered relatively easygoing compared to his successor Yuwanapo, who was truly terrifying. In Nanda's words,

> The leadership of Yuwanapo was fierce. He was a bad person. Poison and sorcery, he did it all. His talk was red hot. He chased the kids away and shot them with a bow and arrow. At the door of the church down there, you see, there is a big stone. When some other kids and I caused trouble, he took us over there and told us to scratch the stone. The kids surrounded this big stone at the base of where the goalposts are now. . . . We scraped that stone, on top of the stone. While we did that, he held a stick and went around behind us. We scraped away our fingernails. Our fingernails were scraped down to the base. He was a bad leader. But he spoke powerfully, and because of that people respected and feared him. They worked and the village changed. It changed. If they left, Yuwanapo would beat them. Because of that they were afraid. "If we leave, he's going to beat us terribly." That's what they thought, and so they were afraid and showed up to work. They respected him and did some work, and they improved the village.

It is hard to know whether Yuwanapo really wielded such a despotic grip on the community. None of the community leaders I encountered had anything close to the control over the community that Nanda describes here. But the threats of poison and sorcery that Yuwanapo wielded so effectively are no longer used as a tool of governance. The spread of Christianity has led people to eschew poison, sorcery, and other forms of "bad magic," at least publicly. Considered inimical to a modern, Christian, harmonious way of life, these seemingly effective tools of leadership have been removed from the toolkit of contemporary leaders. Though no one I spoke with hoped that community leaders would resume using threats of occult violence, many noted that it is harder to get things done without such means of coercion.

As both the "good magic" of a leader like Bagwo and the more disturbing sorcery of a leader like Yuwanapo indicate, an expert knowledge of occult powers was a vital tool of leadership. In a political context where people were willful and placed a high value on their self-determination, mastery of such special powers was a means of subduing a fractious community and coercing them to act. But as the mix of admiration and condemnation in Nanda's account of Yuwanapo highlights, the use of these powers involved a trade-off. Yuwanapo is admired for getting things done; he spoke powerfully, people listened to him, and he improved the village. Despotism has its benefits, especially when it comes to orchestrating collective projects. But it flies in the face of the kind of anarchic values that are so central to Yopno political life. Yuwanapo tortured people, attacked them with a bow and arrow, and wielded the threat of sorcery to force people to do things against their will. To be effective, leaders must push others to do things they often do not want to do. Yet the use of violence and threats has its downside: the ability to influence others comes at the expense of community members' self-determination, and this creates resentment.[1] Indeed, leaders often appear to have suffered the consequences for exercising power over others in this way. Yuwanapo, like his predecessor Minibao and many other leaders, is said to have been killed by sorcery, as retribution for his threats, violence, and impositions.

In every one of the villages in the Yopno Valley I have visited, there are men who are recognized as leaders. Although people value their self-determination and the anarchic (i.e., leaderless) character of village politics, people also appreciate a powerful leader's ability to get things done: to improve the community, build institutions, organize events, and pull in resources that many in the community want. They chafe at community leaders' impositions but recognize that getting things done requires leaders to be bossy and worse. This is a tension at the heart of Yopno village politics: people enjoy the fruits of the community's collective efforts; but collective projects typically require leaders to coerce community members to work together.

Today, leaders negotiate the contradictions of "anarchic leadership" in a much gentler manner than forebearers like Yuwanapo and Minibao. Violence and threats of it have been replaced by other techniques of control. One of the most ubiquitous techniques in use today is the focus of this chapter: the communication of expertise.

A notable feature of much of the political oratory in the Yopno Valley is its didactic character. Speeches of community leaders are filled with explanations: spelling out in detail how the provincial education bureaucracy works, for instance, or how the conservation NGO awards scholarships. In contrast to many parts of Papua New Guinea where oratory involves the mastery of elaborate styles of verbal artistry, political oratory in the Yopno Valley is notably prosaic and even pedagogical.[2] It aims to instruct its audience, to communicate the insights of a knowledgeable expert on some matter to an audience that lacks an understanding of it. Why political oratory takes this form in the Yopno Valley has much to do with the incongruity inherent in anarchic leadership, as I hope to show in this chapter

Much of the scholarship about expertise over the past few decades has stressed its role as an technique of control. Expert knowledge operates as a potent, if often disguised, means of shaping the way people think and act: it does not merely describe reality, it constructs reality. Foucault's accounts of the role of expertise in regimes of discipline and governmentality have been particularly influential on this point, giving rise to probing accounts of the kinds of effects that psychological and psychiatric, criminological, economic, orientalist, and other forms of expertise have on the conduct of people and populations.[3] Experts in these fields shape the way non-experts understand themselves and others, their natures, and the causes of their behavior. They offer standards for measuring behavior, classifying some as normal or model specimens to be imitated and others as deviant. In refashioning non-experts' conceptions of themselves and others in these ways, experts provide an impetus for people to adjust their own conduct and that of others to achieve ends that they desire or that they are told they should desire.[4]

In much the same way, community leaders in the Yopno Valley share their expertise with others as a way to shape their conduct, as we will see in this chapter. But there is more to the politics of expertise in the Yopno Valley. Looked at from the perspective of the anarchic listener, expertise serves a second purpose: listeners seek out expertise to empower themselves. By gaining a better understanding of reality from experts, they are able to exercise greater control over their own future.

Too often, this perspective is overlooked in scholarly accounts of the politics of expertise. In giving equal attention to the listener's point of view, I hope to show that expertise thrives as a medium of politics in Yopno villages because it has the potential to serve multiple interests simultaneously—those of speakers and listeners, experts and non-experts. It supports the efforts of anarchic listeners to advance their self-determination even as it serves as a technique of control for community leaders. In that respect, the communication of expertise provides a way to navigate the contradiction inherent in anarchic leadership and renders domination an integral part of anarchic politics.

To begin this exploration of the politics of expertise in Yopno villages, I start on the other side of the word, with the perspective of listeners. Not only is that perspective typically overlooked but it is also the foundation of the politics of expertise in the Yopno Valley: if there were no people interested in listening to the expertise of others, there would be no politics of expertise to speak of.

Expertise from the Listener's Point of View

In 2014, I joined Peter, one of the leaders of the Nian congregation, on a visit to a house outside the main village settlement. Peter had been invited to bless a new pig pen, the sort of task that Christian leaders are often called on to perform. After the blessing was completed, the two women living in the house disclosed a second reason for their invitation: they were having problems (*jikŋɨ*; <u>hevi</u>) that they hoped Peter could help them solve. Kauso, the more vocal of the two, was married and approaching middle age. She had given birth to a daughter several years before but had no sons. This was a matter of growing concern for her and her husband, who was hoping for a male heir. The other woman, Kauso's cousin, too had no sons: both women hoped that Peter would help them uncover the reason why they were seemingly unable to produce male children.

Peter is often called out on tasks like this. At the time in his fifties, he had worked with other Nian villagers on coastal plantations in the late 1980s. There, they had developed a deeper knowledge of Christianity through regular study and interaction with people from other areas of Papua New Guinea, who had been interacting with Christian missionaries for a longer time. On returning to Nian with a deeper knowledge of the religion, Peter and an older man whom he had traveled with were named congregation leaders by the village headmen, and they have retained these leadership roles ever since.

Like other Christian spiritual experts in the community—the evangelist and the congregation chairman, in particular—Peter oversees church services on Sundays and travels to people's homes during the week to mediate conflicts, hold private ceremonies to bless houses and gardens, and diagnose the causes of people's problems. When problems arise in people's lives, experts are often called on to help. As we saw in chapter 2, people are trained from an early age to regard reality as deeply obscure and their understanding of it to be limited. But some—whom I call "experts" here (*nandak nandak amɨn*; <u>saveman</u>)[5]—are regarded as having a greater understanding of the workings of the world than others.

Formerly, this social stratification of expertise was most clearly institutionalized in the men's house (*bema yut*), where senior men taught initiates the histories, esoteric formulas, and rituals that would enable success in warfare, gardening, pig rearing, marriage, and more. Today, experts are found in virtually all domains of life. There are experts in Christian matters like Peter, who are typically clerical and lay leaders of Lutheran churches in the valley. There are experts versed in the ways of sorcery and witchcraft, who learned from others how to identify the cause of an illness or death.[6] There are those known for their knowledge of clan histories, who offer support for their clan's claims to land.

There are people knowledgeable about ceremonial dances, who teach others the tunes and prepare the decorations. And, of course, there are teachers, conservation workers, and others whose expertise is linked with their positions in national and international organizations.

At times, people turn to experts to perform services that they themselves cannot do, from murdering someone with sorcery to preparing the decorations for a ceremonial dance to blessing a new pig pen. But one of the main tasks that experts perform is to provide people with knowledge (*nandak nandak*). When people are feeling uncertain about the situation they find themselves in or are unsure how to act to resolve their problems, experts provide them with more accurate and comprehensive representations of the world around them and explain how to act effectively in that world.[7]

It was to obtain knowledge of this sort that Kauso and her cousin had asked Peter to visit them. As she explained to Peter, there were various possible reasons why she and her cousin were having trouble giving birth to male children, and they did not know which was the correct one. It might be because her mother and father were not married according to custom, i.e., the marriage should have been arranged by the families and bridewealth paid to the bride's family. Or it might be because her father and mother belonged to "partner clans" (*gapma-gapma*), which regard one another reciprocally as a source of blessings—as each other's gods.[8]

In explaining why she had asked Peter to come, Kauso began by stressing her uncertainty:

> Our lives are messed up. We wonder, "Is it because we did this? Is it because of that?" . . . We have wondered about this and now we are going to talk about it. . . . My own mother and father did not get married in the right way. People didn't arrange their marriage. They married without bridewealth being paid. Are our lives messed up because of that? Is it because of that that we have problems? We wonder about that sort of thing, and we asked you to come. You have come, so you can listen to us talk and end our problems. For that we asked you to come.

At that point, Peter asked the two women to explain their situation more clearly so that he could help resolve their problems. Kauso continued,

> My father took his god as a wife. He married his god so is it because of that that difficulties have come? Those two violated the prohibition on marrying one's *gapma*. Is it because of this that difficulties keep coming? Is it because of that that the two of us are troubled or is it something else? It's that sort of thing we wonder about.

Kauso emphasizes her own uncertainty here: Is she cursed because her parents were married without the payment of bridewealth, or is it because her parents were members of each other's partner clan (*gapma*) and thus improper marriage partners? Or is there another cause for her misfortune?

Obscurity surrounds Kauso's problems, which often plagues people's efforts to diagnose the source of their difficulties. Present-day misfortunes are frequently taken to be the result of actions by deceased ancestors that have long been forgotten by most people. In addition, there are almost always multiple possible ancestral misdeeds that might be the source of current problems. Alternatively, a person's difficulties might be caused by others in the community, who are retaliating with curses or sorcery for things distant relations have done. Given all these possible causes, the source of people's problems is often murky, and experts like Peter must be called in.

After Kauso expressed her confusion, Peter declared definitively that the source of their problems was the fact that her parents were each other's *gapma*. Because Kauso's mother violated the prohibition on marrying her *gapma*, treating her god with disrespect by marrying him, her *gapma* has kept her from having male offspring. And this inability to give birth to sons has continued to curse the family in the next generation too. In Peter's words,

> If you mess up the *gapma* relationship, you will truly see it in the kind of life you are living. Up and down, sickness and sores, anxieties, difficulties. Things will be difficult, you will find things hard to do, your body will hurt.
>
> "Are there some people who have died? Am I experiencing this because of the death of some people?" you will ask. You will say, "I'm like this because someone has been killed" [i.e., you are experiencing difficulties because someone has put a curse on you or attacked you with sorcery in revenge for another person's death].
>
> But, if you look closely, the reason for the difficulties is that a *gapma* is something important.
>
> . . .
>
> Your *gapma* kept your mother from having a boy with a curse: "You yourself have blocked the road for a boy, so I won't give you a boy. I give you only girls." Your *gapma* said this, and as a result you do not have plenty of children, just one.
>
> . . .
>
> We'll blame evil spirits and all sorts of things, but it's not that. It is really because *gapma* married each other that these problems arise.[9]

Like Kauso, Peter also stresses how hard it is for people to understand the situation they find themselves in. He notes that people will blame their misfortunes on others' revenge attacks or on evil spirits. But in the end, Peter offers his expert understanding of the situation: the source of the women's difficulty is that their parents were each other's *gapma*.

One piece of evidence Peter draws on to determine the source of Kauso's problem is a dream that she had mentioned earlier in the conversation, when she was explaining the situation to him. In the dream, Kauso finds a giant rat in her house that was rubbing its face; this kind of rat is called *karan*, and Peter notes that it is closely connected with the *gapma* relationship. Men would cook this rat in the men's house with their *gapma*, to feed the spirit (*koŋ*) that lived in its vicinity.

According to Peter, this dream indicates that the source of the women's difficulty is the marriage between *gapma*. But there is more to it. The way the rat rubs its face in the dream points to a second cause of the women's difficulties. As Peter puts it, "Rubbing its face like that, that shows there is dirt in your eyes. You two need to remove it and see clearly. There is dirt in your eyes and you two can't see clearly. Rub them and your life will improve. You need to look clearly." The dream indicates that the women's difficulty is the result not only of their parents' wrong actions but also of their own inability to understand what is going on in their life. Their lack of understanding is one of the causes of their problems.

This point is made often: people's failure to understand the context in which they are acting leads them to act ineffectively. In the preceding chapters, we saw it in historical tales and preschool lessons, in dream interpretations and political discussions. People cannot exert control over their future if they do not understand the reality that confronts them.

After diagnosing the cause of their problem, Peter explained that Kauso and her cousin should give an offering to the church during the Easter service, which will then be given to the national church as a way to move the *gapma*'s curse far away from the women and the village. They agreed to make that offering in the hopes that it would clear up their difficulty. But before they could do so—before they could try to address the problems they were having—they needed to understand the nature of their difficulties, and for that, the insight of an expert is essential.

There are many topics on which people purport to offer expertise in Yopno villages—the secret workings of nature spirits and educational bureaucrats, the conservation NGO and the Christian God. But a common denominator is that expert insight about such subjects will enable those who hold onto it to take greater control over their own lives. The communication of expertise and the self-determination of the listener go hand in hand—ideally, at least.

Of course, the communication of expertise often does not live up to this ideal. As we will see in later chapters (particularly chapter 4), a common source of trouble is that purported expertise is in fact deceptive, which *threatens* rather than enhances the self-determination of listeners. Audiences are aware of the potential that those peddling expertise are offering up tricks and lies. But still people seek out experts to help them, at times quite desperately.

A friend of mine, Kabwum, spent well over a year trying to get experts in his clan to provide him the esoteric knowledge he needed to interact with a spirit that lived on land he was claiming as his own. His family had fled Nian during a feud two generations earlier, and he was raised in a neighboring valley. He lived for a period in urban Papua New Guinea when his father took up work as a medical assistant, but after running into trouble as a member of an urban gang he returned to Nian, his homeland. Interacting with the spirit that lived on his father's land would help Kabwum secure his ownership of the land and gain other benefits that powerful forest spirits provide. But he needed to know the spirit's name and how to interact with it effectively. As he recounted to me in tears, not one of his clan mates would reveal knowledge of this spirit to him. He eventually left the village.

In a context where reality is so often hard to grasp, expert knowledge is something that people need if they are to create the futures they want. And it is this desire for expert knowledge that makes such knowledge particularly well suited to serve as a medium of politics in the anarchic villages of the Yopno Valley.

The Gift of Expertise

For village leaders, it can be hard to gain a hearing in the anarchically minded communities of the valley. Community members readily disregard their directions and suggestions, and if leaders push too hard, they risk reprisals from people who feel imposed on. By communicating expertise, however, leaders are able to reframe their role in community affairs. By sharing expert knowledge, they are not *subverting* the self-determination of their audience; they are working to *enhance* it, to support their audience in achieving their desires, a point they routinely insist on. As a medium of political communication, expertise provides a way for leaders to present their efforts to influence community members as fundamentally altruistic and, somewhat incongruously, even anarchic in spirit.

A younger man in his thirties, Muyan, offered a particularly rich portrayal of the altruistic leader sharing the "gift of expertise." For years he had been trying to encourage people in the community to support the US-based conservation NGO working to protect tree-kangaroos in the valley. In speeches during the thrice-weekly village market in Nian and at other events, he had explained again and again that people in the valley would benefit from working with the NGO. But few listened to his advice.

So, in 2014, when the NGO hosted a workshop in Nian village to teach people how to grow high-end coffee for distribution in the United States, he was vindicated. The NGO had found a US distributor that would market this coffee as "conservation coffee," fetching prices that would allow villagers to harvest coffee, transport it by air to processing facilities in the city of Lae, ship it on to the United States, and still receive a decent return for their efforts. But to participate, people needed to produce higher-quality coffee than they had in the past. By the time of the workshop, most people's coffee gardens had been abandoned because of the low prices they had received for their coffee and the difficulties of transporting coffee to market in this mountainous region without roads. Here, then, was an opportunity to revitalize what had once been the prime cash crop in the valley, and quite a number of people showed up for the workshop.

As the workshop wrapped up and the closing speeches and thank-yous were ending, Muyan took the floor. The son of Bagwo and a lively public speaker in his own right, he began innocuously, asking how everyone was doing. "Great!" came the reply. "You feel great?" "Yes." And then the tone shifted. What seemed like the beginnings of a pep rally for the coffee workshop and the conservation NGO turned into something else. His voice rising to a fevered pitch, Muyan demanded of people in the audience: "I want to see you tell me the fruit of compassion. Tell me now! Tell me! I'm an annoying bird calling out in the plaza. I think you are children of Thomas." From there he went on to say that for years he had been trying to explain the benefits of working with the conservation NGO; that is, he has been "an annoying bird calling out in the plaza. . . . For your own good, you people of Nian and Nokopo, I talk endlessly. I suffer for you. I don't sleep, and the result of this is that now you are at peace."

The line is a standard one; leaders often insist that they are offering their expertise and knowledgeable advice for the benefit of their audience. But Muyan takes the point further. In an elaborate metaphor, he compared people in Nian to "doubting Thomases," a metaphor in which, not incidentally, Muyan plays the role of Jesus. People had not believed the truth of what Muyan was telling them until now, when they see the benefits of the conservation work with their own eyes. As he puts it, "You all thought, 'He's lying, he's lying.' So, you ignored me, thinking to yourselves 'when the benefits of conservation come, we will see them and do something about it.'" And now that the people of Nian have received this benefit, they will not remember that it was Muyan—the Christ-like sacrifice—who had tried to steer them in this direction all along. He continued,

I want you to get hold of this good thing [i.e., benefits from the conservation NGO] and so I speak out. I speak so that you, lots of people, will be
satisfied. I have died for you. I have given my life for you, so your hearts
will be satisfied. I speak out for you and have given my life; now it has
come to an end, and I'm done. You have gotten important knowledge
during this coffee course. You will use it to do things. You will receive the
fruits of this but you won't think of me. That's your problem. You will
be big shots. I speak and you don't listen. I struggle and run around until
the work is finished, and you all get peace; your hearts are easy.

Muyan's impassioned speech was greeted with considerable applause, which surprised me. It was rare to hear people publicly berate others in this way and be
applauded for it.

But Muyan's righteous anger seems to have struck a chord in his audience.
Part of the speech's effectiveness is the way he framed himself as the aggrieved
party. The underlying premise of Muyan's tirade is that he gave something valuable to people. He acted altruistically toward others—"I have given my life for
you"—by trying to get people to support the work of the conservation NGO. He
tirelessly explained the benefits that would come from supporting the conservation work. But people in Nian had not listened, as is so often the case, leaving
him to cultivate a relationship with the NGO largely on his own, pledging land
to the conservation area that was being developed and organizing events like
the coffee workshop. And now the community at large was reaping the benefits
of all of his work: "I speak and you don't listen. I struggle and run around until
the work is finished so you all get peace."

One aspect of his complaint anticipates the future failure of people to reciprocate all that he has done. The community will fail to recognize that it was his
efforts to support the conservation NGO that led them to receive these benefits.
As he puts it, "You make a lot of money; you won't think of me, that country
bumpkin." The idiom "to not think about (a person)" is used to remark on the
failure to recognize others and satisfy obligations to them.[10] Christians are accused of not thinking about God when they do not follow biblical command-
ments. When someone fails to reciprocate contributions to a bridewealth payment,
they are said to have not thought about the original donor. And here, Muyan anticipates that people will also fail to return the favor once they make their fortune
as coffee growers.

But he is also complaining about the fact that people did not listen to him. In
effect, they rejected the gift of expertise he offered them. There was much debate at the time about whether people should engage with the conservation NGO
and if so, how they should do so (discussed in more detail in chapters 4 and 5).

What was the conservation NGO up to? Was it there to help the people of the region or to steal their land? What does one need to do to receive the benefits the conservation NGO was providing: scholarships to teachers' training college, health patrols, and now a connection with an overseas coffee buyer?

In providing people with a better understanding of how to gain benefits from the conservation NGO, Muyan offered them knowledge that would help them. In contrast, by disregarding his insight and advice, people nearly lost out on something they all desired. As I discussed in chapter 1, disregarding the words of community leaders is a routine way that people exercise their self-determination in Yopno villages. But the vision of the politics of expertise voiced here by Muyan flips this on its head. In this framing, expertise is a gift, one that will benefit those who listen, receive, and hold onto it. Leaders often make this point, saying "We speak until our mouths hurt for the benefit of everyone." From this perspective, by holding onto the expert insights and advice they hear in public speeches, listeners will enhance their ability to control their future and get hold of the things they desire. Church workers help people understand the reasons they are unable to have children so that they can right past wrongs and have the children they desire. Experts in ritual designs explain the nature of money so that community members can give gifts to politicians that will lead money to flow into the valley. Teachers explain the workings of the Christian God so that children will flourish in this life and the next. And others like Muyan explain the advantages of working with the conservation NGO, enabling listeners who hold onto what he says to gain the wealth they desire.

In the Yopno politics of expertise, community leaders fashion themselves as altruists and patrons of anarchic values, advancing the self-determination and equality of community members. This is a politics quite different from days past, when leaders used threats of occult violence to coerce people to act against their own wills. Of course, community members often do not accept the offer of expertise, as Muyan's diatribe testifies. But in the end, disregarding Muyan's words did not prove to be a very effective way of asserting control over their future for people in Nian: they almost lost out on benefits that they desired because of it. The applause that Muyan's diatribe received suggests that in retrospect the audience members realized that they should have held onto his talk about the conservation efforts.

In the politics of expertise, leaders seek to overcome the recalcitrance of community members by offering them something they want: expertise that will aid them in their efforts to determine their own future. At the same time, as we see in the next section, expertise is also an instrument of control: a means of exerting influence and control over community members. In that respect, expertise-laden oratory is not as purely altruistic as leaders often claim it to be.[11] Yet talk of expertise as a kind of gift should not be regarded as a complete ruse. I do not doubt the sincerity of Muyan's claim that he has been trying to help his family and fellow villagers by sharing his knowledgeable advice with them (though that may not be *all* that he is up to).

Rather than regard the politics of expertise as an either/or proposition—either expertise is offered altruistically or self-servingly—it may be better understood as a medium of politics that has the potential to serve both ends simultaneously. Unlike the despotic mode of politics, in which the will of leaders and that of community members are pitched against one another, the communication of expertise is capable of supporting the self-determination of community members while also serving as a tool for directing their activities. To see how those distinct and even contradictory ends are fused, we need to look more closely at the content of the sort of expertise-laden oratory common in Yopno politics.

Expertise as a Technique of Control

During the coffee workshop in Nian village, people in the audience raised questions about the operations of the NGO: What were the rules for the use of land in the conservation area, what did people need to do to receive benefits from the NGO, and what was the NGO ultimately trying to accomplish? These questions were continually circulating around the villages I lived in and visited. Sensing there was a misunderstanding about the aims of the conservation NGO, Franklin, a young man from the region who worked as one of its field assistants, shared a bit of his own expertise with the people of Nian. During a question-and-answer session, he sought to clarify the relationship between the conservation work and "nature"—or, rather, netsa. Although the Tok Pisin term netsa is cognate with the English word "nature," it has a different meaning from its English counterpart, one that lies at the heart of a "working misunderstanding" between residents of the Yopno Valley and the conservation NGO that is at times productive and at other times confounding.

Netsa denotes not only "forest," "animals," "streams," and the like but also the spirits that live in and control them. Many in the Yopno Valley understand the efforts of the conservation NGO to protect their "nature"—the forest, animals, and streams of people in the Yopno Valley—as also an effort to protect their netsa. Supporters of the conservation work appreciate the NGO's efforts to protect the spirits of the forest, who are an important source of power and a potential source of wealth for people in the valley. At times, however, the conservation NGO can appear too interested in Yopno netsa, leading people to wonder whether the NGO is in fact there to steal this source of power and wealth.

In his speech, Franklin offers his own expert account of how <u>netsa</u> views the conservation work, contrasting his own esoteric perspective on the matter with others' exoteric perspective in the sort of play of perspectives we have seen before (see chapter 2):

> No matter what you thought before, for instance, that the conservation workers are going around visiting the spirits who live on our land. I am a true Yopno person, I'm telling you directly, it's not true. I have not seen one spirit in the forest. They don't come to me. But they celebrate, when I walk around, they feel peace. . . . There are all sorts of enemies who are coming here. We don't know how to control them. When we don't know how to manage things, all of this forest, land, they are in pain, they worry. When you conserve them, then they are at peace, they feel calm. And they see you, this proprietor of the forest and ground or YUS man [i.e., a man from the Yopno-Uruwa-Som area], they see you as their powerful king. That's how <u>netsa</u>/nature now see you all. . . . So now, as a Yopno child, I myself say: the rumors about spirits are wrong. False thinking. Cargo cult thinking. It goes against this Garden of Eden we want to walk around in. If we conserve it, we go back to Genesis. So watch out, God's Word also will indict you.

In this brief excerpt, Franklin juxtaposes esoteric and exoteric perspectives concerning the workings of <u>netsa</u> and the conservation NGO. On the one hand, some in his audience believe that the conservation NGO is trying to interact with forest spirits and use the spirits' power for their own purposes. As a result, Yopno landowners have shied away from involvement with the NGO and their conservation area.

To this "false account"—this "cargo cult thinking"—Franklin juxtaposes his own expert account, underwritten by his close involvement with the NGO, his long-term work in the forest, and his local origins. During his time in the forest working for the conservation NGO, he has not interacted with any spirits; but the spirits do feel grateful for the presence of the NGO, which is protecting them from mining companies and others who threaten them.

Here, Franklin not only distinguishes his knowledgeable perspective from that of his audience, but he also offers them an expert account of the relationship of forest spirits to the conservation NGO that promises to enhance their control over their forest spirits: "When you conserve your <u>netsa</u>, then they are at peace, they feel calm. And they see you . . . as their powerful king." In contrast, Franklin points out, if community members operate with a mistaken understanding, they will in effect lose a measure of self-determination, acting in ways they do not understand with consequences they do not intend: people will endanger the Garden of Eden that they want to create and they will bring down the wrath of God on themselves. They make their <u>netsa</u> feel pain and worry at the threat of "enemies" (e.g., mining companies) who are coming to the area.

But Franklin is not only altruistically seeking to enhance his listeners' self-determination with this "gift" of expertise; he is also using this bit of expert knowledge to steer his audience to support the conservation work, which he is deeply involved in. Like many orators, he offers up expertise that highlights the benefits of activities that he is trying to encourage people to participate in. In this way, expertise-laden oratory provides leaders a way to exert a measure of control over others without, seemingly, subverting their self-determination. Rather than pitting the will of community leaders against the will of community members, communicating expertise entangles the two.

We can see how this happens in a series of conditional statements that Franklin makes linking means to ends: "If we conserve it" (means), "then we go back to Genesis" (end). In contrast, "when we don't know how to manage things" (means), "all of this forest, land, they are in pain, they worry" (end). In short, when you work with the conservation NGO (means), then you gain control over your nature spirits (end). In these conditional statements, control over <u>netsa</u>—which is the end his audience presumably has in view—is said to be conditional on supporting the conservation work, an end that Franklin has in mind. His audience's interest in gaining power from spirits becomes linked to—premised on—acting in ways that Franklin is seeking to promote.

This is an example of a means-end formula common in expertise-laden oratory in the valley. Put schematically, the means-ends format of expertise takes the following form: experts explain to their audience that if they want to achieve a particular end, they must employ certain means. In that way, experts offer to further people's ability to achieve the ends they desire. But they steer audience members toward using certain means to do so—and these means are typically the very activities that community leaders are trying to encourage people to perform for their own reasons. In this way, the power and self-determination of listeners are entangled with the aims and the control of leaders. If you want to control your <u>netsa</u>, you must support the conservation NGO, says a man working for the conservation NGO. If you want to have male children, give an offering to the Lutheran church, says a congregational leader. If you have problems in your life, giving a pig as an offering to a church celebration will help, say the organizers of the celebration who need pigs (see chapter 1). In short, listeners can achieve the future they want but only if they do the things that orators want them to do.

We should not take this to mean that the communication of expertise is merely a ruse to trick audiences into performing actions they otherwise would not. At least, we need not be any more cynical than listeners in the Yopno Valley, who are quite alert to the possibility that community leaders are offering them deceptive expertise. As I noted in the previous section, it is possible to be both altruistic and self-serving at the same time when sharing expertise. Franklin can urge people to support the conservation NGO he works for while also advancing his audience's control over their <u>netsa</u>. Through the means-ends formula I focus on in this section, altruism and self-interest, community members' self-determination and village leaders' power have the potential to coexist. Franklin may indeed be helping his audience gain greater control over their future while also steering them to support the conservation NGO he is trying to drum up support for. In the politics of expertise, the means to community members' ends and the ends that a leader seeks to promote are portrayed as one and the same.

Expertise and the Parasitic Power of Leaders

Expertise is a form of verbal power, as we have seen; a way for community leaders to influence the actions of community members in a context where influence can be hard to come by. In the Yopno Valley, community leaders often lack effective means of coercion to back up their words and give them force. Announcements go unheeded; discussions continue at length. Threats of sorcery may be effective but have significant drawbacks. In this relatively anarchic political context, the communication of expertise provides leaders with a way to influence audiences to act. At the same time, this power *over* listeners is tempered by the power that the communication of expertise provides *to* listeners.

Ultimately, this power that both experts and their audiences partake of in the politics of expertise springs from elsewhere. Up until this point I have focused on orators and audiences, two parties who clearly have a stake in the communication of expertise. But there is typically a third figure who makes an appearance in the politics of expertise, not as a participant but as an object of expertise—a powerful actor or organization that is often distant from daily life or is otherwise inscrutable: the conservation NGO, <u>netsa</u> spirits, the national government, or the Christian God. In the politics of expertise, orators leverage the power of these third parties to vest their own words with the power to influence listeners to act. We might say that the power of leaders here is *parasitic* on the power of these distant, inscrutable others. Expertise provides a way for relatively powerless leaders in the anarchic villages of the valley to gird their words with power.

To see how this works, it is helpful to compare the parasitic power of expertise with another common strategy that community leaders use to give power to their words: the promise of reciprocity. At the start of the 2008 school year, as community members were off in the forest collecting pandanus nuts, the work to prepare the school for the year ahead was not being done (see chapter 1). Several weeks after the school year was supposed to have started, the head of the school walked up to Nian village and gave a speech urging people to complete these essential tasks: build a new classroom and house for a teacher, register their children, and pay the registration fee for the year. In the following extract from this speech, the headmaster places the work he is requesting people do in a framework of reciprocity: you do the work, and I will open the school.

> The teachers have come and we would like to start work, but we can't. Yesterday I told the school inspector that you are going to finish up some work on the school and after that we'll start school. He said that was okay. . . . When we give the word, the school will open. . . . So, on Monday, don't sit around. Leave your pandanus nuts in the forest. If you think your children are important, bring them down to the school and sign them up. . . . There's a lot of work to do. Do this work and I'll send a report about this down to the school inspector's office. Let's just do this. Parents, I'm giving you room to do your part. Go sign your kids up and prepare what you need to. We can't open the doors of the school until you do. You get everything ready first and when we tell you, we'll all have a meeting, make an offering to God and start school. So, don't think that tomorrow we're going to start school. Get the registration list prepared, add your children's names, and pay the registration fee.

The headmaster links the opening of the school to the completion of the work. Only after the work is complete will he and the school inspector give the okay for the school year to start. In effect, the headmaster leverages his own power over the school to give force to his words. Community members cannot send their kids to school unless they do what he tells them to.

This is the kind of rhetoric one hears from leaders who have control over significant resources, such as functionaries who control the operation of schools or who run programs for the conservation NGO, people who have a large number of pigs, or those who have control over powerful sorcery. They leverage their control over resources to encourage people to do what they say, couching their threats or promises in terms of exchange and reciprocity. Of course, their ability to influence others depends on their ability to control the disposition of things that people want (rewards) or do not want (punishments). When the headmaster threatens to keep the school closed, for instance, his power to influence people's behavior is parasitic on his control over the school and children's education.

These threats and promises often do work (although not in the case of the headmaster's speech). After a student insulted a teacher at the primary school in Gua, for instance, the teacher demanded an apology, which the student refused to give. So, the teacher withheld end-of-the-year grades for his class. In effect, he went on strike (see chapter 1), preventing the students in his class from moving on to the next grade. The school board and headmaster quickly got involved, and the teacher got the apology he wanted.

Likewise, men gain an audience for their directives if they have the wherewithal to contribute to people's school fees, bridewealth payments, funerary gifts, and other exchange obligations. The promise of potential gifts—and the threat of not providing them—earns them an attentive and willing audience. In the classic "big man" style, men gain power by creating obligations through wealth exchange. In the past, aspiring leaders built up influence especially through bridewealth transactions, providing pigs and money for the bridewealth payments of relatives and others in the community.[12] They continue to do so and provide other means of support as well, such as paying school fees for other people's children. In return, these aspiring leaders retain influence over those who receive these gifts. They can call on young people whose school fees they paid or whose bridewealth they contributed to to support their positions in meetings, menace their rivals, and lend them material support or labor when needed. Gifts given and promised lend force to the words of a big man, who will remind his audience of all he has done for them or will do for them if they heed his requests.[13]

In all these cases, speakers use promises and threats of future reciprocity or reminders of past gifts to induce people to listen to them. They leverage their control over resources to vest their words with power. The rhetoric of expertise works somewhat differently. Compare the headmaster's speech to this address given by the school board chairman at a Parent-Child Association (PCA) meeting for the Nokopo-Nian primary school. As the 2008 school year wore on, an increasing number of students had stopped regularly attending classes. The headmaster had made up a list of students who had many absences and asked that the parents of those children come speak with him about how to remedy the situation. But these parents failed to do so, and at the PCA meeting, he and the school board chairman urged them to come. The following excerpt from the school board chairman's speech provides a sense of how they did so:

> A major issue the headmaster mentioned is that the government will help Nokopo school, but they won't just send us money. They will count the number of children and give us support based on that. . . . If we remove children's names from our school roster, the number of students

will go down. Change will not happen as a result [i.e., the primary school will not add an additional seventh and eighth grade as people hoped that it would]. Why? The number of students will decide. We think that we are going to grow and add new grades. But if the number of children is small, we won't be able to quickly add grades. Why? We think that next year we will add on seventh grade. That is our dream. We gave a report about this to the school inspector. He came and said the number of students has gone down so we won't be able to add on seventh grade. Parents, what can we say? The children have run away from school, so what are we going to say?

The power to add additional grades to the Nokopo school, they say, lies with the school inspector and the provincial educational bureaucracy. It is not the school board chairman himself who is threatening to block expansion of the school if parents do not help improve student attendance (in contrast to the headmaster's threat to keep the school closed until work on the school is completed). Neither the school board chairman nor the headmaster claims the power to do so. Rather, the school board chairman points up the power of distant educational authorities, claiming *they* have the power to provide or withhold resources that the community is interested in. To harness that power, people in the community need to understand how the educational bureaucracy works.

There is a kind of reciprocal give-and-take here, but it is not between the local school leaders and their audience. The reciprocity is between the community and the provincial educational bureaucracy: if the community increases the number of students, then the educational bureaucracy will allow the school to grow. The bureaucracy is the ultimate source of power here, not the orator. But the orator *is* involved in this give-and-take as a mediator, providing the community with *knowledge* of how to engage effectively with this power. In sharing knowledge about the workings of the educational bureaucracy, the school board chairman is giving his audience a measure of power. They now have the knowledge they need to interact effectively with the educational authorities and bring about the future they desire. The power of the school board chairman's words to influence the behavior of his audience is *parasitic* on the power of distant authorities to do something for his audience.

The parasitic nature of this power is a distinctive feature of expertise as a medium of political communication: orators vest their words with power not by leveraging their own control over resources or their own capabilities (e.g., by threatening to use sorcery) but by drawing parasitically on the power of third parties, typically distant others that are regarded as particularly potent.[14] Experts offer their audience an understanding of how these actors—conservation

NGOs, forest spirits, *gapma*, the Christian God—operate, in effect giving audience members a measure of control over them. We have already seen this in numerous examples. There is Peter who explains the power of *gapma* to curse people and the power of church offerings to undo the effects of such curses. There is Po'o, an expert on ancestral designs who explains the power of national politicians to print money with local sacra on it (see chapter 2). There is Franklin who explains that if you support the conservation NGO, you will retain control of your <u>netsa</u> and receive benefits from the NGO. Community leaders in Nian point out that if you give pigs to a church celebration, then the Christian God will bless your life (see chapter 1), and so on and so on.

In conveying expert knowledge to listeners, orators provide listeners with the ability to use the powers of these powerful actors and institutions to benefit themselves. At the same time, orators use the promise of control over these powerful actors to influence audience members to act—to support the conservation work, to give pigs to the church celebration, to give offerings to the church and sacred designs to national politicians.

In the politics of expertise in the Yopno Valley, experts present themselves as mediators between listeners and powerful others inhabiting the dim margins of existence. Leaders channel control over these distant and powerful third parties and give it to listeners, lending themselves a measure of power and influence along the way. In an anarchic political environment where community leaders have limited means of coercion at their disposal, expertise provides a source of power that leaders can draw on parasitically. Leaders need not have wealth or other resources to offer their audiences to encourage them to listen; instead, they provide knowledge of others that have extensive resources and powerful capabilities, allowing relatively powerless "anarchic leaders" to gain a measure of power in the process.

Truth and the Pragmatics of Listening

Leadership in the anarchic villages of the Yopno Valley is a fraught business. Leaders are expected to organize the collective efforts of community members to pursue widely valued projects—building schools and churches, hosting public events, ensuring the spiritual health of the community, providing opportunities for development and the like. But they must do this in a context where community members carefully guard their self-determination and routinely ignore leaders' dictates.

As I showed in this chapter, the communication of expertise provides a way to navigate the tension between effective leadership and the anarchic ethos prominent in Yopno politics. Lacking coercive power or resources of their own, community leaders leverage their purported esoteric knowledge of distant and powerful third parties. By providing much-needed insight into the workings of these powerful actors, leaders promise to give listeners greater power and control over their future, even as they shape the conduct of those who listen: spurring them to fix up schools, provide pigs for celebrations, and support the conservation NGO, among other collective projects.

In achieving a delicate balance between the self-determination of community members and the controlling hand of village leaders, much hinges on the *truth* of the expertise that leaders offer. False representations of how the world works do not empower listeners. Indeed, they have the power to rob them of their control over the future (a point discussed in more detail in the next chapter).[15] In the politics of expertise in the Yopno Valley, truth is of the essence, which raises a particularly thorny issue.

Over the past several decades, a number of influential accounts of expertise and the social life of knowledge have deliberately and productively sidestepped questions of truth. Some, in an "archaeological" vein (in the Foucauldian sense), focus not on the truth of the knowledges or discourses they consider but instead on their internal logic—the presuppositions they harbor and codify about the world and how it works. Edward Said's (1978, 5) study of orientalism is a classic example, where his concern is "not with correspondence between Orientalism and Orient, but with the internal consistency of Orientalism and its ideas about the Orient . . . despite or beyond any correspondence or lack thereof, with a 'real' Orient."[16]

Others, in a more "genealogical" vein (again in the Foucauldian sense), are "primarily interested, not in whether our representations are in good epistemic standing, but . . . in what our representations do" (Srinivasan 2019, 141).[17] Here too, attention to the truth of knowledges and discourses is bracketed in favor of looking at what might be called the "social pragmatics of knowledge": both the ways in which knowledge and expertise are socially produced and the effects that particular forms of knowledge and expertise have on the social world. As Amia Srinivasan (141) points out, these critical genealogists tend to dwell on the oppressive function of expert knowledges. Becoming an object of knowledge—through the medical gaze, Christian confession, or the carceral panopticon, for instance—is to become an object of domination (Foucault 1997, 179). To be "interpellated" in schools and churches—identified and located within a particular ideological vision of reality—is to be rendered a subject fit for domination and exploitation (Althusser 1971). This emphasis on the oppressive function of representations not only brackets questions of truth but also makes it hard to understand why people willingly seek out expert advice and knowledge—unless of course they are dupes.

But can we divorce questions of truth from the social pragmatics of knowledge in this way? Can we analyze the effects of knowledge and expertise without reference to the veracity of that knowledge and expertise? When we adopt the listener's point of view, as I sought to do in this chapter, the possibility of such a neat split seems questionable. Certainly, in the Yopno politics of expertise, the accuracy of expert representations and their social effects appear indissociable from the listener's point of view. Whether listeners are empowered by the expertise they hear or robbed of their self-determination depends fundamentally on the truth of what they are told. If the conservation NGO really will provide benefits to people, as Muyan claims, then Muyan's "gift of expertise" really is that: it provides the listener with knowledge they can use to enhance their control over their future. But if it turns out that Muyan is wrong or lying, the effect of sharing this bit of "expert" advice is quite the opposite: it effectively robs the gullible listener of their self-determination, leading them to help the NGO only to receive nothing in return.

From the listener's perspective, what expert representations *do*—the effects they have—hinge on their veracity. In that respect, questions of truth are pragmatic through and through. And I would venture that in many instances this is the case for audiences beyond the Yopno Valley who seek out the advice and instruction of experts to gain a better grip on reality.[18] As Bernard Williams (2010, 42–43) among others has pointed out, an epistemic division of labor is likely a universal aspect of human social life: in a very basic sense, "each person in a collective group needs information which he or she is not in the best position to acquire." Communication enables people better positioned to acquire information to share it with others who might have a use for it. The veracity of the communicated information may or may not be a particular concern of those who supply it to others—after all, there is value in deceiving one's audience. But from the listeners' point of view, the pragmatic value of accurate information is quite clear. True representations are "invaluable instruments of action" (James 1978, 97), providing those who hold them the means to understand and interact more effectively with the world around them—including those powerful and distant third parties with which the expertise circulating in the Yopno Valley is particularly concerned.

Representations have power to do things, as the scholarship on expertise and the social life of knowledge has amply demonstrated. They have the "world-making" power to shape reality, influencing how people think of and act on themselves and the world around them. But from the listener's point of view, expert representations have another kind of power. Anarchic listeners in the Yopno Valley do not turn to experts to have worlds constructed for them; they turn to experts to gain access to better, more accurate and comprehensive insight into the world around them.[19] They are interested not in the "world-making" power of representations but in the "world-disclosing" power of *true* representations. By holding onto accurate insights into distant, often inscrutable third parties, anarchic listeners are empowered; they gain some control over those powerful third parties, which in turn enables them to take greater control of their own future.[20] It is hopes for empowerment of this sort that lead anarchic listeners to participate in the Yopno politics of expertise, as I showed in this chapter. And it is hopes of this sort that, perhaps ironically, leave anarchic listeners open to the influence and controlling hand of community leaders offering the "gift" of expertise. In this way, expertise renders domination and leadership part and parcel of the anarchic politics of Yopno villages.

DECEPTION AND THE DANGERS OF LISTENING

Deception is a prevalent concern in the Yopno Valley and for good reason: it is a routine part of life. From an early age, children are subject to lies and tricks to get them to behave. They are led to fear monsters that are not there and promised goodies that they never end up getting. Once I was surprised to hear a young girl offer to buy a bag of chips for her screaming little brother. I had never seen anyone in the valley buy something as superfluous as a bag of chips. When I expressed my surprise, she explained that she was just tricking him into being quiet.[1]

Children respond to this trickery in kind, tricking each other and the adults around them. A five-year-old boy spent one evening meal pointing up at the wall of the house and saying to me, "That, up there" (*asu*). Looking and seeing nothing, I asked him what he was pointing at. He just repeated the expression, over and over in varying tones of voice. After repeatedly failing to see anything, I finally asked his parents what he was pointing at. They said he was just tricking me.

Subjected to tricks throughout childhood—and hearing plenty of stories about others being tricked (see the historical tales discussed in chapter 2)—people learn that deception is a regular part of communicative life.[2] And they learn to be vigilant. Among the most common terms of abuse children hurl at each other is *tɨpgo tɨkɲɨ* ("you're full of it" or "bullshit!"). Adults are no less on guard against the tricks of others, though they are less bold about making overt accusations of this sort.

Both the prevalence of deception and people's wariness of it strike at the heart of the efforts of anarchic listeners to shape their future by holding onto the words of others. A prime reason people seek out and listen to others, as I showed in chapter 3, is to gain a better understanding of an obscure reality. Deceptive communication and even expertise that proves unintentionally misleading offer none of these benefits. Indeed, they *detract* from listeners' control over the world around them. When a child is tricked into thinking they will get some chips if they stop crying, their compliance does not produce the future—and the chips—they want.

Of course, with children the ethics and politics of deception are typically not something that worries people much; children's intense willfulness needs tempering. But deception poses a serious threat to adults' sense of self-determination. Community leaders, spirits, neighbors, and people from outside the valley are all suspected of using deception to trick people into acting against their will. A friend of mine, Wonka, for instance, reported to me with evident grief how others in his village mocked him for helping a phone company clear land to install a mobile phone tower. "People gossiped about us," he told me, "saying things like: 'They think their efforts will bring cellphone service to the valley but there's nothing that's going to come of it. They all are just the company's work boys [*amɨn dakon oman*; "the laborers of those people"]. They are worthless old men.'" As he told me this in 2014, the communities in the valley were enjoying mobile phone service for the first time, thanks to the tower that did in fact get built. He had not been deceived after all, although the bitterness of being called the "work boy" of a mobile phone company clearly lingered.

Deception brings with it disempowerment, shame, and subordination; it cuts at the heart of the aims of anarchic listening. But in a way, the threat of deception *enhances* the importance of listening in the anarchic politics of the valley. On guard against the ever-present possibility of deception, people evaluate the words of others carefully to determine whether they are genuine. And to do that effectively requires listening even more, as I hope to show in this chapter.

In the realm of scientific practice, Bruno Latour (1987, 39) has shown that controversies about scientific facts result in the proliferation of discourse: "The controversy swells. More and more [scientific] papers are involved in the mêlée, each of them positioning all the others (fact, fiction, technical details), but no one being able to fix these positions *without the help of the others*. So, more and more papers, enrolling more and more papers, are needed at each stage of the discussion—and the disorder increases in proportion." A controversial paper gives rise to a host of new papers, commenting on and critiquing the controversial one. These make reference to a host of other papers, enlisting even more texts to support their argument. In this way, scientific disputes result in a proliferation of discourse.

In the Yopno Valley, the threat of deception leads to a proliferation of discourse in much the same way Latour describes for scientific controversies. Worried that the advice of community leaders or the proposals of the conservation

NGO may be deceptive, people talk them over with family and clan mates in discussions, where they evaluate (*silip a-*) whether they are true or false, genuine or deceptive. Then they talk them over again with others from their village in more conversations. They even evaluate the evaluations of others they have heard in previous discussions.

All of this is discourse of a particular kind; it is intertextual or interdiscursive, in the sense that discourse or texts in one context (e.g., a controversial research paper, a proposal made by the conservation NGO) are linked to those in another (e.g., the critique of the controversial paper, a later evaluation of the NGO's proposal). As noted by linguistic anthropologists, literary theorists, and others, quoting, paraphrasing, commenting on, critiquing, and otherwise reiterating the words of others are pervasive aspects of discourse.[3] These are techniques that enable speakers to interact, in effect, with others in different contexts—identifying with them, distancing themselves from them, or otherwise adopting a stance toward them. And it is through these sorts of intertextual connections that broader institutional processes and political projects take shape in discourse. Scientific knowledge emerges, Latour argues, as proliferating critiques of a research paper give way to consensus in the scientific community. Scientific facts and truths emerge in the *relationship* between texts. They are not the work of an individual scientist; instead they are the result of a *collective* process of scientists producing texts critiquing, commenting on, and ultimately building on the texts of other scientists (Latour 1987, 29, passim).

In a similar vein, intertextually linked discussions in the Yopno Valley transform the evaluation of others' words from an individual activity into a collective one. Faced with the possibility of deception, people turn to others—family members, friends, and knowledgeable experts—to help them listen better. They talk over the proposals of community leaders, the conservation NGO, and others, listening to how others in the community have evaluated them in an effort to avoid being deceived. Although deceptive and misleading speech poses a threat to the anarchic listener, it does not stop people from listening to others. Rather, it pushes people to listen *more*, in effect transforming listening into a collective endeavor.

The Virtues of Deception

Much as the workings of the world are often taken to be obscure in the Yopno Valley, so too is people's speech. This is because speech often is, in fact, opaque. Lies (*top*; giaman) make it difficult to discern the difference between speech that is true and speech that is false. Speech that disguises and dissimulates (*gen pasulu*; hait tok, 'hidden speech') makes it difficult to see the speaker's true thoughts, feelings, and motives. Such speech is not a transparent lens on the world it purports to describe or on the subjectivity of the speaker who speaks it. Instead, it is an opaque barrier that limits auditors' ability to understand the true significance of what is said and the intentions of those who say it.

Often, the prevalence of such opaque forms of speech is, as in many other parts of Papua New Guinea, the result of political considerations. "Straightforward speech" (*noman gen*)—the very opposite of deception and dissimulation, ambiguity and vagueness—can be counterproductive and dangerous. It poses a threat to village harmony and the well-being of speakers.[4] Far from being the object of condemnation, lies and dissimulation are recognized as playing an essential role in sustaining village life.

When I asked people why women did not play more of a role in leading villages, the most common answer I received was that they were not capable of deception. They did not know how to hide (*pasul*) talk and were too direct (*noman*): they said what was on their mind.[5] Several times I heard men caution their wives to stay quiet lest they stir up trouble. On one occasion, my host in Weskokop Mangau arrived home upset because she had discovered that a pig had been rummaging around in one of her gardens. She started issuing loud threats from the house and promised to take the issue up later with the owners of the pig. Her husband Nanda tried to calm her down, pointing out that nothing would come of her threats but trouble. The person she blamed would shift the blame to someone else, and everyone would end up bickering. Better to hide these feelings than to create social tensions that would be hard to resolve.

The stereotype of women stirring up trouble does not offer an accurate account of the nature of gender differences. There are many women with very cool heads and men who voice their anger and complaints publicly. But it is true that community leaders are expected to be mediators and should not be hotheads.[6] The men who publicly speak out about their true thoughts and feelings tend not to be people who end up as community leaders. That kind of talk stirs up trouble and is ultimately counterproductive, leading people to feel shame (*mayektok*) and lose their strength to act.[7] The preschool teacher in Nian, for instance, threatened to shut down the local preschool when he learned that people were claiming behind his back (*manjip gen*; tok baksait) that he had failed to pay school fees for his children even as he was publicly asking others to do so. After catching word of this gossip, the preschool teacher lashed out one day at market:

> This is how you all are talking about me: "He's asking for school fees when he himself hasn't paid them. So, we're not going to pay our school fees." But I did pay them. . . . This is not my business [i.e., I do not make money from the school]. You point your finger at me . . . and all of my

> strength collapses. With what strength will I do my work? . . . The consequence of this is that after this year what is going to happen? . . . You can pay a teacher from somewhere else to come speak for Nian village and do something for Nian village.

Making use of a common expression here, the teacher notes how accusations sap people of their strength ("all of my strength collapses"). In this way, criticisms and other kinds of too direct speech lead to a breakdown of community life, as those who are its targets withdraw from community affairs. One solution is to keep straight talk hidden, speaking it behind people's backs; but if it becomes public, as it did in this case, problems arise.

Even more worrisome, engaging in straight talk risks making oneself a target for those upset by what they heard.[8] In an uncommonly public instance of anger, Konu—a community leader from Gua—went so far as to place a curse (jobɨt) on a critic, who had complained about his efforts to organize a fundraiser in the neighboring village of Ganggalut. Konu and the other organizers of this fundraiser for the elementary school in Ganggalut were, curiously, people from the neighboring village of Gua, who explained to me that they were helping organize the event because Ganngalut had no effective leaders of its own.[9] The fact that Ganggalut locals were excluded rankled a number of people in the village, and on the final day of the fundraiser people awoke to find a set of complaints posted publicly on a sign staked in the middle of the village.

At a church service held after the sign was discovered, Konu demanded that people bring it to him. Konu displayed it for everyone to see and, with a rising voice, began to denounce the author:

> You believers here in this plaza. You have gathered your belief together. Something to break up that belief has come. Do you see it? Here. You see it clearly. You who made this, you think you are really smart? You think, "I am capable of doing these things [i.e., organizing an event like this]," and you put up this sign? Hey, you wrote my name here. I didn't do anything wrong.

Growing more and more furious, he then publicly cursed the author of the sign:

> We are trying to help you. This is not good talk. It is awful talk. I'm going to evaluate you and tell you what I see. This sort of thing is the way to destroy our efforts. I gather God and Satan together to decide what will happen to your life. Hear that! I gather God and Satan to decide what will happen to your life. You, the one who made this sign. You who wrote this, your death, whatever happens to you, I'm going to say "no" to you. You have destroyed the school there. You have destroyed the school.

The egg we place there you have broken. You who've done this, you're smart. I beat you down to the bones. You are last of everything, hear that! You who've done this, you are last of all things. Before heaven and earth, I declare this: "The door is closed."

Not only did the chairman of the organizing committee rail against the anonymous author for undermining the collective efforts of the community but also, to the applause of the assembled crowd, he then placed a curse publicly on the creator of the sign.

The publicly-voiced criticism on the sign not only threatened to dampen the determination of those who read it, but also led to retaliation. It is notable that in the two instances I discuss here, those who made frank comments about others attempted to mask their identity from the people they were talking about, either by speaking behind their back or posting a sign anonymously. The stakes of saying what one thinks and how one feels can be quite high.

As the ones attempting to influence the conduct of often recalcitrant community members, village leaders are particularly alert to the dangers of straight talk. They tend to be adept at masking their thoughts and feelings by using deception and dissimulation. Gathering ahead of time to discuss how they can most effectively persuade community members to support their proposals, they also carefully consider how to talk about issues so as not to raise the hackles of their audience—papering over conflicts, disguising their true intentions, and generally speaking in less direct ways.

Consider how community leaders from Weskokop village and the Lutheran parish discussed the challenge posed by Foape. Foape was a longtime resident of Weskokop, who had come to the village decades earlier to start a mission school. At the time, he was given land to build a house and plant gardens, and he had gone on to raise children, who were themselves raising children there. He is revered in the community for bringing education to Weskokop, but the population of the village had increased and space for housing was running short. In particular, the community needed space to build houses for newly arriving elementary schoolteachers, who would be coming to start a new elementary school.[10]

As someone who was not a member of a clan or patriline with rights to land in the village, Foape had built a house and planted gardens at the pleasure of the true landowners in the village, who had designated land for him to use. This is a common way in which outside workers—church workers, school workers, government workers—are supported by communities in the valley. In Foape's case, he was widely respected and appreciated by the community, and he was allowed to stay in the village even after his time working there was done.

Yet people in the community were starting to complain about his use of village land. He had annexed some neighboring land over the years, and his children and grandchildren were continuing to live there. This rankled the villagers, who needed the land for the new elementary school. People talked about these land issues behind Foape's back, but they were scared of saying anything to him directly. As one person put it, "He's an old man, so if he wants to give you a blessing he'll do it. If he wants to give you a curse, he'll do that. We are afraid of this and tremble." The curses of older people are particularly frightening, because after a person dies it is difficult to get them to retract them.

So, leaders from Weskokop and from the local Lutheran church parish gathered to discuss the issue. Taningkeo, the president of the parish, had previously tried to talk to Foape about needing his land, but as he put it in the meeting, he spoke too directly (*nakda wo nomansi esat*; "I went up and told him quite directly"), accusing Foape of appropriating more land than the ancestors in Weskokop had given him. Foape rebuffed him, saying that he knew all about the issue and would make room for the elementary teachers once they arrived. But there were doubts. People in the community had been complaining about Foape's presence and the expansion of his fence line for a while. These complaints had gotten his back up, which is in part why he was so prickly when the parish president suggested he move. The question for the participants in this discussion was how to get Foape to move without bringing down a curse on themselves or ramping up the tensions between Foape and other villagers.

The solution they came up with was to paper over the conflict and their true motives:

> NANDA: That's the thing, by what means will you inspire him to adjust the boundary of his homestead? You must talk about the positive side of things. Don't talk about the sorts of things where there is conflict, saying things like: "Because of disputes about land you can't stay here." Don't talk like that. We will speak to him about the positive side of things. You go to the positive side, and he will feel at ease. He will judge that it is true, and he will adjust the boundary. Let's do this all together.
>
> TANINGKEO: The elementary school, it was Foape himself who had the desire and had sex. He was pregnant, and now his child wants to walk. That kind of talk I will tell him later.
>
> PASTOR: The fruit of your work; it's a blessing that has come so you look after it.
>
> [UNKNOWN]: You can't lie to him. You will tell him the truth.

> DRONGO: It wants to come so if you adjust the boundary, it will come.
>
> TANINGKEO: Like that. When it was a young sapling, you didn't crush it. Why did you speak out for it and care for it?

Like many discussions of this sort, the participants carefully considered how the listener—Foape—would respond to their entreaties. Nanda claims that the old man would judge what they have to say, see that it is true, and then proceed to make way for the elementary school. They cannot lie, as one of the participants points out; Foape is a smart old man, and he is already wary of their efforts to get him to adjust the boundaries of his land. Instead, they hatch a plan to turn to the "positive side," disguising their underlying intention; namely, to get him to move his fence line.

The approach they come up with is to play up his role as the "mother of education" in the village: Foape gave birth to the school by bringing the first mission school to the village, so he would not want to keep it from growing now by keeping elementary schoolteachers from coming, would he? Dissembling offers a way to steer clear of critical, disparaging, and forceful rhetoric that would foment conflict. Instead of talking straightforwardly about how he annexed other people's land and his family overstayed their welcome, they plan to take a more circuitous route to their true objective: they would point out a way he could enhance his legacy in the village, focusing on the positive side of things. In this way, they hoped to tamp down on the simmering conflict.

As Nanda puts it later in this discussion,

> Don't disparage him. Build a trap and catch him. . . . You've seen, I often explain how to influence people. For that, you speak gently and squeeze their testicles and they'll pee. . . . If you speak directly, he'll tell you "essss" [a sign of angry dismissal]. Our hair is already standing up on end! [because they fear that anger will lead him to curse them].

Although this approach may not constitute a lie per se, there is something deceptive about it: the strategy masks an underlying effort to get Foape to do something he does not want to do. It also masks the frustration and anger at him that have emerged in the community. That there might be such emotions and motives lying behind people's carefully crafted words is an ever-present reality. Indeed, everyone in the valley has participated in events like this one where people collectively craft modes of indirection. The result is that everyone is aware that words are often misleading.

In the anarchic politics of Yopno villages, where people are keenly sensitive to slights and intrusions in their affairs, deception, dissimulation, and indirection have an important role to play in public speech.[11] They are tools that community leaders use to try to influence people to adjust their behavior while also trying not to spark further conflict. To sustain peace within a village and to ensure leaders' own safety, speech needs to be deceptive at times.

Deception flourishes not only in these sort of careful efforts to formulate rhetoric: it is also part of everyday interaction. The moment when it really hit home for me how much deception is built into day-to-day speech occurred during a morning I spent with one of my hosts in Nian village. He was the treasurer of the local school and spent much of the morning talking about school finances with other school board members. Money was missing from the accounts, and my host complained to other board members that the headmaster was misappropriating funds. The conversation got quite heated as school board members lambasted the headmaster for stealing.

When that conversation ended, my host and I headed down to the school area to meet with the headmaster. I assumed that the point of the meeting was to talk about the missing funds. When the topic finally came up, they both genially agreed that the funds must have been misappropriated by the school board chairman. On the way back to our house, I asked who really had misappropriated the funds. My host said without hesitation that the headmaster had taken them, that he was an untrustworthy fellow, and that he should not be allowed to run the school.

I was startled by his straightforward assessment and the easy way in which he had acted deceptively. He moved from offering one view of the situation to suggesting another, all the while being quite certain about who was the guilty party. Indeed, who knew whether what he told me was, in fact, his true view of the matter. That is the seed of doubt that creeps in when one observes the regular deceptions perpetrated by others and when one is so adept at being deceptive oneself. The aim of all this deception is to keep the peace and keep oneself out of trouble, but it renders speech opaque, masking people's genuine thoughts, feelings, and intentions. After all, how can anyone's word be believed or actions trusted when deception is such a regular part of daily interaction? In a context where everyone has experience with deceiving and being deceived, the possibility of deception is baked into people's expectations when they interact with others.[12]

Anarchic Listening and the Dangers of Deception

Deceptive, indirect, and otherwise opaque forms of speech, as I just showed, serve as ways to promote social harmony. In a context where people closely guard their self-determination and their worth in the eyes of others, opaque speech enables speakers to mask issues that would give rise to conflict. But the opacity of speech also poses a danger. Deception and indirection can be used not only as means of fostering peace in the community but also to manipulate and subjugate others. In the stories currently told of the men's house regime, for instance, the power of men was premised on an elaborate deception. Women were told that a powerful spirit was calling for food, when in fact it was the men turning a bull roarer. To appease the spirit, the women would bring pork that the men themselves would eat. Deception served as a way for men to control both women and pork.

Given the potential for deception to be used in this way, listeners are understandably on guard against the dangers that it poses. Recall the story of the conversion of Nian village, which I discussed in the introduction. Historically, the neighboring villages of Nian and Nokopo were enemies. These two villages engaged in periods of open hostility, fighting with bows and arrows, as well as occult violence. (Open warfare, with bows and arrows, was reserved for intervillage conflict; occult violence was directed both within and between different villages.) As the Christian gospel spread throughout the valley in the middle of the twentieth century, missionaries established themselves in Nokopo and from there tried to coax people in Nian to join the church. The missionaries sent Nokopo villagers as messengers, particularly those whose mothers or other female relatives came from Nian. These were the kind of intermediaries who often played an important role in easing hostilities between neighboring villages. And it was these relatives of Nian who were sent to tell people of the coming of Christianity and to try to get them to come down to Nokopo to learn more about the new religion.

In the way the story was depicted at the tenth anniversary celebration of the church building in Nian, messengers from Nokopo called out to the still heathen Nian villagers, who cowered in fear, holding up their bows and arrows. A narrator described the action:

> The call from God tells the first missionary from Nokopo: "Find your friends, the people of Nian!" The missionary goes up to Nian, looks for them, and calls out to them. And the people in Nian respond: "Don't go to Nokopo! If you go there, you will die!"
> The missionary from Nokopo talked and talked but got nowhere.
> He gave up. He talked a great deal and he gave up. He left the people in Nian and he turned back for home. [The actor walks back across the village plaza.] So let's follow him back. He goes to his village and what is going to happen? What will they say, what will they do? Let's take a look and see what happens.

At this point, the actor playing the first missionary, who has returned to the No-kopo side of the plaza, says to the people there:

> Our friends were afraid of the call of God. They went far away from me. So, I brought the call with me. I put it in your hands and you go try.

The call of God was symbolized in the skit by a conch shell, which people used to blow to call people for church services. It is another example of the kind of metaphorical objects that are often used in skits and gift exchanges (see chapter 2).

The next missionary then walks across the plaza to "Nian" and talks with the people there (talk that was out of range of my audio recorder). When the missionary is finished, the people of Nian run away. The narrator describes what has just occurred:

> The people in Nian say: "The missionary from Nokopo is tricking you so that you will go close to him, and he will take a piece of your food and poison you." That's what the people in Nian say, so they are afraid and run away. People in Nian say: "You lie and trick us. When we go down to Nokopo and you leave us, the people in No-kopo will kill us. You leave by yourself!" To each other they say: "He's a trickster who will take you and kill you; he is tempting us so we ran away from him."

This continues for several more rounds until, finally, the people in Nian are swayed when one man in Nian decides that what the messengers are saying is true and agrees to follow them.

The skit offers a recognizable (if a bit over-the-top) portrayal of the vigilance of listeners who are trying to avoid being deceived. Just as people have every reason to distrust the words of community leaders, expecting that an ulterior motive lurks behind them, the people of Nian had every reason to disbelieve the people from Nokopo. Tricks of this sort were part of the ongoing hostilities between the communities, and people had to take care not to be deceived.

At the same time, however, the vigilance of listeners in Nian threatens to keep people from learning about Christianity, which most people in the valley would now consider to be a disastrous outcome. The audience watching the drama knows full well that Nokopo was not trying to deceive Nian: the Christianized present testifies to the good intentions of Nokopo and the foolishness of people in Nian. As in many skits, the butts of the joke are the heathen ancestors, who in this instance are so foolish that they do not listen to the missionaries when they bring the Word of God. Like so many historical narratives and so much public instruction, this skit dwells on the theme of people who do not understand the context they are in and end up acting foolishly—even dangerously—as a result.

But in this case, it is listeners' efforts to avoid being deceived that leads them to, in essence, deceive themselves.

The skit neatly dramatizes the dangers of anarchic listening in a context where the trustworthiness, sincerity, and truth of speech are often in question. Deception can lead to subjugation and even cost people their lives. Routinely, people mask their true thoughts and feelings, and community leaders inveigle people to act in ways they otherwise would not. Yet as this skit makes plain, the solution is not simply to ignore the words of others, assuming that they are all duplicitous. Listeners need to be prepared to hold onto words that will help them get a grip on the realities that confront them; doing so will help them improve their lives and even get into heaven. Anarchic listeners must do more than just evaluate the words of others; they must evaluate the words of others *well*, correctly distinguishing deception from truth. But how?

At the time the skit was performed, a similar predicament confronted people in their dealings with the US-based conservation NGO operating in the valley. The NGOs signature accomplishment was the establishment of a national conservation area in the Yopno and neighboring valleys in January 2009, the largest of its kind in the country. The conservation area included roughly three hundred square miles of land pledged by landowners in the Yopno, Uruwa, and Som (YUS) Valleys, land that could no longer be used for hunting and harvesting materials. For the roughly 11,000 people living in the YUS region who find food, housing materials, and firewood in the forests surrounding their villages and whose land is home to powerful forest spirits, these pledges were not made lightly.

Some in the valley were quite vocal about the importance of supporting the conservation efforts, but many more were uncertain about what would come of pledging their land to the conservation area. Would they receive money in exchange for their pledges of land? Would the conservation NGO keep poachers off their land if it became part of the conservation area? How could they use the land that they pledged? More generally, why was this US-based NGO so interested in their land in the first place? The conservation NGO made efforts to explain what they were doing and why, but questions persisted. I was routinely quizzed about the NGO's work and did my best to respond to people's questions, sharing what I knew of the conservation project. But often my responses did not seem to satisfy people, and discussions of the matter continued.

People were particularly interested in—and confused about—the benefits the conservation NGO was providing people in the valley. One particularly important benefit was a program to sponsor young people from the YUS region to attend the teachers' training college in Lae, the city closest to the valley. Every other year, a number of students from the region would be selected, their schooling would be paid for, and afterward they would be expected to return to the

YUS Valleys as (paid) teachers for a number of years. However, people were unclear about the selection process for these scholarships. Many parents wondered whether their children would receive this benefit in exchange for pledging their land. Others expected that their support for conservation-related events would help earn their children a place in this program. What, they wondered, did they have to do to receive these scholarships?

These questions ramped up as people in the villages around the government station at Teptep (Gua, Ganggalut, Taeng, and Weskokop villages) prepared to host a celebration marking the establishment of the conservation area in April 2009. National and provincial leaders, including the prime minister, were expected to attend, and villagers were anticipating an event like none seen before in the region. For months, they had been preparing accommodations, collecting garden produce, securing pigs, and gathering firewood for the influx of visitors expected from other villages in the region, as well as politicians, representatives of conservation organizations, and the press (see figure 8).

FIGURE 8.   A representative of the YUS area schools gives gifts to the Hon. Benny Allan, minister for Environment and Conservation, at the celebration marking the establishment of the YUS Conservation Area.

Photograph by author.

As the preparations proceeded, there were extended discussions about the benefits people would receive for helping with the conservation work. One claim often made by the event's organizers was that volunteering to help prepare for the celebration was a way to secure benefits from the NGO. In the village of Ganggalut, community leaders made the point repeatedly as well. One day, after most people failed to show up to help build a dining area for the event, the men and women in the community gathered and community leaders urged people to support the efforts. One leader, Maŋnu, summarized much of what the other leaders had been saying in the meeting:

> Our eyes don't see the benefits of helping with conservation work. So we think, "What sort of thing is this we are doing?" While we think that way and are doubtful, other villages do the work because they have already seen the fruits of this work [i.e., they have received scholarships to the teachers' training college].
>
> You do the work, and afterward, you will see the benefit. In a short time, you will see it, and what will you think then? It's because you do the work now, that's what we're saying.
>
> You see Kumbul and Weskokop villages. Tomorrow they will come down and work on the grandstand, decorating it. Tomorrow we'll go up and see them. They are clear about the way the conservation NGO works. They have seen it with their eyes so they will bring things from their villages and offer them. They will surpass you. What have you been doing? Playing around? They have seen it with their eyes so they are working hard. Benefits have come to them from this. They have experienced the benefit, and they beat their chest proudly and do the work. We have seen it, but it's like we haven't seen. It's a new thing. It seems to me that we want to hide, but let's not hide.
>
> For the good of everyone, we speak until our mouth hurts. We are talking so that you understand. We speak until our mouths hurt for the good of everyone. It's not for us. That's not why we are talking. We are talking for the good of everyone. What did Kumbul village do so that now everyone there gets the benefit? The benefit of conservation has come to them. Tomorrow, you'll see, they will be out working.

Maŋnu's contribution bears many of the hallmarks of the politics of expertise discussed in the previous chapter. He emphasizes the difficulty people have "seeing" how to reap the benefits that the conservation NGO was offering people in the valley, contrasting that with the more expert perspective of people in other villages. Other villages understood the workings of the conservation NGO because they had already received its benefits. They had, as Maŋnu puts it, "seen

it with their eyes." Because people in Ganggalut had not seen it, they were uncertain about whether to participate in the preparations for the celebration.

The difficulty of confirming with one's own eyes the knowledge that self-styled
experts share is a cornerstone of the politics of expertise. Reality is often regarded as
opaque to human perception. People cannot simply look at the world around them
and understand how the Christian God works, or how the national government
produces money, or indeed how the conservation NGO deals out benefits. It is
this sense of the opacity of reality that necessitates and motivates people to listen
and hold onto the knowledge of others; unable to see the way reality works, they
turn to experts who have insight into these matters.

But the widespread perception that speech itself is often opaque and deceit-
ful complicates the situation. The expertise offered by community leaders may
itself be deceptive, or it may be simply incorrect.[13] Either way, it poses a danger
to the audience. What if people help with the preparations for the conservation
celebration (as Maŋnu and other leaders are clearly trying to encourage them to
do), and they do not end up receiving any benefit from it? They would effectively
have become the wokboi ("cheap labor") of the conservation NGO and the community leaders. Indeed, people in the village had expressed this concern, and
Maŋnu responds here by emphasizing that he is speaking out about the conservation work not for his own benefit but "for the good of everyone."

Listeners must be on guard against being deceived, but at the same time, they
must remain open to listening and holding onto the words of others. It is a complex position to be in, caught between the opacity of reality and the opacity of
speech, unable to see reality clearly on their own or to rely on the unreliable words
of others. The predicament is a common one in contexts where specialized knowledge is in question outside of the Yopno Valley as well: How can people effectively
evaluate expertise if they are not themselves experts? The issue is particularly
acute in liberal democracies, where on many issues—from climate change and
public health to finance and education—people lack the expertise to evaluate the
proposals and advice of scientists, doctors, engineers, and other specialists. And
yet, to accept the advice of experts without evaluating their expertise for its biases,
limitations, inaccuracies, and entailments is to surrender the sovereignty of "the
people" to the "rule of experts."[14] As political theorist Stephen Turner (2003, 12)
puts it, "*Recognizing* expertise is a problem. . . . It is intrinsic to the notion of expertise that the expert knows something that the consumer of expert knowledge does
not and cannot know."

People turn to experts to get a grip on an opaque reality. But if it is possible
that these self-styled experts are not in fact experts—that they are offering deceptive or mistaken accounts of the world—then, how is one to know? In the
Yopno Valley, the typical way of dealing with this predicament is to engage in

even more discussion: people talk about and collectively evaluate the purported insights of experts with other experts, friends, and family. In effect, they listen to how others listen.

Listening to the Way Others Listen

In the village of Weskokop, at around the same time as the meeting in Ganggalut, people were discussing many of the same concerns: If they give land to the conservation area, or if they helped with preparations for the celebration, would they receive sponsorships to the teachers' training college? At one of the many discussions concerning these issues, a leader in that community, Nanda—who we have seen several times, including earlier in this chapter—took the lead:

> NANDA: We will bring firewood. We will get material for torches. We are going to support the celebration for the conservation area. We are going to prepare the village in order to get the reward for doing so [i.e., a scholarship to the teachers' training college]. You support the celebration, you better educate your child at the same time. If you do that, a conservation worker will come here and say, "I see your child is prepared. They will go to teachers' training college." If not, if we haven't educated our children, we will see the reward go to others, and we will sit down, our hopes dashed. "Some people have taken the reward for my hard work. I am devastated." Will each of us think like that?
>
> TEK: Previously, I saw our friends in Kumbul village talk like that. "Before we gave land to the conservation area, what land and resources have the people selected for scholarships from other villages given?" That's what they said. After making a huge stink, I bet they used some sorcery or witchcraft.
>
> NANDA: But they didn't produce any educated children. The conservation NGO saw that the children were not well educated. "You all are not up to it." That's what the conservation NGO told the people in Kumbul and their hopes were dashed.

This is the very stuff of community discussions: a meta-discourse evaluating the words of others, sorting out the true and genuine from the false and the deceptive. Yet, unlike the illustrative community discussion presented in chapter 1, Nanda comments not only on the speech of others taking part in the discussion, such as Tek; here, words of others *outside* the meeting itself are also subject to evaluation (like those spoken in the village of Kumbul). That is, in fact, par for the course in community discussions: the words of people from outside the valley, people elsewhere in the valley, and people speaking at other times (including in earlier events of discussion) are all mulled over publicly.

Nanda is particularly keen to critique a view that was circulating widely at the time: the notion that supporting the work of the conservation NGO or pledging land to the conservation area is the way to acquire benefits from the NGO. According to Nanda, the relationship with the NGO does not involve the kind of reciprocity that is common in the Yopno Valley. It is not a matter of giving something to them—land or labor—to build a relationship with them that will bring benefits in the future. Rather, Nanda claims that benefits are given to students who are well educated. It is meritocratic achievement, not reciprocity, that will determine who receives the benefits.[15]

Evaluating a common understanding of the workings of the NGO in this way—one expressed by people in Kumbul, as well as by many in Weskokop, Ganggalut, and elsewhere in the Yopno Valley—Nanda presents himself as helping others avoid being misled; in essence, he presents himself as helping others listen better to the claims of those working with the conservation NGO. This evaluative work had a profound effect on at least one of his listeners, a young man named Monji. When Nanda finished, Monji responded by reevaluating his own involvement with the conservation area, to which his clan had pledged land:

> This is some important talk, did you hear it? This poses a challenge to those of us who have joined the conservation area. . . . I didn't understand any of this. Who explained it to me? Is this what I wanted? Who encouraged me to join? If they lied to me and misled me, then I'm in big trouble. You [i.e., those who have promoted the conservation area] have steered me into trouble. I'm not able to deal with this challenge. I'm not able to get the benefits being offered. So, why are you pushing me to join?

At this point, people in the audience start laughing. Monji's surprisingly overt expression of his feelings of confusion and dismay is not the normal stuff of discussions of this sort. When Monji then tells Nanda not to laugh at him, Nanda explains that he is laughing because he understands what Monji is driving at. The headman of the village adds, "We're laughing because you're speaking the truth." Monji continues,

> I didn't understand. My thoughts weren't clear, and you [i.e., those who have promoted the conservation area] deceived me, saying, "Come, let's work together." And now I have fallen into a hole. . . . This is no small point Nanda has made.

Ongoing discussions in the community like this one give people the opportunity to listen *more*, to hear how those in their community—especially people seen as knowledgeable like Nanda—evaluate the speeches of others. Ideally, they also provide an opportunity for people to listen *better*, as they listen to evaluations that reveal the deceptions and misleading claims of others or that highlight their veracity and trustworthiness.

Monji continues by elaborating on Nanda's words and adding support to his evaluation of what the NGO's spokespeople have been saying (all with a tongue-in-cheek claim that it is he, Monji, who is the expert identifying the deceptions of the celebration organizers):

> This work [for the conservation celebration] that you are going to do, what will you get out of it? . . . It wouldn't be good if we work hard and other people receive the benefit. I'm telling you, we are really other communities' laborers. . . . Their representatives will speak to you, and you are excited and clap about it. Don't just cheer. You don't want to cheer and strengthen their lies. You see me there at the meetings. If I feel it's not OK, I don't laugh and clap my hands. When the talk I hear is not satisfactory in my mind, when I hear something questionable, and I think it's not OK, I just sit there. You are excited for no reason. This has become your way of doing things. Stop it and clarify your thinking. You think, "If we talk like that, they will like us." . . . I don't have pigs and money, but my thinking is excellent! [laughter]. . . . Weskokop, they deceive you with kind words. They call you their slaves and pat you on the back and you keep doing it [laughter].

As Nanda did earlier, what Monji is doing here is evaluating the talk of the celebration's organizers, who are said to be deceiving the people of Weskokop, giving them a false account of what their support will get them.

At the same time, Monji is evaluating the words of Nanda, an evaluation that lends support to what Nanda has been saying. In essence, Monji purports to help his audience listen better to both Nanda's words and those of the conservation celebration organizers. Indeed, Monji complains that people have not appreciated what Nanda has been telling them—"I feel you haven't 'broken up' and 'evaluated' that important talk Nanda made" (*gen tepi tɨmɨ dɨ yusok, pɨdaŋ sɨlɨpmoro mi nandisat*)—and his speech is an effort to get them to hear it more clearly.

At the same time, by clarifying Nanda's evaluation, Monji joins Nanda in offering to help people at the meeting listen better to the celebration organizers. Instead of holding onto the words of the conservation organizers and cleaning up the area for the celebration as the organizers had said—and as people had been wont to do—people in Weskokop should disregard what they have heard, which was in fact meant to mislead them. As Nanda put it, "Those people over there who have already received the benefits from conservation, they order us about. . . . They tell you to clean up their area for the conservation celebration. If you want to get the benefit, the place to do so is there [pointing to the school]." By listening to the organizers, people were reducing themselves to their laborers or slaves. Nanda and Monji purport to be supporting people in their anarchic listening, helping them listen better and not be deceived.

Monji and Nanda's evaluation provides a good example of how the danger posed by deceptive and misleading speech is intertwined with the practice of discussion. One way to deal with the threats that deceit and falsehood pose to listeners is to listen to others, who can help evaluate claims that have been made and advice that has been given. In this way, mistrust of speech leads to more speech; the danger of listening to more listening.

Of course, these evaluations need to be evaluated too; they are not a panacea for the danger posed by deception and falsehood. But even though people may not be able to evaluate the purported expertise they hear, they do have a sense of others who are likely to offer them a truthful and trustworthy evaluation of that knowledge. As Steven Shapin (1994) has noted, the "knowledge of things" is thoroughly entangled with a "knowledge of people"; early modern English natural philosophers sorted fact from fiction on the basis of their sense of the kind of people whose reports they could trust. In the Yopno Valley, the knowledge of people often leads people to turn inward, discussing matters with close relatives and village mates, whom they feel better able to trust.[16] Nanda and Monji, for instance, highlight their identity as fellow residents of Weskokop, unmasking the deceptions of organizers from other villages. In the case of the missionization of Nian discussed in the previous section, it was a man with kinship connections to Nokopo who finally accepted the invitation to go there to learn about the new religion. Historically, as we have seen, villages were enemies with one another, and they continue to compete with one another for prestige and power. Under such conditions, concerns about deception are heightened, and people often turn to kin and fellow villagers as more trustworthy sources of knowledge.

In that way, concerns about deception shape the way the collective process of listening unfolds. Villagers turn to co-villagers for help evaluating things they have heard from outsiders. Clan mates and relatives help evaluate the words of others for each other. But looking inward is not always sufficient. With the conservation NGO, for instance, people not only turned to family and neighbors but also frequently looked further afield—to people who worked with the conservation NGO (like Franklin in chapter 3) and even to me. As someone regarded as an educated person from the United States, I was seen to be well positioned to know something about the workings of NGOs and particularly this NGO, which was based in the United States. Many of the most pressing questions in the valley today involve actors and organizations from outside the valley; to gain truthful knowledge about them at times requires looking beyond neighbors and relatives to people whose trustworthiness may be more uncertain.

People like Nanda, who are locals with considerable schooling and experience outside the valley, play a particularly important role when discussion turns to actors and organizations like the NGO. In his forties at the time of my research, Nanda was among the most educated men of his generation in Weskokop, having completed twelfth grade at Rai Coast High School. He had gone on to serve as the local level government counselor at a young age, in part because of his educational background. But his larger political ambitions stalled out after that, and he returned to Weskokop to live the life of a subsistence agriculturalist and to devote himself to village affairs. He was knowledgeable about government and current affairs, spoke some English, and was quite well read. At the same time, he was native to Weskokop and had a wide circle of friends and relatives there. Balancing knowledgeability and trustworthiness, he had a good deal of influence with many in the village.

But still, he clearly had an agenda. At the time of this discussion, he was the local elementary school board chairman, so it is perhaps no surprise that he was telling people that educating their children was essential for receiving benefits from the NGO. He was clearly using the conservation benefits to promote the school, and a number of people in the community readily disregarded what he had to say.

Listeners, as we have seen, have good reason to suspect that what they are being told may not be correct, may not be the full story, or may mask hidden motives and feelings. And when they suspect deceit, they respond by disregarding the words of others. People in Nian initially failed to heed the call of the missionaries from Nokopo because of fears that they would be killed. Likewise, people in Nian ignored Muyan when he urged them to support the conservation NGO (see chapter 3). As he put it in his diatribe, "You all thought, 'He's lying, he's lying.' So, you ignored me, thinking 'when the benefits of conservation come, we will see them and do something about it.'" Worries about deception lead listeners to disregard the words of others.

But if the threat of deception shuts down some avenues of listening, it also pushes people to listen more. The way to deal with the danger of deception is not to simply disregard what people say; there is danger in that too. Much of the time, people deal with the danger by participating in discussions, where they can listen to others' evaluations of what they have heard, and in the collective process of listening to and evaluating the words of others, do a better job of anarchic listening than they would on their own.

Listening as a Collective Activity

Listening is a dangerous activity in the Yopno Valley. The ever-present possibility of deception and dissimulation in Yopno communicative life threatens to turn anarchic listeners into the unwitting laborers and servants of others. Even *unintentionally* false speech is dangerous. Holding onto false expertise and incorrect advice, even when it is not meant to deceive, can lead listeners to lose their grip on reality and their control over their future. Then, there is the possibility that listeners themselves may not pay close attention to or be able to understand what it is they are hearing. In chapter 1, I briefly discussed the words of an NGO worker from the Yopno Valley, who warned people about the dangers that mining-related development poses to them. As he said, "You want to say yes to some big mining exploration effort? Be careful. They'll give you forty pages of a contract to read and sign. We're Papua New Guineans. We won't finish those forty pages. . . . You'll thrill at the prospect of money and say, 'OK, I'll sign.'"

In all these ways, listening proves to be a dangerous activity. It can give rise to misunderstandings and false ideas about the way things work, ultimately putting the self-determination of listeners at risk. But leery of the danger that deception, falsehoods, and misunderstandings pose to them, people do not abandon the political work of listening. Often, they listen more, participating in discussions where fellow villagers, conservation workers, community leaders, teachers, pastors, and others offer to help them listen better. There, they listen to how family, friends, and experts of various sorts evaluate the words of others—listening to the way others listen.

Resolving questions of truth often involves this sort of proliferation of discourse. This is true in scientific practice, as Latour points out. It is also true in the legal system, which is organized as an elaborate intertextual edifice: verbal evidence (statements, testimony, documents, audiovisual recordings), much of it collected in the course of an investigation, is presented and commented on in trials, where competing views of the matter are debated and judged. Throughout the process, more and more discourse about discourse piles up, as part of an effort to get at the facts of the matter.[17] We find a similar proliferation of discourse in the political domain. The purported upsurge of lies and misleading statements in the "post-truth era" of contemporary politics in the United States, for example, has led to a commensurate upsurge of fact checking and journalistic exposés that seek to get at the truth of the matter.[18] In the commercial sphere, financial audits are conducted to evaluate and ensure the accuracy of "the books," as a kind of accounting of accounting; after financial scandals, there are even audits of audits.[19]

Yet, there is a persistent sense—at least among some in the European philosophical tradition—that words, language, and representations are the very things that prevent people from grasping the truth. The mediating role of signs is distorting, blinding people to the material reality present in the immediacy of experience. What is needed is sensuous contact with things themselves, not more talk. But as a practical matter, questions about the nature of reality are often resolved not by setting aside representations and approaching reality itself more closely. They are settled by talk, talk about talk, talk about *that* talk, and so on.

And of course, all of this talk also involves listening. In the Yopno Valley, speech is often deceptive, but there is little expectation that the workings of reality will reveal themselves under closer inspection. It is more talk to which people turn to sort the true and the useful from the deceptive and the dangerous. The threat of deception does not stop people from listening in the Yopno Valley: it transforms listening into a collective endeavor. People turn to family and friends to help them evaluate the words of others. And there is a willingness to turn to new sources of insight too, especially when family and friends may not have the expertise to help navigate the sort of issues that face people, such as the workings of an unfamiliar conservation NGO.

In a classic article, Erving Goffman (1979) illustrated how the act of speaking is, at times, a collective activity. Speech may involve the contributions of several participants. It may be composed by one person (the author), delivered by another person (the animator), and express the views of yet another person (the principal); for instance, when a spokesperson (the animator) reads a statement prepared by the Press Office (the authors) detailing the views of the President (the principal). Speaking, as Goffman shows, is often not the act of an individual; the production of speech can involve a multiplicity of participants.

As we see in this chapter, the reception of speech can have the same collective character. Instructions to prepare for the conservation celebration are heard and evaluated by many people. Some of these listeners share their evaluations with others, in effect serving as an analyst or interpreter for others. Others evaluate the evaluations of others to assess whose evaluations to trust or to put forward yet another evaluation of their own. In effect, people listen to the ways in which others have listened, evaluating their evaluations, holding onto some and disregarding others—all in an effort to sort out how to understand and whether to act on the words of others.

Deception threatens to undermine anarchic listening, but it does not stop people from listening. In the face of deception, listening becomes a collective endeavor, as elaborate and layered as the act of speaking at times can be.

LISTENING AT THE ENDS OF THE EARTH

Over the past century, churches and schools have come to stand at the center of Yopno villages, both literally and figuratively. It would be hard to identify institutions that have had a more transformative effect on life in the valley over that time. In the decades after they first arrived in 1928, Lutheran missionaries—most of them Papua New Guineans from the eastern portions of the Huon Peninsula—reshaped villages, gathering people together in settlements built around mission schools and churches. They suppressed the men's houses and introduced villagers to a new cosmology—a new history of the world filled with new actors and new possibilities. They instituted a host of ritual forms—church services, prayers, blessings, offerings—that people came to use to interact with these new actors. They taught people a new language—Kâte, a lingua franca used by the Lutheran church for missionization—which they used to preach to them and educate them and in which people learned to read the Bible. And they trained people as teachers and pastors, who continue to instruct people in the Christian gospel on a daily and weekly basis in villages throughout the valley.

Many of the schools in the valley are still associated with the Lutheran church, although they no longer concentrate on religious instruction. Focusing instead on the familiar subjects of Western-style education—math, English, science, and social studies—Lutheran schools and government schools alike have found a place alongside Lutheran churches at the center of village life. Community members devote a good deal of their time, energy, and resources to their schools and churches: building and maintaining them, supporting teachers and pastors, and giving offerings to the church and paying school fees, the latter being the largest regular monetary expense for most families in the valley. Village leadership is now largely linked to these institutions as well: teachers and pastors, school board members and congregation leaders make up the core leadership of Yopno villages today.

Of course, as we saw in the preceding chapters, support for these institutions and their leaders is hardly assured. Pigs needed for the celebration of a church event can be hard to come by; people do not always show up on days designated to build classrooms and teachers' housing; and many students do not attend school regularly. There is an ambivalence about schools and churches that is evident in the vacillating interest and support they receive. They are, on the one hand, thoroughly hierarchical institutions; students and community members chafe at the dictates, instructions, rules, and discipline to which teachers and pastors, school board members and congregation leaders subject them. Many students routinely skip and eventually quit school. Most adults at the time of my research had not completed more than the sixth grade, typically citing either a lack of school fees or a desire to marry and start an independent household as their reason for leaving school. Community members too are often absent from church and school events. Resenting being told what to do and being asked for so much of their time and energy, they withdraw from involvement in community activities.

All in all, however, these institutions do receive a great deal of support from community members (see figure 9). Although organizers struggled to find pigs for the Nian church anniversary (see chapter 1), donors eventually were found, and the anniversary celebration was considered a big success, attracting hundreds of people from throughout and beyond the valley. Although villagers were slow to begin work on the new classroom and the teacher's house for the Nokopo school, these were both finished not too long after the school year started. By the time I left the valley in 2009, a new double classroom had been constructed with sawn timber and tin roofing; and, in the following years, the school added seventh and eighth grades (see chapter 3).

From my first weeks in the valley, it was clear that these institutions play an outsized role in people's lives: from the prayers that accompany virtually every activity to the blessings that are sought from God for new babies, new fences, and new ventures in general; from the time students devote to schoolwork to the shame people felt that their local school was not the equal of others in the valley. But the importance of these institutions really hit home for me when one of my language instructors, Kokwasu, told me he was returning to complete primary school. A man of about my age (twenty-nine at the time), he had quit school to marry and start a household as many young people do. But after a few years and now the father of two young children, he and his clanmates decided that he

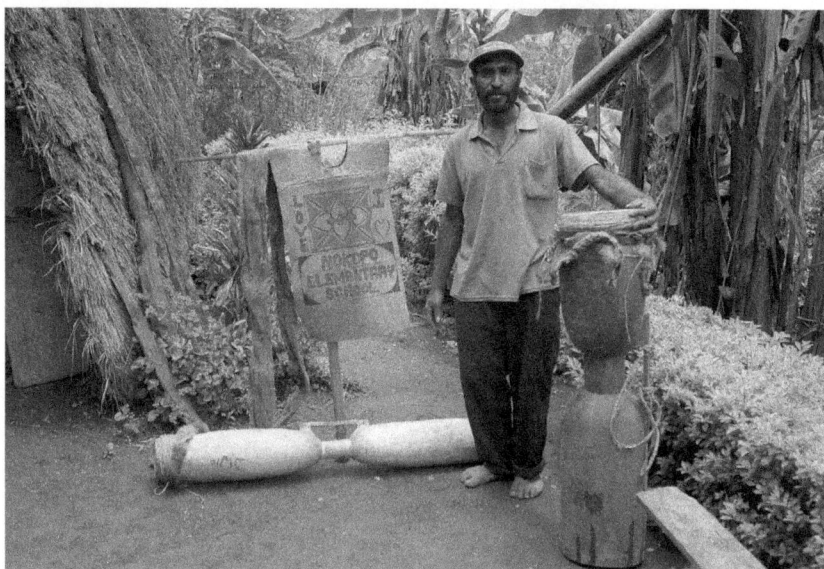

FIGURE 9.   An expert in designs and traditional crafts, Yuman, displays some of his creations.

Photograph by author.

should go back to school to finish sixth grade with the hope of eventually completing high school. At the time, he was one of four "family men" in the village of Nian—men with wives and children—who had plans to return to primary school to complete their education. They were doing this despite the disapproval they faced for focusing on their own education (and spending hard-to-come-by money on it) when they should have been focusing on their children's education. Although not all these young men did return to school, my language instructor did, eventually completing the eighth grade.

Like Kokwasu, people at times pull away from schools and churches. But over the past century, they have increasingly embraced them, as Kokwasu himself ended up doing. By the 1990s most villages had built a Western-style church of their own, made of sawn timber and tin roofing. During the period of my research, new schools were spreading in a similar fashion, thanks to increased government funding and to a growing demand for schools in the region. In the early 1970s, just before Papua New Guinea gained independence, the first government-run school was built in the valley: a community school located at Teptep that educated students up to sixth grade. By 2014, five primary schools had been built in different parts of the valley, most of them educating students up to eighth grade. Many villages were also in the process of building their own elementary schools as part of a change in educational policy.[1] Several communities in the valley had even started piloting kindergarten programs of their own. And in 2018, Saonu Lutheran High School, the first high school, with ninth and tenth grades, was opened: it provided students the opportunity to continue their education without having to leave the valley.

To appreciate why these institutions have come to play such a prominent role in contemporary life in the valley, we need to understand them as venues for listening. Schools and churches are valued for many reasons, of course. As physical structures, they are a mark of a much-valued "modernity"; often, they are the only structures in a Yopno village built with sawn timber and tin roofing. As political emblems, they indicate the strength of communities and their leadership; the growth of churches and schools and the success of events they host are opportunities for leaders and villages to gain renown.

But to a significant extent, schools and churches are institutions where people in the valley play the role of listeners; there, they listen to the precepts, advice, and knowledge of others. This is a reason why, at times, people keep their distance from these institutions; in schools and churches, students and community members alike are subject to the direction and the critical judgment of others. Yet, access to this expert knowledge and advice is also a prime reason why people embrace these institutions. Schools and churches are prime venues for the kind of anarchic listening described in the previous chapters: they are places where listeners can gain greater control over their future and a greater measure of equality with the rest of the world by holding onto the words of teachers and pastors.

In practice, however, these institutions comprise an incongruous mix of anarchic ideals and hierarchical realities, egalitarian aspirations and growing inequality. People's efforts to enhance their self-determination motivate them to embrace these thoroughly hierarchical institutions, where they are subject to the dictates and discipline of others. Their efforts to achieve greater equality with others in the valley and beyond lead them to support these institutions, which are introducing new forms of inequality in Yopno villages.

In many parts of Papua New Guinea, the growth of resource extraction industries and the emergence of markets for labor and land are giving rise to new modes of socioeconomic stratification.[2] In the Yopno Valley, it has primarily been knowledge-centered institutions—churches and schools—that have fostered the emergence of a regional elite and incipient class divisions. We might say, then, that at present, anarchic listening in schools and churches is helping produce a situation that is anything but anarchic and egalitarian.

To see why that is, we need to situate the practice of listening in churches and schools in a larger context; indeed, in a world-historical context. Up to this point, I have contextualized events of listening—in discussions, preschool lessons, public speeches, and the like—in a relatively localized way, focusing largely on face-to-face encounters set within the context of Yopno village politics. But to understand some of the most consequential transformations in the valley, it is necessary to look at listening in churches and schools in the way people in the Yopno Valley often do: as a moment in a global history of knowledge and power in circulation, a history in which people in the Yopno Valley are among the last in the world to learn about the workings of distant powers. Contextualized in this way, listening in schools and churches becomes a way for people to insert themselves into this "world-system" of knowledge in circulation, which will enable them to create the future they desire. But at the same time, listening in churches and schools is domesticating and entrenching these national and global institutions in the villages of the valley and the new forms of inequality that they bring with them.

Living in the *Las Ples*

Sailing off the north coast of the island of New Guinea in 1827, the French explorer Jules Dumont d'Urville saw an immense mountain range in the distance, "drawn like a bluish line" across the horizon. He gave that range the name it bears today: Finisterre, "the ends of the earth." D'Urville never set foot in those mountains, home to the Yopno Valley; for him, they truly were the ends of the earth. But the name he gave them echoes uncannily in the way people today living in the valley speak of their place in the world.

As in many other parts of Papua New Guinea, people describe their region as the *las ples*—the "last place" to undergo development, to receive government services, and more generally to gain access to the wealth and power that others in Papua New Guinea and especially the global north have long enjoyed.[3] The expression is in part a comment on the extreme global inequalities that are visible from this rural area of the global south, highlighting the stark divide between life in the countries of the global north (Australia, New Zealand, Japan, the United States, and Europe) and their own.[4] As people in the valley routinely pointed out to me and to each other, they live like "pigs and dogs," while people in Australia and the United States drive everywhere in cars and never have to work. They pitied me for leaving such a life behind to come live with them.[5] Similar (though less dramatic) disparities are often noted with people elsewhere in Papua New Guinea, who own businesses, cars, and Western-style houses and have access to roads and the cash economy.

The cause of these inequalities is a topic of regular comment. Recall the dream interpretation in chapter 2. In that event, the wealth of other parts of Papua New

Guinea was linked to the way sacred objects from those regions are pictured on the national currency. If only people from the Yopno Valley could get their sacra on the national currency, they too would be able to acquire wealth, much like people elsewhere had.

Among the array of explanations for these national and global disparities, it is a commonplace that inequalities of wealth and power are related to the way knowledge (*nandak nandak*; <u>save</u>) has spread through the world. The dissemination of Christianity is paradigmatic in this regard. Everyone in the valley is familiar with the basic outlines of this history: knowledge of the ways of the Christian God, which first appears in the words of Jesus, prophets, disciples, and others recorded in the Bible, spreads with the Bible to Europe, America, and Australia through the work of Martin Luther and other church workers before finding its way to Papua New Guinea with the arrival of the first missionaries. For the Lutherans in the Yopno Valley, the Word of God (*Piŋkop gen*) was brought to Papua New Guinea by the Lutheran missionary Johannes Flierl in 1886, an event celebrated annually in Lutheran churches throughout the valley and the country. It then spread through the work of foreign and Papua New Guinean missionaries, ultimately reaching the village of Isan in the Yopno Valley in 1928. From Isan, the history of the gospel's dissemination diverges as people tell of the comings and goings of the gospel from village to village.

This history is often retold in the valley. It is repeated in church services and the speeches of community leaders; it is taught to children in confirmation classes and schools; and it is a story I was told on many occasions when traveling around the valley. On my most recent visit it surfaced in the graduation ceremony for the eighth-grade students at the Nokopo primary school. After a church service and the speeches of several community leaders, the headmaster of the school concluded the event with a speech of his own, setting the moment in historical perspective:

> Traveling from Germany to Simbang [the location of the first Lutheran mission in Papua New Guinea], John Flierl came with lots of things so that you and I would see the power of God's Word. If the Word came alone, people would think it was nothing of significance. So to strengthen people's belief, to show that God's Word must be put to work, that it has power, he came with education. Education isn't something of this earth; it is something from heaven.

In this telling, the power of God's Word and the power of education both come from the same source: heaven. They have traveled through the world, appearing first in the eastern Mediterranean in the time of Jesus, then going to Europe, and eventually to Papua New Guinea with John Flierl. On this day it passed into the hands of the students at the graduation: "You have learned a great deal of knowledge," the headmaster told them. "So, this knowledge you have learned, you can't waste it. You have to go and use it."

In my conversation with the headmaster after this ceremony, he elaborated on this history, noting that the missionaries did not start educating people right away after arriving in the Yopno Valley but began with the Word of God:

> At the time, people in the Yopno Valley were confused (ɨŋtok aŋ). They did not know the Word of God, so the missionaries brought it and worked very hard. God's Word first. Before they baptized people, they spoke the Good News to them and taught them how to be church leaders. They taught them how to be teachers. They brought lots of books, and they educated them with God's Word.

In the headmaster's telling of the history, both secular and religious education are intimately connected to one another. Both arrived in the valley with the Lutheran missionaries, but religious education was imparted first.

This history of the circulation of God's Word and Western-style education serves as a commonly invoked explanation for the wealth and power of people in the global north, who have leveraged their long-standing knowledge of the Christian God to their benefit. Yopno ancestors, as the headmaster noted, were ignorant of this god, and so white people (kwakŋɨ) have received the blessings of God, whereas their Yopno ancestors did not. That is not to say that the Yopno ancestors did not have knowledge of powerful beings. Their knowledge of spirits that inhabit the valley—knowledge that was passed down from generation to generation in the men's houses and within families—served and continues to serve as an important source of power for people there.[6] But because the Christian God was unknown to their ancestors, its power was not available to them. It is only recently (and fitfully) that people in the Yopno Valley have been able to leverage knowledge of the Christian God for their own benefit.

A similar story is also told of secular education. When it comes to school-based education, people in the valley feel themselves to be behind not only people in the global north but also those in other parts of Papua New Guinea, who gained access to schools long before they did. There is even a heated competition between the educational offerings of different regions of the valley; people in Nian often expressed feeling shame because their school had been shut down for years and, at the time of my initial research, still only served students through sixth grade. Other schools in the valley, by contrast, educated students through eighth grade and even had a few graduates who went on to high school and got high-status jobs with mining companies and the US-based conservation NGO operating in the valley.

Being among the last areas to receive Christianity and Western-style educa-tion provides an explanation for the place in the world that people in the valley feel they inhabit: the *las ples*, at the bottom of a global hierarchy of wealth and power. But this explanation also suggests that schools and churches are a way out of this place, a way for people to become the equals of people in other parts of the valley, the country, and the world. The sense of being the *las ples* to re-ceive power-giving knowledge serves as what might be called a "communicative imaginary" that contextualizes the listening that happens in schools and churches; it is a conception of a wider world of communicative activity that gives significance to individual events of communication. Set within this imaginary, listening in schools and churches becomes a way for people to insert themselves into global networks of communication that have brought knowledge and, with it, wealth and power to much of the rest of Papua New Guinea and the world.

In speaking of an imaginary here, I am borrowing from Charles Taylor's (2003) discussion of the social imaginaries of modernity, those large-scale so-cial formations like markets, nations, and publics that far outstrip any partici-pant's personal experience. As Benedict Anderson (2006, 26) writes about the nation, "An American will never meet, or even know the names of, more than a handful of his 240,000,000-odd fellow Americans. He has no idea of what they are up to at any one time. But he has complete confidence in their steady, anon-ymous, simultaneous activity." Participants' imaginaries of these large-scale formations—their sense of the kinds of persons that comprise them and the sorts of activities they typically engage in—is vital to the existence of these social for-mations. These imaginaries form the context for people's activities, giving meaning to their actions and shaping their conduct.[7] Contextualized within an imaginary of public sphere discourse, for instance, a person's speech is trans-formed; it becomes a moment in a "national conversation" carried on by a mass of strangers unknown to one another, who discuss matters of public concern and in the process forge the public whose opinions should influence the policies of governing authorities. For those who share in this imaginary, it serves as the backdrop that contextualizes and gives meaning to their speech.[8]

In much the same way, the imaginary of the global circulation of the Christian gospel and of Western-style education gives meaning to a particularly consequen-tial regime of listening in the Yopno Valley. It renders acts of listening—particularly acts of listening in schools and churches—a moment within a global history of power-giving knowledge in circulation. In this imaginary, listening is an activity of the marginal and the inferior—of the *las ples*. It is a vision of global communi-cations that recalls the kind of top-down view of globalization summarized pithily by Ulf Hannerz (1989, 67): "When the center speaks, the periphery listens, and on the whole does not talk back."[9] In this top-down view, the peripherality of people in the global south is manifest in their position on the receiving end of global flows of knowledge and culture. As in the Yopno imaginary sketched here, it is a communicative imaginary in which listening is a mark of marginality.

But in the Yopno Valley, listening in schools and churches is more than that. It is part of an imaginary concerned with more than the way in which knowledge and power have circulated around the world in the past. It is part of an imaginary that also includes a vision of the future, one that comes into being, in part, through the work of listening. By listening in schools and churches, people in the valley gain access to the knowledge of powerful figures that has long been known to others and that is now being communicated to them. Contextualized within this imaginary, listening in schools and churches is rendered a means of empowerment that enhances listeners' ability to shape their future and achieve equality with others both within and beyond the valley; in short, it is rendered a species of anarchic listening.

To illustrate how this imaginary materializes in day-to-day life, I turn in the next section to one of the routine communicative events of Yopno life: a church service, and particularly the homily that stands at its center. In this mundane event, we can see how this global imaginary of knowledge in circulation comes to contextualize everyday communicative activities in the Yopno Valley and gives meaning to the practice of listening that goes on in them.

Listening in the *Las Ples*

At least once a week, and sometimes as frequently as every night, people gather in Lutheran churches or in their own houses to sing Christian songs, read the Bible, and hear a homily, the high point of Yopno church services. Homilies are generally careful explanations of the day's Bible readings, taken from a calendar produced by the Evangelical Lutheran Church of Papua New Guinea. The day's readings are translated line by line from the Tok Pisin Bible into Yopno, parables are elucidated by discussing situations more familiar to Yopno life, other salient Bible passages are discussed, and ultimately the day's text is boiled down to a straightforward maxim that bears on people's daily conduct. In essence, homilies portray both God's ways and God's Word as something obscure and difficult to understand, requiring the insight of church-trained pastors and lay leaders to make it accessible to uncertain and unknowing parishioner addressees. In that respect, homilies involve the sort of communication of expertise that is a common part of political life in the Yopno Valley. By carefully evaluating (*sɨlɨp aŋ*) the biblical text, the homilist renders it comprehensible to his or her audience.

But centered as they are on elucidating biblical texts, homilies inevitably point up more than just the expertise of the homilist, who often is a pastor or evangelist trained in Bible schools and Lutheran seminaries; they also point up a larger history of communication and knowledge in circulation. Homilies take up the words of prophets, disciples, and even God, which were spoken in the distant past and which since traveled around the world through the work of missionaries. And they put that knowledge into circulation in the here and now, ideally moving it from the homilist's mouth to the audience's ears. In that respect, homilies not only depict a history of knowledge in circulation but they are also the latest moment in that history—*if* listeners hold onto the knowledge that is being offered to them.

To get a sense of how the act of listening is contextualized in a church service, let us examine one homily in detail, which was delivered in a midweek church service held in a house in the village of Ganggalut. A few relatives and friends gathered there in the evening, and the leader of the community Sunday School led the service. Yabikbe was a younger man in his thirties, respected for his devotion to the church and for sharing the gospel with others. His role in the local church was not a significant one, but he was still young and was positioned to take on greater responsibility in the years to come. Though not a trained pastor or evangelist, the homily he delivered blended biblical text, present-day context, and future repercussions in the way they typically do.

The Bible text for that day in the Lutheran church calendar was Matthew 14: 22–33, the story of Jesus and his disciple Peter walking on water. In the story, Jesus walks across the water to his disciples, who were offshore in a boat. At first, seeing him walk across the water, the disciples think he is a ghost. Jesus tells them not to fear, and Peter replies, "Lord, if it's you . . . tell me to come to you on the water." Jesus does, and when Peter starts across the water, he grows fearful and starts to sink. He asks Jesus to save him, and Jesus does, chiding, "You of little faith . . . why did you doubt?"

That night Yabikbe presented these events as part of Jesus's plan to teach Peter a lesson. According to the homily, after traveling around performing miracles alongside Jesus, Peter began to develop a misplaced sense of his own powers: he thought that he himself was the source of his miracle-working power. As in the historical tales discussed in chapter 2, the homily is organized around the differing perspectives of the characters. The major contrast in it is between Peter's and Jesus's perspectives: Peter thinks he is the source of his own power, whereas Jesus recognizes that belief in God is the true source of power. Like the historical tales, the tension between these contrasting perspectives is resolved over the course of the homily, which unsurprisingly identifies Jesus's perspective as the true account. Peter's failure to walk on water testifies to his false understanding of the nature of power. After Peter attempts to walk on water only to sink into the sea, Jesus drives this point home in Yabikbe's elucidation of the story:

> Jesus said to Peter: "I told you 'come!' and you started to come by means of your own strength. Why did you sink into the water? . . . Peter, your understanding is lacking. What kind of person are you? You are lacking in belief."

Peter's misperception of reality is demonstrated and the truth revealed to him through Jesus's ruse. The homily construes Peter's attempt to walk on water as part of a process of instruction. Jesus tests him, and Peter's failure opens the way for Jesus to provide an esoteric and truer representation of the nature of power to his disciple.

But this story is not merely presented as an account of events that happened long ago. It is presented as an act of instruction in the here-and-now telling of it, a lesson directed at "us" in the audience:

> Now in the present time, who are we like in this story? Are we like Jesus or Peter? Now we here are all like Peter . . . We obey the Word of God, but . . . We do the work of the gospel, but . . . We act right, but . . . We share the Word of God, but . . . We do many things. We think about ourselves like this: "I do the work of the gospel. I obey the Word of God. So, I will definitely go to heaven. I do the right things."

In effect, people today see their own actions as the route to salvation. They think that they have the power to save themselves through good works; like Peter, they think that power rests with them. But as Yabikbe goes on to point out, they, like Peter, lack belief in God, which is the true source of salvation.

This is a standard move in Lutheran homilies in the valley. As part of their instruction, pastors, evangelists, and other church leaders are taught that they should connect Bible stories to the present lives of their audience. The effect this produces is one in which Jesus teaches a lesson not only to characters in the Bible but also to the audience of the homily. In the homily we examined, Jesus not only reveals to Peter that belief in God is the ultimate source of our capabilities but also reveals this truth to "us." In this communicative framework, homilists are the middlemen. They do not present themself as the original source of the message they are conveying; that message comes from the Bible, the prophets, the disciples, or Jesus himself. In Goffman's terms (1979), homilists serve merely as the "animator" of the lesson, whose "author" is found in the Bible.

Here, the Word of God seems to circulate through the words of the homily; it seems to have moved from the Sea of Galilee millennia ago into the Yopno Valley of 2009. People in the valley are well versed in the history of how the Word of God has circulated through the world, from past to present, from the global north into Papua New Guinea. That same history materializes in the way homilists link Bible stories set in other times and places to the present. Explicating a Bible verse, homilists incorporate the speech of characters from distant contexts into their own, creating a sense of speech in circulation that mirrors the histories told of the circulation of God's Word.

Take the following reported speech construction from the homily just discussed:

> "Jesus told Peter: 'Peter, your understanding is lacking. What kind of person are you? You are lacking in belief.'"

The initial part of this bit of quoted speech ("Jesus told Peter") tells us something about the way this talk has circulated. The speech comes originally from a different speaker: not the homilist saying these words today, but Jesus. And the past tense of the verb "told" in both the English translation and the Yopno original locates that original speech event sometime in the past, prior to the moment in 2009 when we heard it in a house in Ganggalut. Through the reporting of Jesus's words, the speech of Jesus is seemingly taken out of its original context of utterance generations ago and dropped into Ganggalut village in 2009, where it provides instruction to the homily's audience. The movement of Jesus's words across time and space is depicted in this reported speech construction.[10]

Even in this seemingly minor example, a barebones sketch of a communicative history is developed. This sketch is fleshed out in the copious reported speech constructions that make up any one homily and, more broadly, in each person's experience of the Bible in a lifetime of churchgoing, as pastors and others cite and explicate biblical texts again and again. This sketch is filled in even more with the help of the histories of missionization and biblical times that occur alongside these reported speech constructions—the kind of history discussed in the previous section of this chapter. Through the histories of missionization and the use of reported speech constructions, a communicative imaginary takes shape, one in which words travel from Jesus's mouth to the homilist's ear through the efforts of missionaries, teachers, seminaries, bible colleges, and any number of other mediators. Notably, the homily is itself a moment in this communicative imaginary—one in which the words that traveled from Jesus's mouth on the Sea of Galilee continue to circulate onward from the homilist's mouth to the ear of the present-day listener. By sharing Jesus's words with their audience, the homilist incorporates the audience into a long history of communication as the latest to hear that message.

Of course, Bible texts are repeated regularly, so listeners have typically heard them all many times. The issue is not that they have not heard those words but that they have not listened *well* to that speech. As pastors and evangelists point out, people routinely fail to hold onto the words they hear; they do not keep them in mind and let them shape their actions as they should. Even more, they do not properly grasp the meaning and the implications of God's Word. In homilies, Bible texts are presented as a source of esoteric knowledge about the nature of reality and the workings of the Christian God. By "breaking up" and "evaluating" the Word of God, homilist help their audience grasp the knowledge that lies hidden in it.

That esoteric knowledge, in turn, enables those who listen and hold onto it to draw on the power of the Christian God in their endeavors. The point is often emphasized in sermons: by holding onto the Word of God and the evaluation of it provided by homilists, listeners gain power. Here is how Yabikbe puts it in the homily we have been considering:

> Jesus asked God to give him all his strength, and God said to him, "All right, you can walk on the water." And so Jesus did. He got up and walked on the water. Us too, if we give all of our mind and body to who? If we give it to Jesus, we will be able to walk on water and go where? . . . This Bible reading tells us that we will be able to walk on top of the water. This Bible reading tells us that you'll be able to fly up in the air.

The Bible offers knowledge of an otherwise inscrutable source of great power—the Christian God—which can empower the listener to walk on water, to fly in the air, to get into heaven, and much else besides. Like many other kinds of expertise (see chapter 3), the words of Jesus transmitted and elucidated by missionaries, pastors, and homilists convey esoteric knowledge to listeners and, with it, a measure of control over distant and powerful others.

Homilies serve in this way as a vehicle for circulating power. As such, they render the act of listening to them a pivot point between a past of being the *las ples* and a future of enhanced capabilities—one in which people in the Yopno Valley will be able to enjoy the blessings of the Christian God that people elsewhere in the world have long enjoyed. Between a past marked by inequality and inferiority and a future of greater equality and power lies the listener who holds onto the Word of God: who grasps the knowledge hidden in it, who keeps it in mind, and who allows it to shape their behavior. Contextualized within this imaginary, the act of listening in churches is rendered a species of the sort of anarchic listening we have seen in the politics of expertise—a way for people to insert themselves into global flows of knowledge and power to take greater control over their future.

Pursuing Equality, Entrenching Hierarchy

Alongside churches, schools play a pivotal role in an imaginary that sees the Yopno Valley as the "last place" to receive power-giving knowledge. In the way students, parents, teachers, and community leaders often talk about them, schools provide knowledge that people need to engage effectively with powerful and wealthy others from outside the valley: the government, NGOs, mining companies, potential employers, and even foreign governments.[11] Other regions of Papua New Guinea and even other villages in the valley have educated their children and gained access to this knowledge, the lament often goes—but "we" in Nian or Weskokop or the Yopno Valley as a whole have not.

Here is Nanda, the head of the local elementary school board in Weskokop village whom we encountered in the last chapter, offering one of his standard speeches about the future facing the children of the valley. In this dystopian vision, the government will come to register the land, marking out which clans own what land:

> Soon when we want to speak about our land, the educated among us will talk. Now we aren't educated, so we just blow hot air. Soon the government will prepare documents and tell us to get out, you see? We will be lost. I see this and I'm afraid . . . If an educated man comes and uses his knowledge against us, what will we do? . . . The neighboring village of Ganggalut has produced plenty of educated people. They have produced a pilot, an engineer, a high school teacher. And another neighboring village Gua has also done that. Gua has outpaced us. . . . If we produced a lawyer that would be good. They would defend our land and we would be all right. Soon, the population will grow, which will give rise to disputes over land. If you have a lawyer, they will speak for you. If not, Gua will take our land. . . . So, we must fear for our children. We've brought them into this world and placed them in a hard position.

Like the powerful Christian God, the ways of the government—its documents and its laws—are often unclear. School-based education provides a way for people to learn about the workings of the government and to use that knowledge to take control over their destiny. Without it, educated outsiders and neighboring villages will take advantage of them, stealing their land and their livelihood.

In the way it is often talked about, school-based education is a bulwark against a dystopian future of the sort Nanda presents here—a future in which people remain powerless and poor, the inferiors of others, even of others living in the Yopno Valley. Here is another dystopian vision, which was offered up by the evangelist in Nian at the start of the 2008 school year as he urged community members to build a new classroom and teacher's house in preparation for the year ahead:

> It's the work at the school that I'm talking about. Let's listen and com-
> plete it. Do you think that these children of ours are going to amount to
> something? If you think so, then you should worry about our children.
> Tomorrow, they will be—you don't know . . . Tomorrow there will only
> be educated people. After our time now, there will only be educated
> people. Or, if you want the children of Nian to be the ones who wash the
> clothes of people from other villages, all right, you can keep doing things
> this way [i.e., continue to not prepare the school for the new school
> year]. . . . Tomorrow, there will only be educated people. We don't want
> some of us to end up pitiful and ignorant. You all aren't made fearful by
> this sort of talk. You aren't afraid. Let's change. That's it. Let's tend to the
> school.

In this portrait of the future, young people without an education end up wash-
ing the clothes of people from other communities: they are their "work boys."[12]
Dystopian visions often feature the sort of inequalities that people are familiar
with from the stories they hear of life in other parts of the world or from their
time living in urban squatter settlements or working in towns. Yet, in these dystopian portraits, such inequities are "domesticated"—they have become part of
life in the Yopno Valley itself. People take ownership of their neighbor's land,
they employ one another as servants, and some go off and get jobs while others
are left homeless and without food. Schooling is presented as the way young
people can take control of their destiny and escape this fate.

These dystopian portraits also indicate something of the role schools are playing in the *growth* of inequality in the valley. Present-day educational inequalities between villages, for instance, play a prominent part in this rhetoric, no
doubt drawing on a long history of animosity between villages.[13] In their efforts
to revitalize the local Nokopo school, community leaders, teachers, and several
parents all harped on the fact that children in other regions could complete
eighth grade in their own villages, whereas the Nokopo school only went up to
the sixth grade. The result, they pointed out, was that these other villages had
sent many more students to high school, and their children had secured jobs and
political positions.

Schools are giving rise to other forms of hierarchy and inequality in the valley
as well. Yopno communities never have been truly egalitarian.[14] In the past, they
were stratified along lines of gender and age, with adult men for the most part
controlling the land, material wealth, and valuable knowledge. But schools and
churches have introduced a host of new positions of authority into Yopno com-

munities, which are themselves embedded in wider institutional hierarchies. Congregants attend church and listen to homilies where they are told how to act by Jesus and the prophets, by evangelists, and by pastors who are trained by seminary instructors and theologians and overseen by parish, circuit, district, and national-level presidents and bishops. In much the same way, students and community members find themselves on the lowest rung of the educational hierarchy, instructed and directed by teachers who themselves are overseen by headmasters and school board members, who are monitored by provincial and national education officials.

The sort of gender inequality that was institutionalized in the men's house largely continues in schools and churches today. There were no female pastors in the valley at the time of my research, and the vast majority of teachers were men. The one female teacher who came to teach at the Nokopo school married shortly after arriving and stopped teaching to start an independent household. That illustrates one of the prime reasons why there are so few female pastors and teachers: women are expected to leave their jobs when they marry, which makes the expense of educating them to be a teacher or pastor a risky investment.[15]

Schools are also introducing class divisions within Yopno villages. In a region where virtually everyone is a subsistence agriculturalist, a small but growing number of people today have moved somewhat or entirely out of the subsistence economy, having found employment that affords them a wage or even a salary.[16] This group includes the teachers in the five primary schools in the valley, most of whom hailed from the Yopno Valley at the time of my research. In addition, a small group of young people have completed college and landed white-collar jobs, working with mining companies or with the conservation NGO operating in the valley. And then there are a few politicians and government officials in the provincial bureaucracy.

Many who make up this economic and political elite are, in fact, descendants of the first people in the valley to be trained as teachers and church workers. The early Lutheran missionaries, who came to the valley from other Papua New Guinean communities to the east, sought to cultivate a group of local men who would take over the work of teaching and missionization. This first generation of Yopno church workers fanned out through the valley and up into the Central Highlands of Papua New Guinea, spreading the gospel and, with it, literacy in churches and mission schools.

Currently, many of the teachers in the valley are children of these men and of later generations of church workers. As one teacher, himself the child of a pastor, put it to me, "Church workers raise teachers." The children and grandchildren of these early missionaries also make up a disproportionate share of the white-collar workers, government officials, and politicians who come from the valley. Notable among this group is Ginson Saonu, who served as the member of Parliament for the Kabwum district where the Yopno Valley is located (and who, at the time of writing, is once again a member of Parliament, as well as the governor of Morobe Province, the most populous province in the country). His father was born in the Yopno Valley and served as a missionary, bringing the gospel in 1949 to the village of Gua, which was not far from his own. He became a teacher, studying at Goroka Teachers College and teaching in various schools around Morobe Province before launching his political career.

Others—many of whose parents served as Lutheran missionaries—have followed similar paths: they attended teachers' college or seminary, becoming pastors and teachers, politicians, and government officials. They are among the best-educated people in the valley—often having attended or completed high school, when most people of their generation dropped out by sixth grade. Today, they play a central role in local and regional politics as village leaders of various sorts such as school board members or congregation leaders, as employees of the provincial government, or as politicians in the local-level government.

Thus, there is a discrepancy between the imaginary and the reality of schooling. In the imaginary, schools are heralded as vital to the future of young people, the source of power-giving knowledge that will bring with it greater empowerment and an end to being the *las ples*. In reality, however, schools are a prime source of inequality: they are places where students and community members find themselves at the bottom of institutional hierarchies and emerging class divisions.

For many students and parents I spoke with, this increasing inequality actually helps confirm their sense that schooling is a source of valuable knowledge. When I asked older students why they stuck it out in school after others dropped out, the hope of jobs was generally the first reason they gave. Often, these students pointed to the growing cadre of young people from the Yopno Valley who completed teachers' training college and were now working as teachers. Wamat, a young man from Ganggalut whom I got to know particularly well as I helped him study for his high school entrance exam, spoke of his desire to follow in the footsteps of a slightly older man in Ganngalut, who had just completed college and was working for a mining company. For young women, who had fewer role models from their communities to point to, hoped-for jobs in nursing and teaching provided the chance to escape from burdens of agricultural work that fall largely on women. For these students, the regional elite produced by education serves as proof that schools are a route to greater opportunity.

Most parents I spoke to support their children's education with an eye to its future dividends as well. This perspective was epitomized for me by Topa, the owner of the small store in Nian (another route to participation in the cash economy, even though Topa still lived a largely subsistence-based lifestyle). He paid the school fees not only for his own sons and daughter but also for his brother's son and daughter, as well as several other children in the community. He explained that it was like playing laki ("lucky"), a betting game of chance. Some of these children would get jobs as teachers and provide him with money when he was older and unable to care for himself. Maybe one of the young women he supported would marry a wealthy family from outside the valley, and he would get a piece of the bridewealth. But it was impossible now to tell which ones would succeed, and so, he needed to spread his investment out widely. Though his phrasing was particularly colorful, the perspective was common. Education is an investment: a means to generate wealth.

The growing disparities of wealth and power that schooling has fostered actually seem to attract people to schools. Consider the story of my language teacher Kokwasu, who was introduced at the start of this chapter. As a "family man" with a wife and two children, he returned to school to finish sixth grade. At the time, I was baffled: what would he get out of completing grade six? When I returned to the village for a visit in 2013, the answer became clear: he had returned to school to make himself a viable candidate for a position of leadership in the community. He was the member of one of the smaller clans in the village, but one that claimed an outsized importance in the history of the village. Yet none of his clan members were in a leadership position in the community or had a particularly distinguished background in the church or in school. So, he went back to school as a full-grown man, sitting with children who were almost twenty years his junior. He finished grades six, seven, and eight, after which he became the school board secretary, securing a position in the village leadership for his clan.

For many like Kokwasu, Wamat, and Topa, schooling creates new opportunities, enhances their power and wealth, and helps them achieve a measure of equality with others on local, national, and global scales. Schooling is a route to a future in which today's children can gain jobs, defend their land from predatory outsiders, and drive around in cars like Americans. But listening in schools, much like listening in churches, is doubled-edged: it not only holds out hope for greater power and equality in the future but it also means accepting submission and inequality in the present. By participating in these institutions, people in the valley are—fitfully—being incorporated into national and global institutions that are hierarchical through and through. They find themselves parishioners in churches, receiving instruction and injunctions from pastors and congregation chairmen, parish and circuit presidents, bishops, and, of course, the Christian God.[17] The same is true in schools. In this way, these institutions are conduits for new forms of inequality in the Yopno Valley, stratifying communities into teachers and students, pastors and parishioners while licensing some to direct the activities of others.[18]

These distinctions of institutional status are accompanied by incipient class divisions. In the rural villages of the Yopno Valley, wage-earning teachers are a conspicuously distinct class, able to buy food at the market, to pay people to build pig fences, and to purchase computers and phones. To the limited extent that class-based stratification is emerging in the Yopno Valley, the divide is primarily between the small number of government-paid educators and the subsistence agriculturalists whom they are paid to educate. In a sense, the distinctions people see between the global north and global south are being reproduced in the valley: educated/uneducated, rich/poor, powerful/powerless.[19] Schools and churches are domesticating global and national inequalities, bringing them into the villages of the valley itself.

Of course, people resist the direction of church and school leaders, as we have seen; there is also grumbling about teachers who do not share their wages widely enough, about a pastor who calls on the community to build a pig fence for his large herd of pigs, about politicians who do little for the communities they represent and use their office to benefit themselves instead. But this pushback should not be overemphasized. Many parents hope *their* children will be teachers or pastors or politicians someday, even if that means living with institutional hierarchies and economic stratification in the present.

Contextualized within an imaginary of the Yopno Valley as the *las ples*, the hierarchy and inequality that schools and churches introduce into Yopno villages are nothing new. Living in the *las ples,* the past is characterized by marginality and lack. Schools and churches may be stratifying Yopno communities along lines of knowledge, wealth, and power, but they also provide hope for a different future—one in which people in the valley are no longer marginal and lacking.

At the heart of that hope is the act of listening—of joining in a global system of communication that will provide access to power-giving knowledge. By listening well and learning in schools and churches, people are working to produce a future in which they are more powerful and more equal to others in their own communities and the rest of the world. In the context of this imaginary, the act of listening in schools and churches unfolds in what Elizabeth Povinelli (2011, 2–3) has termed the future anterior "social tense": "The future anterior is what will have been the ultimate truth, good, and justice of this existing action, event and experience, after every last man has had his experience and his say. This truth might only become available with the point of view of the last man." The future jobs, increased wealth and power, growing parity with the outside world, and ability to keep up with others in the valley "will have been" the ultimate goods that render listening in schools and churches worthwhile.

Of course, students drop out along the way "when they do not find what they are looking for," as the chairman of the Nokopo school board once put it. But others persist, submitting themselves to teachers, paying school fees, repairing and building schools, and in general sustaining the institution and its hierarchical structure. Much the same is true of the church, where the hoped-for blessings on earth and a heavenly afterlife motivate submission to the dictates of pastors and church leaders.

In the imaginary I explore in this chapter, the present and future are intertwined such that present submission is a source of future empowerment, and future equality legitimates present inequality. In such a context, the act of listening in schools and churches is rendered equivocal. It is a hopeful species of anarchic listening that looks to a future of greater self-determination and equality to be brought about by this listening. But it is simultaneously an act of submission that is giving life to hierarchical institutions in the present and to new forms of inequality in the villages of the valley.

The Future of Listening in the Last Place on Earth

To celebrate Papua New Guinea's Independence Day in September 2009, people from the villages of Nian and Nokopo gathered at the local school for a day of games and speeches. One of the teachers presented a history of Papua New Guinea, its colonization by the Germans and the Australians, and the years leading up to independence in 1975. Another spoke about the celebrations happening that day in Port Moresby, the nation's capital. The day's events there, he said, had begun at 5 a.m. with a church service; only after that did people in the capital proceed with the Independence Day ceremonies. That, he pointed out, was as it should be: "1886 comes before 1975," as he put it. The arrival of John Flierl and the Lutheran mission in 1886, he explained, is the event of prime importance in the history of the country, coming before even national independence. And so, it was appropriate that people in the capital started the day with a church service.

The teacher's statement—"1886 comes before 1975"—encapsulates a view of history that is the subject of this chapter, in which the key events are moments when knowledge arrives from elsewhere. These are the defining events in a world-historical imaginary of the Yopno Valley as the "last place": the last place in the world to receive power-giving knowledge originally concentrated in distant realms—the global north, the eastern Mediterranean, heaven—before being communicated to people in Papua New Guinea and ultimately the Yopno Valley.

As I show, this is an imaginary that serves as a pervasive context for the knowledge that circulates in the churches and schools of the valley. It is there in the reported speech constructions of homilies and the future promised in school lessons, in the dystopian futures portrayed in public speeches and the histories of the past century that are told on special occasions. This imaginary renders listening in schools and churches a vital means of empowerment and enrichment: it is a way in which anarchic listeners in the valley can gain access to knowledge that will help them bring about the futures they desire. At the same time, schools and churches are conduits for new forms of hierarchy and inequality in the Yopno Valley. They are thoroughly hierarchical institutions themselves, and they are largely responsible for class divisions that are presently developing in the valley. In effect, anarchic listening is helping entrench new forms of inequality and hierarchy in the region.

Although this mixture of anarchic ideals and institutional realities is a source of tension at times, the empowering role of education is corroborated by the growing number of teachers, pastors, white-collar workers, and politicians in the region. People have watched as churches and schools have filled the valley over the past century, and today they see them filled with teachers and pastors and evangelists who come from the valley itself. Clearly, these institutions provide some means of empowerment.

At the time of my research, it was hard to find anyone who challenged this view. One of the very few critiques I heard came from Wonka, my host in the village of Gua. I had asked if he knew any Kâte, the lingua franca used by Lutheran missionaries in the Yopno Valley and in other areas of Papua New Guinea where the mission was active. The early missionaries adapted this language spoken around the Lutheran mission settlement at Finschhafen and used it for missionization throughout New Guinea. The Bible was translated into Kâte, church services were run in Kâte, and students in mission schools were taught the language so they could read the Bible and participate in church. None of the other missions in Papua New Guinea, however, used this language, and the Lutheran church no longer does either.

With a bitterness that surprised me, Wonka told me that Kâte was a trick. The church had led people to believe that Kâte was the language of Christianity and the wider world, when in fact it was little known even in Papua New Guinea. They were taught this language to isolate them and keep them dependent on the church. Wonka told me that it was only with the arrival of government schools that people realized that English was the true language of the wider world. Now that their children were learning English in school, he felt that things were finally moving in the right direction.

It was rare to hear anyone criticize the Lutheran church in this way. Certain pastors or congregational leaders are subject to criticism for various faults—being too judgmental, stealing money from the church, and the like—but the institution itself remains widely respected. But that does not mean it will always be so. Recall the former men's houses. Historically, they were the dominant knowledge institutions in the valley; today they are defunct and often described as an elaborate hoax. It may be that schools and churches too will be subject to a similar fate in the future.

Such a future seems more plausible when we turn our attention from the educational success stories to consider the many young people who have not realized their dreams through schooling. Take my friend Wamat. He passed his eighth-grade exam and went on to high school, with hopes of emulating an older man from Ganggalut who had gotten a job with a mining company. But like many students, he had to drop out of high school because he could not afford the school fees. He returned home to Ganggalut, where he struggled to find a place for himself. He sought a bigger role as a leader in the community but was rebuffed by older men who saw him as a troublemaker. Like many in Ganngalut, he was accused of operating as a sorcerer, using the occult powers of the village spirit to harm others.

On a visit to the valley in 2015, I learned that Wamat had died. People I spoke with blamed his death on the very sorcery that he himself was accused of wielding. Sometimes occult powers "kick back" and kill the people who use them. Although his story is a particularly tragic one, he was far from alone in being well educated and eager for a future that in the end did not come to pass. At the time of my research, the success stories were highly visible. The schools were filled with teachers who are themselves from the valley. The few people who work for companies and NGOs were often trumpeted in public speeches. The then-governor of Morobe himself was a product of the valley's schools. But there have been many others who failed to find similar success—those who had to drop out for lack of funds, those who completed some high school but got no work, those who struggle to find funds to attend teachers' training college or seminary but never do.

In Papua New Guinea, where most people's livelihood depends on subsistence agriculture, I wonder whether most of the Yopno children of today will be able to forge a future in the knowledge economy—as teachers, white-collar workers, and politicians. And I wonder what will happen if they do not—if this generation of children educated in schools ends up tending their fields and pigs in the Yopno Valley like their parents. Will people continue to embrace schools and churches, perhaps even redoubling their efforts to listen well and hold onto the knowledge they receive in those institutions? Or will some begin to question the communicative imaginary I sketch in this chapter? Will they turn to alternative sources of expertise or new knowledge institutions? Might they even turn to a new form of politics—one that involves a different understanding of the nature of global inequalities, one that is not so focused on the power-giving knowledge of others, and one in which different communicative practices become essential to people's efforts to bring about the future they desire?

At the time of my research, such possibilities seemed remote. The activities of politicians, community leaders, anthropologists, mining companies, and NGOs were the subject of much uncertainty and criticism during my time in the Yopno Valley. By contrast, the importance of schools and churches was rarely questioned. This is in part due to the conspicuous successes of school- and church-educated politicians, teachers, and pastors. In part, it is due to a widespread communicative imaginary of the Yopno Valley as the *las ples* to gain access to power-giving knowledge, which schools and churches now provide.

And in part, it is also due to a politics and a pragmatics of listening that, as I show in this book, are pervasive in the valley—one in which people work to enhance their control over their future by holding onto the expertise of knowledgeable others and learning how to carefully evaluate the proposals and projects of powerful others that promise them much but that may not be what they seem.

Earlier in this chapter, I gave some examples of the dystopian futures people see their children having to confront. Mining companies, conservation NGOs, governing authorities, greedy neighbors—these and more threaten future generations' control over their land, their netsa, their independence, and even their lives. Listening in schools and churches is seen as essential to learning how to navigate these dangers and take advantage of the opportunities that powerful actors and institutions both inside and beyond the valley provide.

Monji, a young man whom we met in chapter 4, put it this way in a discussion about the dangers confronting people in the valley:

> When the government comes to talk about the land, what will you say? . . . The conservation NGO has come and gotten pledges of land. When the government comes, the NGO will strengthen their hold on the land. What is it that you have already agreed to by pledging land to the conservation area? Yikes! Oh no! Well, it's true. You will see the consequences of this. . . . They will say, "The land is mine." What will you say? The people in the government who will make decisions about land will come. What will you say? "I gave them land, so what will you give me to compensate?" . . . The government will come. What will you say then? "What will you give me? My existence has always been here. You

have taken it. Now what will I do?" Who is ready for this? You who have agreed to pledge land, you must gain knowledge first, and then you can speak out.

In a mode of democratic politics that is pervasive around the world today, "speaking up" and "speaking back" are privileged means of exercising political agency. Speaking up about injustices, speaking back to those in power, voicing demands and views: these are political activities par excellence in this politics of voice. Monji, by contrast, points to the inadequacy of speech and a politics built around speaking up. Over and over, he poses the question: What will you say? When the government comes to talk about the land, what will you say? When the conservation NGO claims the land, what will you say? He even offers some examples of the sort of pitiful, ineffective speech people might make: "What will you give me? My existence has always been here. You have taken it. Now what will I do?"

Speaking up, Monji insists, is not sufficient to defend their future from the conservation NGO or the government. Speaking up can even be dangerous. Those who pledged land to the conservation NGO already got themselves into trouble with their talk, he points out: "What is it that you have already agreed to by pledging land to the conservation area?" What further trouble might people get into by speaking up more in the future? Speech is, at best, ineffective; at worst, it can be hazardous.

What is needed, according to Monji, is for people to listen and gain knowledge first. In the face of threats to their future, listening up—not speaking up—is essential. And the place to do that, as he and so many others point out, is in school.

LISTENING TO LISTENING, ETHNOGRAPHICALLY

When I returned to the Yopno Valley in 2013, national education reforms were well underway there. Elementary schools were opening in villages throughout the valley; my old house itself had become a classroom in Nian's new elementary school. So, on that visit and visits over the next several years, I stayed in the compound of Topa, the brother of my longtime friend and language instructor Peter. Along with the small store that he ran, Topa had several houses within his fenced compound, and he allowed me the use of one during my visits, joking that it would be the "men's house." Indeed, he and his brother, along with their male children, often slept in the house with me. Even more to the point, the house was a place where I would listen to stories and receive instruction, much as initiates once did in the *bema yut*.

During a stint in that house in October and November 2014, there was one story that I heard over and over: that of Amïnda, Topa's great-uncle. In 1942, Japan invaded the Territory of New Guinea, and Australian and US forces with the support of New Guineans fought in the campaign against them. According to the story told about Amïnda, a US Army officer came to the Yopno Valley to recruit locals to join in the fight against the Japanese. He invited the men in Nian village to try to shoot a target with a rifle, which Amïnda did with great success. The officer took Amïnda with him to battle, and after the war the Americans settled Amïnda on the island of Buka, where he was given a plantation. Amïnda never returned to Nian, but people hear stories of his children, who are all successful, urban dwelling, and middle class: one is a pilot, one a university professor, and so on.

I had heard the story before, but on this visit, it kept coming up. Topa's father told it in the "men's house" to me and an audience of his family members, who remarked afterward how meaningful it was. A few days later, after seeing me set up my video camera in the plaza of Nian village to record a community meeting, Topa—who rarely speaks at such meetings—took the floor and, staring straight at the camera, told the story of Amɨnda again.

Then, a few days later, the story of Amɨnda was repeated at a gathering in Topa's compound, which was both a birthday celebration for me and a preparatory ritual for Topa's and Peter's children, who would be taking their eighth-grade exams several weeks later. They were trying to become the first children in this family to attend high school, and their extended family gathered to hold a church service, pray for them, and give an offering to the Christian God in support of their efforts.

When I asked Topa why the story of Amɨnda had been so much in the air over the past few weeks, it was this high school exam that he mentioned. His children, the great-great-nephews of Amɨnda, were going off to "fight" in the eighth-grade exam, he said, using a war metaphor that I had also heard in other communities in the valley. Just like Amɨnda, they too would prove successful in "battle."

This metaphor made sense of something Topa had said at the meeting in the village plaza a few days earlier, something that had left me both confused and uneasy. After he finished telling the story of Amɨnda, he addressed me specifically:

> James, you know a good deal about hunting animals. I didn't know how to hunt. But an American in my own village told me, "You and I can hunt together." You brought a bow and arrow for me, and I learned how to shoot something valuable. Now I can hunt animals. Thank you.

I know nothing about hunting, as my efforts in the forests around Nian amply demonstrated, and I certainly did not teach anyone to hunt. Topa's remarks are a good example of the sort of metaphorical, allusive, and often inscrutable style of oratory discussed in previous chapters.

But placed in the context of the upcoming high school exam—an exam the students were going off to fight in—the significance of Topa's remarks and the story of Amɨnda made more sense to me. I was being equated to that US officer who had taught Amɨnda how to fight. And Topa's children, nephews, and nieces were being likened to Amɨnda, going off to fight in war (the word Topa used for "hunt" in his address to me, *emat*, is the same word used for fights among humans [i.e., war]). We, in the present, were reprising the story of Amɨnda: his descendants too had learned something from Americans. Amɨnda had learned how to shoot a gun; his descendants had learned important knowledge in Western-style schools and had even gotten occasional help with their schooling from me.

Crucially, just as Amɨnda proved a skillful handler of Western guns in war, so too Amɨnda's descendants would prove to be skillful handlers of Western-style education in the upcoming fight in the eighth-grade exam. Amɨnda's experiences and my own association with this family augured well for their performance on the exam.

Although I now understood the significance of Amɨnda's story, Topa's expression of gratitude in the plaza that day still made me uneasy. If anyone should be thanking someone for the education they had received, surely I should be the one thanking my longtime hosts for sharing their lives and their knowledge with me. I had not taught them how to hunt: they were the ones who had devoted a good deal of their time and energy to helping me with my research.

My feelings of unease that day were hardly new. This was only the latest in a long string of moments when I was cast, uncomfortably, in a role I had not anticipated playing in the valley: the role of instructor, dispenser of knowledge, expert. The first time came shortly after arriving in Nian village, when the organizers of an education awareness rally at the local primary school asked me to give a speech about the importance of education. The school had had some rough years, and the teachers and school board members were concerned that parents would not register their children for school, pay their school fees, and do the work that needed to be done to prepare the school for the year ahead. So, they had planned a rally to inspire support for the school. A regional educational administrator had agreed to come speak, and perhaps I too would share some inspirational words with students and their parents.

This was the first of many such requests I received over the following years: education rallies, graduation ceremonies, pre-exam student blessings, and the like were all occasions when I was asked to dispense wisdom for students, their parents, and members of the community. On this, the first occasion, I demurred. New to the area and uncomfortable taking on such a seemingly prominent and vocal role at the very beginning of my research, I attended the event and recorded the speeches but kept my mouth shut. Still, several of the speeches noted my presence, remarking particularly on my education and where it had gotten me. Who, one speaker at the event asked, would be the first student from the Nokopo school to go to America?

Thus began my introduction to a role that I eventually, begrudgingly, accepted. Having gone to the Yopno Valley to study political oratory, I found myself giving speeches. Having gone to learn about people's lives there, again and again I found myself cast in the role of an expert and asked to dispense knowledge: to give sermons, to host grant-writing workshops, to explain the workings of NGOs and governments, to run English classes, to help with homework—even to confirm the accuracy of people's genealogies and migration histories.

As I discovered over the course of my research, I was caught up in the currents of a global circulation of knowledge that has been reshaping life in the Yopno Valley for at least three generations. Christianity and Western-style education have taken on a central role in Yopno village life, bolstered by a communicative imaginary in which the global north serves as a source of vital, power-giving knowledge for people living in the *las ples*. As an avatar of the global north myself—one who was university educated, a researcher, and even trying to become a teacher—I was pegged as a potential source of expertise.

The chapters of this book offer an extended explanation for why I was often invited to instruct, preach, give speeches, and provide advice. Although I gradually came to understand better the role I was being cast in—and even acquiesced to playing the part, in limited ways—it was an awkward position to be in, ethnographically. In Malinowski's ([1922] 1984, 25) well-known formulation, the goal of the ethnographer is "to grasp the native's point of view, his relation to life, to realise *his* vision of *his* world."[1] Although ethnography is a much more diverse pursuit than Malinowski's account would have it, it still does not typically involve giving speeches advising people what to do and informing them about what is missing from their genealogies and migration histories. Indeed, ethnographers do play a major role in shaping their data, but it would be a caricature of reflexive anthropology to suggest that they should center an ethnography on the speeches they themselves give and the expertise they dispense.

In that respect, ethnographic research continues to strive for a practical ideal in which it is the ethnographers' role to *listen* to others as a way to gain access to their world and their perspective on it.[2] "While the anthropologist is always a necessarily flawed and biased instrument of cultural translation," as Nancy Scheper-Hughes (1995, 417–18) observes, "like every other crafts person we can do the best we can with the limited resources we have at hand: our ability to listen and to observe carefully and with empathy and compassion." The ways that ethnographers listen—who they listen to, how they listen, what they listen for, and why—have clearly changed over time; ethnographic practices of listening differ from school to school, researcher to researcher. But listening to the speech of others in one way or another remains essential.[3] Indeed, it is hard to imagine ethnographic research that does not center on the act of listening (or receiving linguistic messages through another sensory channel).[4] Listening—in interviews and informal conversation, to personal narratives and media broadcasts, and to public speeches and *sotto voce* gossip (not to mention reading the myriad texts that appear in the field)—is, to a large extent, what ethnographers do.

No doubt this helps explain my discomfort at being recruited so often to *speak* publicly and authoritatively in the field. It should be ethnographers' counterparts—their interlocutors in the field—whose speech is the cornerstone of ethnographic research. Whether it serves as a source of information about their lives, or it provides a window on their subjectivity, or it shapes the social world around them, the speech of our interlocutors is essential to the ethnographic endeavor; its indispensability is written on most every page of ethnographic texts, where it is quoted, paraphrased, and summarized.[5] The preceding chapters provide ample illustration of this.

Within this division of communicative labor—in which the ethnographer is first and foremost the one who listens to their interlocutors speak—it is easy to overlook our interlocutors' practices of listening. Yet listening practices, as I show in the preceding chapters, may be as critical to our interlocutors' projects and activities as they are for the ethnographer. Of course, the character of our interlocutors' listening is likely quite different: in many ways the sort of ethnographic listening I did in the field and the anarchic listening I detailed in the preceding chapters are very different activities. Some things that I was eager to listen to—for instance, the meetings of church women's groups—appeared largely insignificant to my male interlocutors. And I struggled to appreciate (at least in the way I think I was supposed to) some things that they urged me to attend to, such as preschool lessons.

As the ethnography of speaking pointed out long ago, speech is intricately intertwined in the social and cultural worlds of language users; the forms that speech takes and the functions that it performs take shape within the particular contexts of people's lives. In this book, I have tried to make the case that the same is true for listening. Listening in the anarchic politics of Yopno villages, listening in the liberal democratic public sphere, listening in the Islamic Revival (Hirschkind 2006), and listening ethnographically in the field are hardly the same activities. They are situated in very different contexts: in different political and economic settings, set against different institutional and historical backdrops, informed by different aspirations and imaginaries. Such conditions shape how people listen, why they listen, who they listen to, under what circumstances they listen, what they listen for, and so on. To get a handle on practices of listening in all their diversity, it is necessary to attend to these conditions: the lived experiences, the institutional contexts, and the ideals and ambitions that give these practices their import. In other words, listening requires the kind of close ethnographic attention to culturally informed, richly contextualized practice that speech has long received.

That is what this ethnography of listening set out to do: to explore a set of interrelated practices of listening that together play an essential role in the anarchic politics of Yopno villages. This anarchic listening takes a variety of forms: holding onto, disregarding, breaking up, and evaluating the words of others. Much of this ethnography has been devoted to exploring the contextual conditions that make each indispensable to the art of anarchic listening. There is the sense of uncertainty, which makes expert insights an essential resource to hold onto if listeners are to act effectively in the future. There is the routine deception that goes on and the dangers that it poses, which make carefully evaluating the words of others a necessity, sorting the true from the false. There is the world-historical imaginary of power-giving knowledge circulating in the *las ples*, which renders schools and churches particularly important venues for listening. And, of course, there is the anarchic politics of Yopno villages, which vests anarchic listening with its particular political ideals.

Political values, social institutions, epistemological sensibilities, and historical consciousnesses all factor in the Yopno pragmatics of anarchic listening—that is, they give shape to a sensibility about how different practices of listening can be used in different contexts to undercut the authority of others, to assert one's self-determination, to enhance one's power, and to achieve a greater measure of equality with others. This sensibility guides people's listening practices and it shapes the wider ecology of communication in the valley. The seemingly endless discussions, the politics of expertise, and, of course, churches and schools all flourish in a communicative environment where anarchic listening is routine.

In that respect, some of the most significant aspects of contemporary life in the Yopno Valley cannot really be appreciated without understanding how people listen and why they listen. That is the case in many other contexts as well. From liberal democracy to the Islamic Revival, practices of listening are integral to political systems, religious movements, economic activities, educational institutions, and media worlds. To understand them, it is necessary to grasp why and how people listen. And that requires listening ethnographically to the ways that others listen.

Notes

INTRODUCTION

1. Yopno words and expressions are italicized in the text; words in Tok Pisin are underlined. See the "Note on Languages, Orthography, Maps and Names" in the front matter for more details about the two languages.

2. Reenactments of first encounters with missionaries are common throughout the region and emphasize many of the same themes found here (Errington and Gewertz 1994; McDougall 2016, chap. 4).

3. The European rhetorical tradition has been central to education, politics, and religious practice in Europe from its codification in ancient Athens to the early modern era. The Greek term *rhêtōr* meant "orator" and was used to describe those in the role of professional speakers in the assemblies and the courts (Arthurs 1994). As a centerpiece of Athenian governance and jurisprudence, public speaking was a particularly conspicuous form of sociopolitical action (Yunis 1996; Cohen 2004; Ober 2009). Harnessing the power of speech for political, religious, courtly, artistic, and commercial ends was the bailiwick of the rhetorician through much of European history, and it resulted in a sizable body of doctrine that centers on the agency of speakers and the power of speech in communicative encounters.

4. The politics of voice extends well beyond the act of speaking proper to include all manner of ways of "sending a message" or "making a statement": protesting, voting, donating money, boycotting, and much else can be understood as forms of "voice," insofar as they are modes of expressing views and articulating demands. For my purposes, the key point is that in the politics of voice, it is the party sending the message—the "speaker," as it were—who is regarded as the locus of political agency, even when that message does not involve verbal communication. On the politics of voice, see Fishkin 1997; Dreher 2009; Green 2010, chap. 3; Kunreuther 2014; Weidman 2014; Schäfers 2017; and Macnamara 2020.

5. Spurred in large measure by the work of Jürgen Habermas ([1962] 1989, 1984), discourse and debate in the public sphere have been held up as important facets of democratic politics, as vital means for citizens to participate in their own governance. See Bohman 1998; Dryzek 2000; and Chambers 2003 for overviews of the framework of deliberative democracy and the motivations behind it.

6. The performative use of speech and other signs to construct identities, social relations, and other aspects of reality has been explored by philosophers of language (e.g., Wittgenstein 1953; Austin 1962), sociolinguists and linguistic anthropologists (e.g., Goffman 1959; Bucholtz and Hall 2005), philosophers of science (e.g., Hacking 1999), and many others. Judith Butler's (1990) argument that gender itself is constructed through the routine performance of gendered signifiers is a particularly influential and well-known example.

7. As Ratcliffe (2005, 20) points out in her work on rhetorical listening, "Western rhetorical theories themselves have traditionally slighted listening. Classical theories foreground a rhetor's speaking and writing as a means of persuading audiences; these theories are only secondarily concerned with how audiences should listen and hardly at all concerned with what Ballif calls the desires of particular audience members." Lacey's

(2013) work on "listening publics" makes a similar point for media studies. Of course, there has been growing attention to the listening side of the communicative equation, as Ratcliffe and Lacey's discussions of the topic indicate.

8. The anthropology of documents, bureaucracy, and the state has made the important point that, in practice, "listening to" and interpreting policies, orders, and records are hardly automatic, simple, or straightforward activities (Hetherington 2011; Hull 2012; Mathur 2016). Agency and power lie in the hands of those interpreting these documents and messages, requiring close ethnographic attention of its own.

9. In contrast to statements that describe the world (e.g., "the cat is on the mat"), John Austin (1962) identified a set of expressions that appear to act on the world—to transform it. These he dubbed "performative utterances." Many of his examples come from the domain of legal, governmental, and institutional discourse but certainly not all of them. There is more discussion of Butler and Austin's views of performative utterances in chapter 1.

10. In the democratic vision of self-sovereignty, sovereign speech has a curious, reflexive character: the people as sovereign speaker addresses itself. Or in Rousseau's well-known formulation, "obedience to the law one has prescribed for oneself is liberty" (1987, 151). Here, citizens play two communicative roles simultaneously. As prescribers of laws (i.e., speakers), they exercise power and sovereignty. As addressees of the laws (i.e., listeners), they are subjected to the power that they themselves exercise (as speakers). Habermas (1996, 120) explicitly delineates the communicative roles: "The idea of self-legislation by citizens . . . requires that those subject to law as its addressees can at the same time understand themselves as authors of law." It is through this communicative arrangement that "the people" achieve self-sovereignty: those subject to the law (as listeners) act also as sovereign speakers.

11. See Thill 2009; Dreher 2010; Butterwick 2012; Oring 2016; and Lawy 2017.

12. Calls to redress inequalities and past injustices often involve demands that the powerful listen in the open, empathetic, and potentially transformative way characteristic of democratic listening. As Bassel (2017, 7) puts it, the question is "[h]ow to make people, powerful people, listen and even transform their views and ways of being with others?" (see also Levin 1989; Calder 2011; and Dobson 2014).

13. Rhetoric and magic were linked to one another but in different ways in ancient Greece (Romilly 1975), the Middle Ages, and the Renaissance (Ward 1988).

14. For a good discussion of the rhetorical sensibility—the "rhetoricality"—of the contemporary humanities and social sciences, see Bender and Wellbery 1990.

15. The aim of harnessing mass communications technologies for propagandistic and marketing purposes was central to the development of the field of communications research (Gitlin 1978; Simpson 1994; Glander 2000; Pooley 2008) and shaped the longstanding interest in the effects of mass communications. As Harold Lasswell (1948, 37) famously put it, the "scientific study of the process of communication" considers "who says what in which channel to whom with what effect." Although the capacity of media messages to influence audiences has been much disputed, the study of the effects of messages relayed through mass media remains an ongoing concern of the field, now increasingly focused on new media and the effects of messages circulating through them.

16. For Habermas and other advocates of deliberative democracy, public sphere discourse crucially involves "rational" and "logical" argumentation, as opposed to what are often termed "rhetorical" forms of discourse. Other political theorists have stressed the essential role of such rhetorical forms in the public sphere, including testimony (Sanders 1997), narrative (Young 2000), and even rhetoric itself (Dryzek 2010). Bryan Garsten (2011) provides an overview of what he dubs the "rhetorical turn" away from rational deliberation and argumentation as the privileged form of public sphere discourse.

17. The Marxist tradition has long regarded symbols as a tool of class conflict, blinding or numbing people to their true interests. Horkheimer and Adorno's (2002) discussion of the culture industry is a classic example. Other well-known renditions include Althusser's (1971) account of the working of Ideological State Apparatuses and their interpellation of subjects, Raymond Williams's (1977) account of culture and hegemony, and Stuart Hall's (e.g., 1977) discussions of media and ideology. Outside the Marxist tradition, there is a vast literature on the role of media in shaping consciousness as well; see, for instance, Abu-Lughod 2005.

18. The naturalizing work of symbols has been an important area of investigation of both feminists and postcolonial critics in their explorations of the symbolic construction of gender and race (e.g., Said 1978; MacKinnon 1983; Butler 1990; Bhabha 1994; Yanagisako and Delaney 1994; and Kramer 2016). It is also the basis for many other varieties of critical social theory (e.g., Barthes 1972).

19. A vast literature inspired by the work of Foucault explores the relationship of knowledge and power, where discourses and regimes of truth shape the way people act and are governed inside and outside institutions (e.g., Rose 1999; Hacking 2002).

20. The psychoanalyst Jacques Lacan's (2002, 55) view of the unconscious as constituted symbolically by the Other—"the subject's unconscious is the other's discourse," as he claims—captures the very fundamental way in which symbolic power has been seen to mold subjects:

> Symbols in fact envelop the life of man with a network so total that they join together those who are going to engender him "by bone and flesh" before he comes into the world; so total that they bring to his birth, along with the gift of the stars, if not with the gifts of the fairies, the shape of his destiny; so total that they provide the words that will make him faithful or renegade, the law of the acts that will follow him right to the very place where he is not yet and beyond his very death; and so total that through them his end finds its meaning in the last judgment, where the Word absolves his being or condemns it—unless he reaches the subjective realization of being-toward-death. (67)

21. See, for instance, Memmi 1967; Ngugi wa Thiong'o 1986; Viswanathan 1989; and hooks 1994. Franz Fanon ([1952] 2008, 112–14) captured the workings of symbolic power as well as anyone in his descriptions of growing up in the context of colonial domination, where comic books and history lessons play an important part in the colonial enterprise and the white supremacy that underpins it.

22. For discussion of the hierarchy of the senses in European modernity, see Schmidt 2000; Erlmann 2004, 2010; Hirschkind 2006. Several biases coalesce to elevate vision and visual experience above hearing as a sense and sound as an object of that sense, including an ocularcentric bias that privileges vision over hearing (Schmidt 2000; Bendix and Brenneis 2005); a textualist bias that takes the written word as an object of primary attention over the spoken word (Ong 1982; Conquergood 2002); and a logocentric bias that privileges language, intellection, and representation over ineffable, sensuous, sonic experience (Stoller 1989; Hirschkind 2006).

23. For excellent examples of work done on listening in the sensory humanities, see Johnson 1995 on music; Peterson 2021 on noise; Smith 2001 on machines; and Rice 2013 on the human body. See Feld and Brenneis 2004; Samuels et al. 2010; Rosenfeld 2011; and Faudree 2012 for overviews of the extensive scholarly literature on listening as a sensory modality.

24. As a growing body of work on sound symbolism, qualia, ideophones, and vocality emphasizes, verbal speech takes sensuous form in sound (e.g., Nuckolls 2004; Inoue 2006; Harkness 2013; Webster 2015; Eisenlohr 2018; Neufeld 2018). My focus here, however, is on listening to the semantic, not sonic, qualities of speech.

25. The practices of listening that have received most attention from scholars have been in domains where listeners do wield power: priests hearing confession (Foucault 1978), psychoanalysts (Marsilli-Vargas 2014), and even sociolinguists (Inoue 2006). Flores and Rosa (2015) point out the powerful role of the white listening subject in educational and other domains of practice (see also Lo 2021). As Susan Gal (1991, 175) notes, "In religious confession, modern psychotherapy, bureaucratic interviews, and in police interrogation, the relations of coercion are reversed: Where self-exposure is required, it is the silent listener who judges, and who thereby exerts power over the one who speaks." For a thought-provoking consideration of listeners who do not wield such power, see Berman 2020.

26. What is meant by the label "egalitarian" varies quite broadly in the ethnographic literature. It is used sometimes to indicate that equality is an ideal in some social domain (among adult men, for instance); at other times, the term is used to indicate actual relations of equality in practice. In addition, the use of the expression is always relative. As Roscoe (2000, 104) notes, "Melanesian societies are commonly said to be egalitarian, for example, even though they include transegalitarian and chiefly societies. Here, the use is casual and the intent relativistic: compared to other, more politically centralized societies, Melanesian communities seem egalitarian. . . . In another casual usage, egalitarian means an absence of hereditary leadership: a chiefdom is ranked or hierarchical, a Big-man society is egalitarian." See McDowell 1990; Robbins 1994; and Rio 2014 for considerations of the different ways that the term "egalitarian" has been used in the region. For a consideration of hierarchy in egalitarian societies more generally, see Flanagan 1989.

27. In Marilyn Strathern's (1987, 2) words: "The peoples of this region are characterisable as 'egalitarian' in world terms: horticulturalists, whose local organisations are small scale, and whose cultural efflorescence is to be found in institutions based on wealth exchanges and life cycle events. Big men and institutionalised ranking flourish to a lesser or greater degree, but nowhere is property ownership in land or the alienability of labour a systematic basis for social discrimination between men. Yet egalitarianism stops short of relations between men and women. Sexual inequality strikes the outside observer." On gender inequality, see also Josephides 1985 and Jolly 1987, among many others.

28. See Sahlins 1963; Chowning 1979; Lindstrom 1984; and Roscoe 2000 for reviews of the literature on leadership in the region.

29. In a description of the "big man" form of leadership long associated with the region, Rena Lederman (2015, 567) characterizes it as one where "political influence is achieved by means of public oratory, informal persuasion, and the skillful conduct of both private and public wealth exchanges." For a discussion of the political importance of oratorical abilities and persuasive speech in Melanesia, see Watson-Gegeo 1986.

30. For discussions of the ineffectiveness or insignificance of political speech in New Guinea, see Lederman 1984; Munn 1986; Brison 1992; Kulick 1992; and Robbins 2001a. On the frequent ineffectiveness of speech in small-scale anarchic and egalitarian societies more broadly, see Rosaldo 1973; Atkinson 1984; Brenneis 1984; and Myers 1986.

31. For instance, in the *kabary* ceremonial speech style in Madagascar, where shows of mutual respect among interlocutors are of the essence (Keenan 1989), orators are closely attuned to the balance of power between speaker and listener. As an interlocutor explained to Jennifer Jackson (2013, 78), "in *kabary* one has to say words which make people think and not impose one's own ideas of truth."

32. See Schieffelin 1990 and Kulick 1992 for discussions of the important role listeners play in communicative ideologies elsewhere in Melanesia.

33. The important role that readers and audiences play in construing the meaning of texts has been highlighted in a number of fields, including feminist literary criticism (e.g., Fetterley 1978; Showalter 1979), reader response criticism (Fish 1980; Iser 2000), the active audiences tradition of media studies (Hall 1980; Morley 1999), and deconstructionist ap-

proaches to literature (Culler 1982). Some have even argued that audiences play the dominant role in construing the meaning of texts (Fiske 1987). Though the point can be taken too far—and it has—audiences clearly bring their own experiences and discourses they are familiar with to bear on the media texts they encounter. The point is important to keep in mind as a counterweight to the power attributed to the rhetorical word (e.g., Gitlin 1979). Unfortunately, much of the discussion of the activity of audiences celebrates the potential for alternative readings of media texts without attending carefully to actual practices of reading (Morley 1993). There are, of course, some notable exceptions (e.g., Radway 1991)

34. The potential power of the rhetorical word makes listening and reading a deeply political activity. "At its best, feminist criticism" as Judith Fetterley (1978, viii) says, "is a political act whose aim is not simply to interpret the world but to change it by changing the consciousness of those who read and their relation to what they read." Postcolonial critics have made much the same point. The historical method of subaltern studies, for instance, focuses on the perspective of the subaltern, a figure that "provides a mode of reading history different from those inscribed in elite accounts. Reading colonial and nationalist archives against their grain and focusing on their blind spots, silences and anxieties, these historians seek to uncover the subaltern's myths, cults, ideologies, and revolts that colonial and nationalist elites sought to appropriate and conventional historiography has laid to waste by their deadly weapon of cause and effect" (Prakash 1992, 9). In a similar vein, postcolonial interpretation in literary studies demands that texts be "read against the grain" (Bhabha 2004, 250). Dissatisfied with the sort of "hermeneutics of suspicion" that motivates such critical readings, a "post-critical turn" has in turn promoted alternative styles of reception: postcritical reading, reading with the grain, reparative reading, and so on (Sedgwick 1997; Bewes 2010; Felski 2015).

35. See Potter 2019 for an overview of the ways media literacy teaches people to read.

36. For an overview of the field of pragmatics, see Slotta 2020. The sort of socioculturally sensitive pragmatics that I am drawing on here focuses on culturally informed, socially contextualized practices of speaking and the norms that guide and give significance to them (e.g., Keenan 1976; Silverstein 1976; Irvine 1998; Bucholtz and Hall 2005).

37. In Boas's words, "It would seem that the essential difference between linguistic phenomena and other ethnological phenomenon is, that the linguistic classifications never rise into consciousness, while in other ethnological phenomena, although the same unconscious origin prevails, these often rise into consciousness, and thus give rise to secondary reasoning and to re-interpretations" (Boas 1911, 63). As a result, according to Boas, language provides an unparalleled window into unconscious associations of concepts, which he regarded as an important and universal aspect of human psychology.

38. On the relation of language ideologies to Boas's view of culture, see Silverstein 1979. On language ideologies, see Schieffelin, Woolard, and Kroskrity 1998; Kroskrity 2000; and Gal and Irvine 2019.

39. For a thoughtful discussion of different forms or genres of listening, see Marsilli-Vargas 2014. Lempert (2022) gives some much-needed attention to the variety of genres of democratic listening in play in the contemporary United States.

40. On the many ways that educational and religious institutions serve as sites of ideological diffusion and subjection, see, among others, Fanon (1952) 2008; Althusser 1971; Ngugi wa Thiong'o 1986; Bourdieu and Passeron 1990; Comaroff and Comaroff 1991; Keane 2006; Hanks 2010; Smith 2012; and Battiste 2013.

41. See Rice 2010 for a very different kind of instruction in listening.

42. There is a vast literature on voice, footing, intertextuality, and interdiscursivity, all ways of analyzing how people employ the speech of others and all useful in thinking about what the use of others' words can tell us about practices and ideologies of listening. Some perspectives on citationality I have found helpful in this book include Goffman

1979; Bakhtin 1981a; Briggs and Bauman 1992; Agha 2003; Bauman 2004; Hastings and Manning 2004; Silverstein 2005; Goodwin and Goodwin 2005; Handman 2010; Nakassis 2013; and Goodman, Tomlinson, and Richland 2014.

43. Discussions of political persuasion often note that persuasive speech must be tailored to the interests and needs of listeners, and in that respect such speech reflects something of the agency and subjectivity of the listener. As Bryan Garsten (2006, xvii) puts it, persuasion has a "dual character," "which consists partly in ruling and partly in following." Insofar as speakers are "following" the interests and desires of their audience, efforts at persuasion can offer insight into the audiences' subjective involvement as listeners in communicative activities. In a similar vein, the "uses and gratifications" tradition of media studies has emphasized the agency of audiences in actively seeking out and consuming particular kinds of media content. As agents, audiences' needs and desires are evident in the media they elect to consume (Katz, Blumler, and Gurevitch 1973; Katz, Haas, and Gurevitch 1973). Of course, this is a model of communication grounded in a consumerist vision of social life that emphasizes consumer choice and agency and operates with a limited psychological vision of needs (Elliott 1974). Clearly, it is not a model to adopt uncritically, but it too highlights how media content—or speech—can tell us something about the listener and their involvement in communication. Indeed, as conversation analysts have shown, even in a single turn at talk in a conversation, it is possible to see evidence of the agency of listeners (Goodwin 1979).

44. On the figure of the "white man" in Papua New Guinea, Bashkow (2006) provides a detailed exegesis of views in another region of Papua New Guinea, one that accords in many respects with my experience in the Yopno Valley.

1. THE ART OF ANARCHIC LISTENING

1. Of particular concern in preparing for the church anniversary celebration were the pigs owned by the Nian church congregation. People often give baby pigs to the church as offerings to mark special occasions, to secure blessings from God, such as ensuring the health and growth of their own pigs or alleviating problems that have arisen in their lives. Pigs given to the church are cared for by members of the community until they are needed for a church event such as this. But sometimes these pigs are borrowed by the community members looking after them if they have a pressing need to give those pigs to someone else; for example, to cement a marriage or to resolve a dispute. These borrowed pigs are supposed to be repaid, but in this instance, several debts were still outstanding, and other debts had been repaid with pigs that were too young to be given as gifts.

2. Clastres's point is one that recurs in the literature on political speech in small-scale anarchic polities; in relatively acephalous or egalitarian societies, leaders cannot simply order others about and often face resistance if they attempt to do so. For some of the literature on political speech in small-scale anarchic polities, see n. 30 in the introduction.

3. A portion of land may be designated for daughters as well as sons, but women cannot pass this land on to their children. Often, women marry men from other villages where they go live after marriage, using their husband's land there, rather than any land given to them by their father.

4. Members of some clans occasionally made claims of ownership to the land used by other clans, telling me that their clan was the first or among the first to arrive in the village. At the time of my research, however, land was plentiful, and nobody pressed these claims publicly, knowing that they would stir up ill will and conflict, which would likely lead to occult or physical violence.

5. For more detailed descriptions of the social organization of Yopno villages, see Kocher Schmid 1991; Keck 2005; Wassmann 2016.

6. As in much of Papua New Guinea (officially, 97%), the land in the Yopno Valley is controlled by its "customary owners," which in this region of the country are patrilineal clans and lineages. The 97% figure can be misleading because land is increasingly appropriated through other means. As Filer (2011, 2) found, "Between the beginning of July 2003 and the end of January 2011, almost 5 million hectares of customary land (11 percent of PNG's total land area) has passed into the hands of national and foreign corporate entities through a legal mechanism known as the 'lease-leaseback scheme.'" The lease-leaseback scheme allows the state to lease land from customary landholders for up to ninety-nine years and then lease it back to them or to other parties. There are no lease-leaseback arrangements in place in the Yopno Valley. But at the time of my research, a conservation area was created there as a result of the efforts of a US-based conservation NGO. Limits were imposed on how landholders could use the land they pledged to the conservation area (see chapter 4 for more discussion).

7. My first stay in the Yopno Valley (2008–9) occurred before the Tuition Fee Free education policy took effect in 2012, which limited school fees throughout the country (Paraide 2015; Walton 2019). Under the policy, however, rural schools were able to impose "project fees" that, in the Yopno Valley, usually equaled the fees that were being charged before implementation of the Tuition Fee Free policy.

8. In this sense of the term, anarchy was an enduring topic of twentieth-century social anthropology (Graeber 2004). Many of the so-called primitive societies of Africa, Australia, Asia, and the Americas that formed the object of much twentieth-century anthropology were, to a large extent, anarchic in this sense. Evans-Pritchard's (1987, 296) description of the Nuer of South Sudan provides a good example: "The Nuer constitution is highly individualistic and libertarian. It is an acephalous state, lacking legislative, judicial, and executive organs. Nevertheless, it is far from chaotic. It has a persistent and coherent form which might be called 'ordered anarchy.' The absence of centralized government and of bureaucracy in the nation, in the tribe, and in tribal segments—for even in the village authority is not vested in anyone—is less remarkable than the absence of any persons who represent the unity and exclusiveness of these groups." The questions that preoccupied social anthropology in the middle decades of the last century were how anarchic societies of this sort were organized and how order was maintained in them—in short, what is the basis of the kind of "ordered anarchy" that Evans-Pritchard described among the Nuer.

9. The Tok Pisin translation of this term, *wok boi* (work boy), has similarly derogatory connotations, which are perhaps evident to an English speaker. It is a term that comes from the era of colonial labor conscription, when adult male laborers were all referred to as "boys," a mark of their racialized subordination. See chapter 4 for additional examples of the use of this term and its Yopno equivalent, *oman amɨn*.

10. People often contrast the ineffectiveness of present leadership with the strength of past leaders, who are at times portrayed as true despots (Salisbury 1964; Strathern 1966). These were men who used their control over resources—especially the pigs needed for bridewealth payments—to gain the support of young men for their projects (Kocher Schmid 1993). Or they used fear of their occult powers—poison and sorcery (*sot mawom*) in particular—to ensure that people listened to their dictates (see Chapter 3 for more discussion of this point; Brison (1992) offers a particularly rich discussion of the issue in another part of New Guinea). People now speak ambivalently about these despotic leaders. They appreciate their ability to get things done, but they also decry their cruel authoritarianism—a tension between the value placed on "strength" and that placed on "equivalence," which has long been noted in ethnographies of the region (Read 1959).

As Christianity gained wide acceptance in the valley, poison and sorcery were no longer consonant with leadership roles and pushed underground. There are still said to be men with the ability to wield these powers, but they exist in the margins of the community, not at the center. It is not clear to me how to take these histories of past leadership. They likely reflect actual historical fact to some extent. But they are also, I suspect, projections based on people's desire for greater order and authority than is typically found in the anarchic villages of the valley. For insightful discussions of the desire for order in other New Guinean communities, see Robbins 2004; Golub 2014.

11. The fragility of villages and other collectives is a recurring theme in ethnographies of the region. Three particularly rich accounts can be found in Stasch 2009; Golub 2014; and Handman 2014. Golub's book not only documents the difficulties of sustaining collectives in the Highlands (in the context of mining activities) but also offers a thoughtful discussion in chapter 4 of the "anti-leviathan tendencies" often reported in ethnographies from the region: the tendencies for people to challenge hierarchical institutions, undermine collective projects, and fracture social groups.

12. These are quite similar to perlocutionary expressions—expressions that indicate the effects of talk—that are used elsewhere in New Guinea (e.g., Goldman 1980 on Huli). For a more detailed presentation of listener-centered perlocutionary expressions in Yopno, see Slotta 2015.

13. The church anniversary celebration was broken into two parts due to scheduling conflicts with other villages that were to attend, lead ceremonies, and perform dances. The first part of the celebration had concluded at this point, but pigs were still needed as gifts for those attending the second part of the celebration.

14. Dobrin (2012) identifies a four-part structure common in Arapesh narratives that might usefully be applied here. The fourth part of the structure is a coda that adds no new information but offers reflections, evaluations, and otherwise emphasizes connections between the narrated events and the event of narration itself. Using this model, the final part of the church leader's speech ("that would be good") adds a fourth part that draws the statement to a close by offering the speaker's evaluation of what he had been talking about.

15. The roughly synonymous verb phrase *kokwin aŋ* ("evaluate, sort, distribute") is used in a similar manner to talk about the work of listeners in examining and evaluating talk.

16. People also emphasize the agentive role of listeners in communicative events in the ways they talk about talk itself. Speaking may be described as "putting" (*yipmaŋ*) speech out there or "moving" it onto the floor of a meeting (*ɨkak*), highlighting that it is up to the listener to complete the communicative circuit: "This is important talk he has presented (*yipmaŋ*), so hold onto (*abɨdaŋ*) it well." Talk, in these cases, is portrayed as something moved into the vicinity of the listeners (pushed or left there), leaving it up to them to do something with it: break it up, examine it, hold onto it, or disregard it. It recalls Robbins's (2001, 906) characterization of a view of speech common among the Urapmin elsewhere in Papua New Guinea: it is a "run-it-up-the-flagpole-and-see-who-salutes" form of communication.

17. Note also that Tim's evaluation of the evangelist's suggestion includes a description of how he thinks the people of the village will evaluate the evangelist's suggestion: "if we talk right away about money then the Congregation will go stand apart from us and say: 'you yourselves do it with money!'" Because participants in this event were plotting a strategy of persuasion, much of how they evaluated each other's talk concerned how the community more widely would evaluate their proposed speeches.

18. Publicly voiced consensus may mask underlying dissensus. If people do not express their views in discussion or if they feel that their contributions have not been properly heard, they exercise their self-determination by not participating in the agreed-on course of action. Don Kulick's (1992, 126) description of oratory in a Papua New Guinean village is largely applicable to Yopno discussions as well: "In oratory, stress is not placed on solving problems or actually achieving concrete results, although this is one

potential outcome of the meetings in the men's house, and it is occasionally realized. More often, however, when the time comes to perform the activity that had been agreed upon, the consensus that had been arrived at in the men's house during oratorical speeches is ignored by some or even most of the individuals who had been present and took part in making the decision in the first place."

19. Goldman's point specifically concerns disputes among the Huli, which he discusses in illuminating detail in his ethnography (see Goldman 1983). Yet it also applies very well to decision-making processes in the Yopno Valley. Dispute resolution too involves lengthy processes of mediation in the Yopno Valley that are similar to those that Goldman describes, though the system of hearing disputes appears to be significantly more elaborate among the Huli.

20. I chose to avoid the term "autonomy" because it is suggestive of the autonomous, possessive individual of the Western liberal tradition (Macpherson 1962), which contrasts with the relational form of personhood much discussed in Melanesian ethnographies (see n. 21). Buitron and Steinmüller (2020) propose "relational autonomy" as a term to describe the kind of relational view of self-determination I discuss here. "Anarchic solidarity" and "cooperative autonomy" have also been proposed (Gibson and Sillander 2011). Blaser and colleagues (2010) thoughtfully attend to the complications that this sort of relationalism introduces in Indigenous people's movements for self-determination.

21. For classic statements of this relationalist view of personhood see Wagner 1977; Strathern 1988. Relationalism has been profitably used to illuminate topics of long-running ethnographic interest, such as land tenure and horticulture (Leach 2003), as well as newer considerations of Christianity (Robbins 2004), prostitution (Wardlow 2006), biomedicine (Street 2014), and incarceration (Reed 2006).

22. See Holly Wardlow's (2006) discussion of "encompassed" and "negative" agency among the Huli for a particularly well-developed analysis and some striking examples of the way women effectively go "on strike," withdrawing from the projects of others when they feel others are not living up to their obligations to them.

23. The *gapma-gapma* relationship is usefully regarded as a species of "coupling" common in Melanesia (Schwimmer 1984).

24. Today, the first fruits go first to the church to acknowledge the Christian God's primacy and to ensure God's blessing. After that, gifts are given to one's *gapma*. In that way, *gapma* have been incorporated into a broader framework of divinity and blessings in which the Christian God is primary.

25. Similar motives for seeking the support of powerful national and international actors are often noted in ethnographies of the region (e.g., Barker 2004; Kirsch 2006; Street 2014). Rupert Stasch's (2021, 270) description of contemporary Korowai as "anarchists for the state" is fitting in the Yopno context; see also Oppermann 2015; Herriman and Winarnita 2016; Tammisto 2016.

26. On the creation and operation of the YUS Conservation Area, see Dabek et al. 2021, part IV.

27. A school board member memorably berated parents in Ganggalut for expecting the government to provide subsidies to support local schools, instead of paying the school fees they owed. He admonished them not to depend on others to help them. But then he added that they should pray to God and God will provide them the resources needed to pay the school fees.

28. On the challenges faced by locals in areas where resource extraction and large-scale agricultural projects were developed, see Filer 1990; Bainton 2004; Errington and Gewertz 2004; Kirsch 2006; Golub 2014.

29. See Leach 2011 and McLeod 2013 for more detailed discussion of this refinery and its effects on the surrounding communities.

30. In addition to talk being "held onto," people also speak of talk as something that may be "protected, looked after" (*kutnaŋ*), like a prize possession or a person in one's care. The expression is used just like "hold" (*abɨdaŋ*) is to talk about keeping the words of others in mind.

31. Not all speech acts in Austin's account are clearly connected with institutions (e.g., thanking, promising), and clearly speakers do not require the backing of the state to exercise linguistic agency (which is evident in the many discussions of the power of words in non-state-centered societies e.g., Bloch 1975b; Stasch 2011a). But it is striking how the agency and power of the listener get elided in the seemingly automatic consequences of speech acts backed by powerful institutional sanctions.

2. SELF-DETERMINATION IN A WORLD OF UNCERTAINTY

1. See Beidelman 1982; Comaroff and Comaroff 1991; Keane 2006; Hanks 2010 for some major landmarks in the development of this view of missionization. Handman (2018) offers a good survey of work in this tradition. For discussions of the way educational and religious institutions have undermined indigenous ontologies and knowledge practices in the Pacific and beyond, see Watson-Gegeo and Gegeo 1992; Adams 1995; Schieffelin 1995; Semali and Kincheloe 1999; Thaman 2003; Pennycook 2005; Marker 2006; Villegas, Neugebauer, and Venegas 2008; Breidlid 2013; Robbins, Schieffelin, and Vilaça 2014.

2. See Barth 1975; Tuzin 1980; Jorgensen 1981; Harrison 1993a; Herdt 2003 for rich accounts of men's houses and their operation elsewhere in Papua New Guinea.

3. See Kocher Schmid 1991 and Wassmann 2016 for more detailed accounts of men's house activities in the Yopno Valley.

4. On the role of deception in men's houses elsewhere in New Guinea, see Langness 1974; Barth 1975; Lattas 1989; Tuzin 1997; and Herdt 2003. Kocher Schmid (1993, 795–96) reports hearing the same story about Yopno men's houses that I did during her research twenty years earlier.

5. This story of the men's house appears highly conducive to the sort of sociological account of secrecy common in the anthropological literature, which focuses analytic attention on the social organization and effects of secrecy: secrecy enhances solidarity, it differentiates social groups, it is a mode of domination, and so on. As a recent review of the literature on secrecy succinctly put it, "Secrets produce value through both the exclusion of outsiders and the inclusion of insiders" (Jones 2014, 54). In this way of treating secrecy, "the object of secrecy—its information—is often less important than the organizational approach to managing it" (Masco 2010, 440). Or, put another way, "From the anthropology of secrecy we learn that what counts is not the content of the secret but the structure it is embedded in" (Verdery 2014, 112). In the context of Melanesia, a review of the role of knowledge in politics remarks that "it is a truism that what is often most important 'is not what is secret, but that it is secret'" (Lindstrom 1984, 301).

In focusing on the social organization of secrecy, however, scholars of secrecy risk losing sight of what interests many of the participants in economies of secret knowledge; namely, the content of the secret knowledge itself. Indeed, certain questions remain intractable without an understanding of the value that secret knowledge holds for people: both those who control it and those who do not. After a review and synthesis of the literature concerning the political economy of knowledge in Melanesia, Lamont Lindstrom (1984, 304) arrives at this problem but unfortunately does not provide any answer: "I have not asked why people are willing to consume specific information or particular interpretive systems. An answer to this question would solve a number of perplexing problems. These include the existence of mystified or 'celestialized' . . . consciousness, the variable attractiveness of so-called cargo cults in Melanesia, why women and more-or-less exploited social classes allow others to define their realities, and why people in general do or do not know what (to us) appears objectively true and, moreover, in their own best interests." Indeed, the sociological effects of secrecy provide, at best, a partial motive for people's interest in secret knowledge; we cannot fully understand economies of secret knowledge if we do not take into consideration people's interest in and desire for the content of secret knowledge in the first place.

6. Tuzin (1980, 212–14), writing about the men's cult among the Ilahita Arapesh in the Sepik region of Papua New Guinea, offers a remarkably similar account of the difficulty in pinning down the nature of the spirit of the men's house. See also the opening of Crook (1999), which describes the dizzying experience of encountering multiple different and even contradictory accounts of the men's cult esoterica.

7. Modernity—and with it, market capitalism, the nation-state, and globalization—are often seen to be a harbinger of uncertainty and doubt (e.g., Giddens 1991). This is a point that Nils Bubandt (2014) highlights and then inverts in his ethnography of doubt in an Indonesian community, where he argues that it is in fact modernity that offers a solution to the doubts that plague social life in Buli.

8. In line with the stress placed on order in the anthropology of the time, the question at issue in much of the debate was the right way to impose order on the hodgepodge of religious elements found in a region near the border of what are today Papua New Guinea and West Papua (Gell 1975; Brunton 1980; Juillerat et al. 1980; Jorgensen and Johnson 1981). Some argued that the human sciences provide the frameworks needed to uncover the coherence in these materials. Brunton himself claimed that the mishmash of religious notions could be explained by attending to the sociopolitical competition that drives religious innovation and differentiation. Others still argued that the solution was to find the often well-hidden Indigenous exegesis that ties up the loose ends.

9. The sense of uncertainty is one that Jorgensen's (1981, 484) consultants dwell on: "Men recall their confusion, uncertainty, and shock in initiations. In the words of one man, 'they turn things turn things, keep turning them, they confuse us until our eyes roll' (*tiin buul*, also means 'to faint')." Among the nearby Baktaman, Frederik Barth (1975, 221–22) reports a similar appreciation of the incompleteness of knowledge: the secrecy of cult knowledge "dramatizes and inculcates a deep emotional experience of the *partial* nature of our understanding compared to the uncharted fullness of reality. The veils of disguise by which the practice of secrecy structures knowledge in successively deeper layers seem to be the conceptual and didactic mechanism whereby this attitude is maintained."

10. There is a widely noted interest among people in the region in foreign material and immaterial culture, which led Margaret Mead to dub the Arapesh of Papua New Guinea an "importing culture" (Mead 1938; Harrison 1993b; Bashkow 2000; Rutherford 2003; Dobrin 2014). Among the reasons people pursue this "commerce in culture" is the hope of gaining new powers from the knowledge and rituals they import. We see a similar search for new and more powerful knowledge in the phenomena widely known as "cargo cults." These movements promise adherents access to wealth and material goods (i.e., "cargo") through the practice of rituals grounded in often elaborate, esoteric "mythical" frameworks. These practices and frameworks are notably highly variegated and relatively short-lived, fading over time only to take on new forms later. In the words of Peter Lawrence (1964, 5), "Cargo beliefs and rituals were never fixed: they could be revised or replaced after failure. Thus, the history of the Cargo Movement represented a succession of different mythological explanations and ritual experiments. Each of these was a cargo *cult*—a complex of ritual activity associated with a particular cargo myth and more or less distinct from other complexes of the same general kind but associated with other myths." Fueled by dissatisfaction with their established cosmologies, rituals and

magic—or a sense that they have been irreversibly diminished (Errington and Gewertz 1986)—people search for new and better ones.

11. Dan Jorgensen notes that if the men's house generates deep uncertainty about truth, "the analyst is ipso facto confronted with two significant facts: he will encounter a multiplicity of indigenous interpretations, often offered in a tentative vein; no single interpretation could ever hope to be exhaustive.... The real problem of misconstrued order, then, is less likely to be a matter of finding sense where none exists than a question of finding too little sense in an embarrassing wealth of meanings" (Jorgensen and Johnson 1981, 472). My only addition would be to say that the "multiplicity of indigenous interpretations" and the difficulty of finding sense "in an embarrassing wealth of meanings" are not only consequences of epistemological uncertainty but are also conditions that generate epistemological uncertainty.

12. For discussion of the difficulties identifying the causes of illness in the Yopno Valley, see Keck 2005.

13. To say that people mostly experience spirits through verbal representations of them is not to say that they also do not experience spirits in the forest, the men's house, or in dreams. But based on my admittedly limited experience, it seems safe to say that people hear narratives about spirits much more frequently than they claim to actually encounter those spirits.

14. A recording and full transcript are available through the Endangered Languages Archive at https://elar.soas.ac.uk/Record/MPI1055791.

15. On the opacity of other minds in the Pacific, see Rumsey and Robbins 2008; Hollan and Throop 2011; Duranti 2015. We have seen examples of talk about other minds already in the discussions among community leaders in chapter 1, as they attempt to predict and shape the thoughts of community members. Many other instances can be found in the examples discussed in this and the following chapters.

16. On the need to investigate the performance of myths in context as a form of culturally mediated social action, see Bauman 1984b; Sherzer 1990; Urban 1991; Silverstein 1996.

17. The conception of babies as effectively self-less is common in Melanesian. The Ambonwari of the Sepik region use a similar idiom to the Yopno one, holding that "children do not have 'insideness' or understanding; they still lack Heart (*wambung*)" (Telban 1997, 313). In the Hagen area, the presence of *noman* ("mind" or "heart") distinguishes human beings from wild animals and adults from children (Strathern 1972, 160–61). Kaluli children are seen as "having no understanding" and so are not treated as communicative partners (Schieffelin 1990, 70–71). Among the Baining, a baby is not spoken to until it is about six months old because "its eye is not clear," an expression meaning that "the child does not know or understand yet" (Fajans 1997, 86). Similar views are found outside Melanesia too, of course (e.g., Mezzenzana 2020).

18. Education in this general sense has a moral purpose: to produce right-acting people who can coexist in social harmony (see Schieffelin 1990 and Kulick 1992 for further discussion). Without this education, people will remain fools and troublemakers. But to achieve this end, people are instructed not only in how to act but also in how the world works. That is, people are instructed in facts as well as values; indeed, instruction in facts is a way to instill values. A moral education cannot be disentangled from an education that provides knowledge of reality.

19. Children learn early to be on the watch for trickery and they come to see it as a basic feature of social interaction: *topgo tɨkŋɨ* (something like "you're full of it") is perhaps the most common retort children use with each other when they feel mistreated.

The generally accepted view that babies are born without understanding means that they are regarded as particularly susceptible to deception. As in other parts of New Guinea (Kulick 1992; Rumsey 2013), deception is used to control children: nonexistent hazards are pointed out, or desirable goods are promised to compel children to behave. I was often presented as one of those threats, with misbehaving children told "the whiteman is going to eat you if you do that," which I presume speakers did not actually believe would happen. Deception is common in children's experience with adults and with each other, and so they watch carefully for it.

20. Through use of the first-person dual or plural pronoun ("we two" or "we"), speakers represent themselves as ignorant members of the community (one of "us"). But their presentation of alternative esoteric perspectives in these events of instruction suggests otherwise. People explained to me that they used "we" (nin) or the dual "we two" (nit) rather than "you" in situations like this so that no one would think they were being treated as inferior. In this way, speakers not only avoid directly singling out people who are in need of enlightenment, but they also avoid highlighting the superiority of their own understanding lest it give rise to resentment.

21. Compare this with the response Rupert Stasch received (quoted earlier in this chapter) when asking why characters in Korowai myths act the way they do. There is a revelatory quality to action in both cases, which begins with an enigma that the audience expects will be clarified. Where Yopno historical narratives emphasize the characters' relative lack of understanding compared with the omniscient perspective of the audience, other events like the acts of instruction described in this section emphasize the audience's lack of understanding and the slow disclosure of what is really going on.

22. The term mibili, which may be translated as "reason, basis, cause, meaning," also signifies the roots of a plant. There is a spatial quality to the term that I try to suggest here by speaking of the "depth" of an event: the reasons and meanings that lie hidden below its surface.

23. When I asked the headmaster of the primary school in Nian why he peppered his public speeches with questions, he explained, "If we ask questions then they have to listen and think."

24. In a sense, this chapter concerns "agnotology," the "cultural production of ignorance" (Proctor 2008). But my emphasis is less on how ignorance itself is produced, and more on the way people reflexively come to see themselves as ignorant, nescient, and uncertain (regardless of their actual state of knowledge). This latter sensibility is what Michael Smithson (1989) has termed "conscious ignorance," distinguishing it from the kind of "meta-ignorance"—the ignorance of being ignorant—that is found in things like the Dunning-Kruger effect (Dunning 2011). Former secretary of defense Donald Rumsfeld offered a pithy typology of this terrain when he distinguished "known unknowns" from "unknown unknowns" (see Proctor 2008, 29). It is this "conscious ignorance"—knowing that one does not know—that is the particular focus of this chapter.

25. As Peter Lawrence (1965, 216) writes of the nearby Ngaing, "Except in minor matters, [the Ngaing] dismiss the principle of human intellectual discovery. All the most valued parts of their culture are believed to have been invented by the deities, who taught men not only the ritual but also the empirical techniques for utilizing them."

26. The importance of listening as a source of knowledge is implicit in ethnographies of knowledge circulation in the region (e.g., Tuzin 1980; Lindstrom 1990). For a very different view of the value of knowledge acquired through listening as opposed to seeing, see Sillitoe 2010.

27. As Jürg Wassmann (2016, 175) notes of Yopno views of dreams, "Dreams can never be directly known; it is the dreamer's task to make their content publicly known. . . . [The actions and objects in dreams] are symbols, and these symbols must be transmitted by the dreaming person to the outside world, and their meaning will be debated publicly."

28. The long-distance exchange networks that connected the Yopno Valley to the north coast and the islands beyond include a number of valuables that are now spoken

of as ancestral "money"—particularly, shells—using the same terms used to describe Papua New Guinea's state currency (the Kina). This ancestral money was produced by spirits, and Po'o draws a similar connection between *kukup kɨdat* (village spirits) and the national currency, though now routed through the Papua New Guinean government. For an account of the trade network along the northeastern coast of New Guinea and the valuables used in it, see Harding 1967. Englund and Leach's (2000) discussion of the nearby Rai Coast bears several striking parallels to the event reported here, from people's questions about the nature of money to Pereng's dream about it. Akin and Robbins (1999)'s edited collection is a particularly interesting look at varied ways that state currencies have been adopted in different parts of the region.

29. Melanesian anthropology has long stressed the role of nurture in giving shape to the most fundamental characteristics of a person's self. Nurturance through feeding (Strathern 1973; Merlan and Rumsey 1991; Fajans 1997), the exchange of fluids (Elliston 1995), and the creation and provisioning of gardens, trees, and land (Leach 2003; Bamford 2007) are constitutive of a person's identity in different Melanesian societies. So too is the nurturance of the mind, perhaps most evident in men's house initiation processes.

30. One hears echoes in the ontological turn of an earlier generation of anthropologists' goal to produce "a world made safe for differences," in Ruth Benedict's (1946, 15) much-cited phrase. An excellent example of how this anthropological concern with cultural diversity intersected with the politics of self-determination can be found in the executive board of the American Anthropological Association's 1947 "Statement on Human Rights."

31. On the failures of modern Western thought—particularly the binary distinction of nature and culture—as they are discussed by proponents of an ontological turn, see Kohn 2013; Cadena 2015; Viveiros de Castro 2015a; and Holbraad and Pedersen 2017. Latour (1993) is a key reference point for these discussions.

32. A recent overview of the ontological turn opens by considering how an anthropology student's conceptualizations are transformed by their encounter with Mauss's argument about the mingling of persons and things in the gift, among other anthropological chestnuts. "To understand Maori gifts, Zande oracles or Balinese calendars, he [*sic*: the student] now realizes, you must be prepared to question some of the most basic things you may have taken for granted. Suddenly, the distinction between people and things [a reference to Mauss's argument about the gift], the assumption that events are best explained by their causes [a reference to Evans-Pritchard's argument about Zande oracles], or the notion that time is something that passes [a reference to Geertz's discussion of Balinese calendars], are all up for grabs. The 'a-ha!-moment' that each of these examples is meant to induce, then, is at once reflexive and profoundly relativizing" (Holbraad and Pedersen 2017, 1–2). Although anthropologists and their students are seen as engaged in this reflexive process of conceptualization—centerpieces of Holbraad and Pedersen's exposition (pp. 9–18) of the core aims of the ontological turn—Indigenous peoples are generally presented as *having* concepts: they are not engaged in a process of reflexive consideration of their own concepts, and certainly not in ways that are tinged with dissatisfaction and doubt. The structuralist roots of the ontological turn are particularly apparent in the way the classic distinction of "hot" and "cold" societies (Lévi-Strauss 1966) is reproduced here. Western ontologies are historically transformed through engagement with the seemingly unchanging ontologies of Indigenous peoples.

33. I have benefited from the insightful use of Gidden's expression in Bubandt 2014. See Bessire and Bond 2014 for related critiques of the model of the Indigenous subject implicit in the ontological turn.

3. ANARCHY, POWER, AND THE POLITICS OF EXPERTISE

1. Kenneth Read long ago pointed out the tension between the value of "strength" and the value of "equivalence," which leaders among the Gahuku-Gama had to navigate. "There is a manifest tension or inconsistency between these ideals, and considering the role of the leader this opposition is likely to be felt most keenly by the man who is attempting to achieve and to maintain authority. But I would state the position more strongly than this. I would say that the character of leadership requires a man who has some feeling for these inconsistencies. It is men who possess this insight—and whose self-control enables them to profit from the knowledge—who are 'selected' as leaders in the traditional sociocultural system" (Read 1959, 434). Expert knowledge, as I hope to show in this chapter, provides leaders with a way to navigate similar tensions of leadership in the relatively anarchic villages of the Yopno Valley.

2. In Papua New Guinea, as in many places, oratory often stands out from everyday speech. In the region around Mt. Hagen in the Central Highlands, for instance, unique intonation patterns and elaborate idiomatic expressions mark out the "arrow talk" (*el ik* or *el ung*) of political leaders (Strathern 1975; Merlan and Rumsey 1991). Among the Manambu of the Sepik region, debates over the ownership of names are political events of significant consequence, requiring the mastery and skillful deployment of a vast amount of esoteric mythological knowledge, including thousands of secret names of totemic ancestors (Harrison 1990). Throughout New Guinea, political oratory often involves "bent," "twisted," "veiled," or "hidden" speech that is elaborately metaphorical, allusive, highly coded, and hard to interpret. We have seen examples of something akin to that in the last chapter, in the didactic skits and gift presentations that are based on complex and often enigmatic metaphors. On the formal, often "poetic" features (in the sense of Jakobson 1960) that distinguish oratory, see Bloch 1975a; Irvine 1979; Silverstein 1981, 2003; and Bate 2009.

By contrast, oratory in the Yopno Valley appears quite plain. The pedagogical character of much Yopno oratory shares with the "plain style" of European rhetoric a greater focus on the referential than the poetic functions of speech. As scholars of English plain style point out, however, that emphasis on the referential function of speech is itself a rhetorical—one might even say poetic—feature of plain style (Jones 1930; Fisch 1952; Bauman 1984a; Vickers and Struever 1985; Skouen and Stark 2014). In this chapter I hope to illuminate some of the rhetorical features of the expert style of oratory in the Yopno context. On the rhetoric of expertise more broadly, see Carr 2010 for a very useful framework.

3. Foucault (1977, 1978) provides canonical accounts of the ways in which expertise in the human sciences functions within disciplinary and governmental regimes of power. Rose (1993) provides a good overview of governmentality and the role of expertise in it. On the role of psychology and psychiatry specifically, see Hacking 1995; Rose 1999; on economics, see Ferguson 1994; Escobar 1995; Mitchell 2002; and on orientalism, see Said's (1978) classic account.

4. As a tool of governmentality used to shape the conduct of people, expert discourses guide the way experts and laypeople alike intervene in the world around them. As Nikolas Rose notes (1993, 289), "Language, from the perspective of governmentality, is not a matter of meanings, but of the ways in which the world is made intelligible and practicable, and domains are constituted such as 'the market', or 'the family' which are amenable to interventions by administrators, politicians, authorities and experts—as well as by the inhabitants of those domains themselves—factory managers, parents and the like."

5. Perhaps I should have followed Dominic Boyer's (2008) suggestion and termed these figures "intellectuals" rather than "experts," insofar as "skilled knowing" rather than "skilled doing" is the focus of my account here. But the term "intellectuals" would suggest too great a distance from the sort of practical concerns that lie at the heart of the politics of expertise in the Yopno Valley. Knowledge serves as the basis of leadership in many parts of New Guinea (Chowning 1979; Lindstrom 1984, 1990; Harrison 1989), but no term equivalent to the well-known appellation "big man" has been developed for those leaders distinguished by their control of knowledge, rather than material wealth (although the Tok Pisin term *saveman* [knowledgeable person] is used broadly in Papua New Guinea for both "experts" and "intellectuals"). Among the Yopno, the term *nandak nandak amïn* ("person with knowledge, understanding") is used. Insofar as this "knowledge" is intimately connected with practical affairs—the topic of this chapter—the translation "expert" seems more appropriate than "intellectual."

6. See Keck 2005 for a rich account of the kinds of expertise that go into diagnosing the causes of illness in the Yopno Valley.

7. In a provocative account of divination, Martin Holbraad (2012) argues that divinatory truth in Cuba is not understood as a representational relationship between signs and reality—i.e., one that might be correct or incorrect. Rather, truth is produced through the causal interaction of several different trajectories of meaning: myths, personal situations, the chance fall of divining tools. From these pieces, a diviner produces a truth claim, which is taken to be necessarily true.

A view of truth as the effect of such a coincidence—without any possibility of falsehood—leads to a serious question that Holbraad (2012, 208) himself poses: "If all transformations of meaning can be considered as revelations of truth, as has been suggested, . . . then in what does the diviner's special claim to truth consist?" In an epistemologically stratified social situation in which some people are viewed as having greater access to correct understanding than others, the issue of representational accuracy is bound to be important (*pace* Holbraad). In a point I return to in the conclusion to this chapter, it is the ability to achieve a greater measure of accuracy that distinguishes experts—or diviners—from laypeople. And the skill of experts is evaluated according to how well they achieve representational accuracy (among other things), as Holbraad's ethnography itself illustrates.

8. See chapter 1 for further discussion of this "partner clan" (*gapma-gapma*) relationship.

9. As a Christian spiritual leader, Peter holds the Christian God up as the primary divinity. But in his discussion of Kauso's problems, he noted that the Christian God created *gapma* as, effectively, a god-on-earth. *Gapma*s are still considered gods by most people I talked with about them, but as gods secondary to the Christian God. Christianity, people often point out, deepened their knowledge of divinity, revealing the (Christian) God that lay behind the gods (*gapma*) and other spirits that their ancestors recognized. The secondary status of the *gapma* is evident in the way first fruits from a new garden or a pandanus nut harvest are now offered. Historically, first fruits would go to a person's *gapma*. Now the first fruits go to the Christian God, and after that the "second fruits" are given to one's *gapma*.

10. The way the Garia "think on" (*nanunanu*) a person is quite similar (Lawrence 1984). There, as in the Yopno Valley, people give gifts and perform rituals in part to get other people and spirits to "think on" them—to recognize them and their obligations to them.

11. In part, the altruistic posture of leaders is a means of trying to attract the attention and willing involvement of community members, no small thing in a political environment where community members readily disregard the words of community leaders. As Muyan's diatribe makes clear, however, expertise certainly does not always succeed in finding an

enthusiastic audience. One of the prime reasons people disregard the gift of expertise is that they deem it deceptive. As Muyan notes, people rejected his advice saying, "You're lying, you're lying." False "expertise" undermines rather than enhances the self-determination of listeners, and people are careful to guard against self-styled experts aiming to trick them into acting against their own will, an issue discussed in detail in chapter 4.

12. See Kocher Schmid 1993 on the former connection between political power and bridewealth exchange in the Yopno Valley. In a classic description of the "big man" style of leadership, Marshall Sahlins (1963, 291) argues that a key feature "is the deployment of one's skills and efforts in a certain direction: towards amassing goods, most often pigs, shell monies and vegetable foods, and distributing them in ways which build a name for cavalier generosity, if not for compassion. A faction is developed by informal private assistance to people of a locale. Tribal rank and renown are developed by great public giveaways sponsored by the rising big man, often on behalf of his faction as well as himself." There has been much debate over the defining characteristics of this type of leadership or whether such a thing as the Melanesian big man exists. For more recent discussions, see Martin 2013 and Lederman 2015.

13. An aspiring leader of this sort who seeks to wield their influence over those in debt to them will "remind" people of all he has done for them. So, for instance, the headmaster in his speech in Nian stressed all the work he had done for the community in rebuilding the school after it was shut down several years earlier: "I brought this school out of the swamp, cleaned it up and fixed it. I left and you all messed it up again, so I came back and cleaned it off and fixed it again. I don't want to do it again." He highlights the debt the community owes him and threatens to withdraw his services at the same time unless the community members pitch in. On the importance of "reminding" people of debts, see Munn 1986 and Schieffelin 1990, 134.

14. That power comes from distant realms is a common view of the matter in the Pacific and beyond (Sahlins 2012).

15. The connection between truth and self-determination that I touch on here is a concern shared by the Western liberal tradition; namely, that an actor's freedom and self-determination are threatened not only by physical obstacles ("geographical conditions or prison walls, armed men or the threat . . . of lack of food or shelter or other necessities of life") but also psychological obstacles ("fears and 'complexes,' ignorance, error, prejudice, illusions, fantasies, compulsions, neuroses and psychoses . . ."; Berlin 1964, 21). According to this liberal view of the matter, people cannot be self-directing agents if they are blind to the reality of their situation as a result of psychological repression, false consciousness, ideological indoctrination, and the like. Indeed, "ideology" poses a particular problem for liberal ideals of freedom and self-determination, insofar as a blinkered consciousness is unable to know what it is truly doing and so ipso facto cannot be self-determining. In its classic sense, as Slavoj Zizek (2008, 27) puts it, ideology is "a matter of a discordance between what people are effectively doing and what they think they are doing—ideology consists in the very fact that the people 'do not know what they are really doing,' that they have a false representation of the social reality to which they belong."

16. On an archaeological approach to knowledge, see Foucault 1972. As Dreyfus and Rabinow (1983, xxiv) note, to treat discourses of the human sciences "archaeologically" is "to avoid becoming involved in arguments about whether what they say is true, or even whether their statements make sense." Much of the archaeology of expertise has focused on sciences that are "dubious," to use Foucault's expression (1979, 131), where "arguments about whether what they say is true" are less interesting perhaps than understanding them in a more philological vein. Under the heading of the "dubious" sciences, we might include psychology and psychiatry (Hacking 1995; Rose 1999), Orientalism (Said 1978), and development economics, (Escobar 1995), among others.

Something like this archaeological approach is also prominent in the way science studies and the history of science approach the hard sciences. As Shapin and Schaffer (1985, 14) describe their method in their classic account of Hobbes and Boyle's debate about the air pump, "'Truth,' 'adequacy,' and 'objectivity' will be dealt with as accomplishments, as historical products, as actors' judgements and categories." Here, the influence of a postpositivist philosophy of science is important (Hanson 1958; Kuhn 1970), a philosophy that, like Foucauldian archaeology, attends to the internal coherence of "paradigms" and "theories" and largely sets aside arguments about their truth.

17. Foucault's genealogical approach to knowledge, as Amia Srinivasan (2019, 140) succinctly summarizes it, "is interested in what our representational systems *do*: which practices they emerge from and help sustain, how they are mobilized by power, what (and whom) they bring into existence, and which possibilities they foreclose." Alongside Foucault, Srinivasan includes Friederich Nietzche, Charles Mills, Uday Mehta, Edward Said, Chandra Mohanty, Simone de Beauvoir, bell hooks, Angela Davis, Catharine MacKinnon, Judith Butler, Quentin Skinner, and Samuel Moyn in a list of critical genealogists more concerned with what representations *do* than whether representations are *true*. We might add many others who share this genealogical interest in the work that representations perform, including many of those cited in the previous footnote, as well as latter-day Marxists (Althusser 1971; Williams 1977; Hall 1986), critics of colonialism (Fanon [1952] 2008; Memmi 1967; Ngugi wa Thiong'o 1986), and other social theorists (Barthes 1972; Bourdieu 1991).

18. Donna Haraway (1988, 579), for one, notes the pragmatic significance of accurate representations in advocating for an approach she calls "feminist empiricism": "Feminists have to insist on a better account of the world; it is not enough to show radical historical contingency and modes of construction for everything. Here, we, as feminists, find ourselves perversely conjoined with the discourse of many practicing scientists, who, when all is said and done, mostly believe they are describing and discovering things *by means of* all their constructing and arguing. . . . Feminists have stakes in a successor science project that offers a more adequate, richer, better account of the world, in order to live in it well." Recognizing the pragmatic significance of truth, however, is not without its complications: "So, I think my problem, and 'our' problem, is how to have *simultaneously* an account of radical historical contingency for all knowledge claims and knowing subjects, a critical practice for recognizing our own "semiotic technologies" for making meanings, *and* a no-nonsense commitment to faithful accounts of a 'real' world" (579). How to resolve these complications remains an open question.

19. In the wake of postpositivist critiques of the possibility of grasping objective truth, Collins and Evans (2002, 236) wonder what roll experts have to play in society: "If it is no longer clear that scientists and technologists have special access to the truth, why should their advice be specially valued?" Insofar as people do turn to experts for insight and advice in the Yopno Valley and beyond, special access to the truth is an important reason why, notwithstanding postpositivist critiques of the notion of truth.

20. This world-disclosing power of representations accords well with the pragmatic, instrumental conception of truth put forward by pragmatists like William James and John Dewey. As William James (1978, 98) puts it, "The possession of truth, so far from being here an end in itself, is only a preliminary means towards other vital satisfactions. If I am lost in the woods and starved, and find what looks like a cow-path, it is of the utmost importance that I should think of a human habitation at the end of it, for if I do so and follow it, I save myself. The true thought is useful here because the house which is its object is useful. The practical value of true ideas is thus primarily derived from the practical importance of their objects to us." In the Yopno politics of expertise, we might

say that the practical value of true representations is primarily derived from the control it gives people over the powerful third parties that are the objects of expert knowledge.

4. DECEPTION AND THE DANGERS OF LISTENING

1. See Schieffelin 1990; Kulick 1992; and Rumsey 2013 for more detailed discussions of the use of deception in childrearing practices in Papua New Guinea and the views of infancy and development that guide the use of deception.

2. In the Trobriands, Gunter Senft (2008) claims that *biga sopa* ("joking, lying or indirect speech") is, in fact, the default speech variety. The important place of deception in the communicative ideologies of people in the Trobriands is highlighted in Weiner 1983 and elsewhere in Papua New Guinea by Munn 1986; Robbins 2001c; and Andersen 2013, among others, as well as the authors cited in the previous footnote.

3. Building on the work of Bakhtin, Derrida, and Goffman in particular, linguistic anthropologists have explored the many ways that the use of others' words constitutes a form of social action (e.g., Briggs and Bauman 1992; Goodwin and Goodwin 2005; Silverstein 2005; Agha 2007; Nakassis 2013).

4. On the dangers of "direct" or "straight" speech in other Melanesian communities, see Weiner 1983; Brison 1992; Kulick 1992; Crook 1999. The use of opaque speech of this sort is commonly remarked throughout Melanesia (e.g., Strathern 1975; Merlan and Rumsey 1991; Josephides 2001), as well as the previous citations. Such remarks apply to actions more generally as well (LiPuma 1998).

5. Kulick (1992) provides a rich look at the way communicative directness is associated with women elsewhere in Papua New Guinea. Keenan (1989) notes a similarly gendered ideology in Madagascar, where women's lack of facility with indirect speech is also used to explain why women do not play a larger role in politics.

6. Wassmann and Dasen (1994) explore the significance of the qualities "hot" and "cold" in the Yopno Valley, which characterize both the temperament of individuals and the way leaders should act.

7. Shame can also be a productive emotion, which speakers cultivate in their audience to encourage them to act. But generally this is not done directly. Rather, shame is induced by offering an outsider's derisive perspective on both the speaker and his audience (e.g., Leroy 1979, 206).

8. Brison (1992) offers a particularly detailed consideration of the ways that the threat of sorcery shapes interactional practice in Kwanga, promoting indirection and gossip. Barth (1975, chap. 14) too contains an insightful discussion of the ways that the threat of sorcery shapes interaction among the Baktaman near the Indonesian border. One of the consequences Barth notes is that fear of sorcery leads people to act with great tact toward others much of the time, lest they be attacked.

9. The local level government counselor (introduced in chapter 2) who had hosted me in Ganggalut in 2008–9 had lost his position and moved to the town of Lae. His older brother had moved to the neighboring village of Gua. By 2014, when the fundraiser occurred, the village had lost most of its leaders as a result of in-fighting among factions and accusations of occult violence. From what people have told me, this has been an ongoing issue in the village.

10. Elementary schools were introduced as part of a new national education policy in 1995, which began to be implemented in the valley during 2008–9. See n. 1 in chapter 5 for further information.

11. Elsewhere too, indirection is often linked to egalitarian-minded political settings, where overt shows of authority are often ineffective and even counterproductive (e.g., Rosaldo 1973; Jackson 2013).

12. The baseline assumption that speech and action more generally are deceptive is, as Alan Rumsey argues, one important reason why other minds are so often treated as opaque in Melanesia. People do not venture guesses about others' intentions and thoughts because people are assumed to be hiding their true thoughts and feelings (Rumsey 2013; see also Weiner 1983; Brison 1992; Robbins 2001c).

13. The distinction between unintentionally misleading and intentionally deceptive speech is not always made in Papua New Guinea (Robbins 2001c) or elsewhere (Danziger 2013). In the Yopno Valley, people are sensitive to the difference between mistaken claims and claims that are made with the aim of misleading others, though it can prove hard in individual instances to decide which is the case. From the perspective of a listener concerned about his or her self-determination, it often does not matter whether a speaker is attempting to be intentionally deceptive or merely offers them mistaken expertise. Both equally threaten to detract from their audience's control over the future.

14. For discussion of the dilemmas that expertise poses to liberal democratic politics, see Bohman 1996; Fischer 2000; Jasanoff 2009; and Callon, Lascoumes, and Barthe 2011. Many of the proposed ways of managing the tension between expert knowledge and popular sovereignty highlight the need for additional "meta-discourse" about expert knowledge in the public sphere.

15. Of course, as the chairman of the elementary school board, it is not surprising that Nanda would be pointing people to the school as the way to secure benefits. As we have seen repeatedly, leaders leverage their purported expertise concerning the power of distant others like the conservation NGO to try to influence the way their audience acts. Maŋnu, who is trying to organize the work for the conservation celebration, instructs his audience that supporting the conservation celebration is the way to receive scholarships to the teachers' training college; Nanda, who is trying to encourage parents to send their kids to school, instructs others that supporting the local school is the means to this end.

16. Trust is a central theme in the work of social epistemologists (e.g., Hardwig 1991; Faulkner 2007). For a classic account of the importance of trust in the development of early modern science, see Shapin's (1994) discussion of the "gentleman" scientists of seventeenth-century England.

17. On the metadiscursive organization of legal proceedings, see Matoesian 2001; Mertz 2007; Goodman, Tomlinson, and Richland 2014; and Komter 2019.

18. On fact checking and its metadiscursive character, see Graves 2016; Slotta 2019.

19. As Power (1999) emphasizes, the institutionalization of audits to check on the veracity of financial and other kinds of statements has been brought about particularly by situations where trust is lacking.

5. LISTENING AT THE ENDS OF THE EARTH

1. According to the Education (Amendment) Act passed in 1995, students were to begin their education in elementary school before moving to primary school in third grade. The introduction of elementary schools rolled out slowly throughout the country and was largely implemented in the Yopno Valley between 2010–14. Before that, many children began their schooling in Tok Ples Preschools (TPPS), a program initiated by an SIL Bible translator and his spouse, who had come to the valley to translate the Bible into Yopno. After students completed TPPS, they would attend community schools from first through sixth grades.

2. For exemplary monographs documenting some of these new forms of inequality, see Gewertz and Errington 1999; Foster 2002; Errington and Gewertz 2004; Wardlow 2006; Martin 2013; and Golub 2014.

3. Talk of being the *las ples* seems particularly concentrated in rural areas of the country that fall largely outside the ambit of state services and economic development proj-

ects. For other examples of this discourse of being the "last place," see Kulick 1992; Englund and Leach 2000; Foster 2002; Hoenigman 2012; Jebens 2012; and Malbrancke 2019. Kocher Schmid (1993, 786) mentions the use of the expression in the Yopno Valley back in the 1990s. "Mipela las boda tru (we are the last border area)," she was told, a lament somewhat unique to the valley, where people often blame the lack of government services on their location on the border of Morobe and Madang Provinces.

4. In the expression *las ples* we hear echoes of a framework of space and time—a chronotope, in the Bakhtinian parlance (1981b)—common to discourses of modernization, development, and missionization (Escobar 1995; Dick 2010; Handman 2010; Stasch 2011b; Koven 2013), which people in the valley have frequently encountered in their schooling and in church services, in the speeches of government officials and local leaders. These discourses distinguish people living in different stages along a temporal trajectory running from tradition to modernity, developing to developed, heathen to saved. In these progressivist chronotopes, people in the "third world," in effect, exist in an earlier stage of history than those in the "first world." Apart from an often-remarked sense that some good ancestral knowledge has been lost, I did not often encounter this chronotope's opposite, the sort of declinist view of history that Tomlinson (2004) describes in Fiji.

5. See Bashkow 2006 for an extended discussion of the way Orokaiva in Papua New Guinea view people living in the countries of the global north, a view that bears a number of similarities to the ways people in the Yopno Valley speak about the lives of "white people."

6. A few people in the Yopno Valley have remarked to me that their power-giving knowledge—the knowledge of forest spirits, magic, ancestral powers, and the like—is not transmitted to people outside the valley to nearly the same degree that foreign knowledge has entered the valley. In acts of exchange—particularly, in acts of exchange with socially distant others like affines or other villages—balance or "being level" (*arɨp arɨp*) is an important consideration. To give as good as one receives is a mark of equality. The lack of balance in the exchange of knowledge is, thus, notable.

In the Waria Valley, another region of Papua New Guinea where I conducted research, one church held that they had esoteric religious knowledge that the rest of Christendom would one day learn from them. I never heard anything at all like that from people in the Yopno Valley. Still, there are concerns that local sources of power like netsa spirits and other sacra might be stolen by outsiders. That is a regular explanation offered for the interest of the conservation NGO in the region, for instance. Occasionally, people expressed worries that Yopno historical tales or magical knowledge are being collected to be sold on the market by me and other anthropologists. I do not doubt that this was a more general concern about my own research than people ever let on in my presence.

7. Communicative imaginaries are not restricted to large-scale social formations. An inspiration for my account here is Judith Irvine's work (1996) on the "shadow conversations" that surround Wolof insult poetry, which elegantly highlights the way cultural presumptions about the circulation of discourse inflect the significance of such poetry. As she shows, such presuppositions are integral to the significance of communicative events whether they turn out to be correct or not. For discussion of other "communicative imaginaries," see Lee and LiPuma 2002; Briggs 2005; Cody 2011; Handman 2018; and Slotta 2019.

8. On the public sphere, see Habermas [1962] 1989, and on its character as an imaginary, see Warner 1992; Lee 1997; Warner 2002.

9. Hannerz and others have argued that this is an inadequate understanding of the way culture flows in the recent era of globalization (e.g., Appadurai 1996; Larkin 1997) But it nonetheless remains a common global imaginary, evident for one in continuing

worries about the cultural homogenization that will result from globalization; the McDonaldization of the world, as it were.

10. As linguistic anthropologists have emphasized, building on the work of Voloshinov 1973; Bakhtin 1981a; and Goffman 1979, communicative events are not isolated occurrences; they are linked to communicative events in other times and places, which they respond to, build on, and foreshadow. Through the use of others' words (as well as other characteristics of others' speech), speakers interact with people across events of communication, establishing a stance, footing, or alignment toward them (for a good overview of this perspective, see Wortham and Reyes 2015). In this respect, bits of language may be said to move through space and time—to circulate—connecting the use of language on one occasion "interdiscursively" to other moments as part of broader institutional processes and political projects through which social identities and relationships, speech genres and registers, and even culture itself are generated, stabilized, and transformed (e.g., Briggs and Bauman 1992; Irvine 1996; Spitulnik 1996; Urban 2001; Agha 2003, 2005; Bauman 2004; Goodwin and Goodwin 2005; Briggs 2013; Lo and Park 2017; Gal 2018).

This interdiscursive perspective on speech events has developed alongside increasing scholarly attention to global flows of commodities, people, and cultural forms (Appadurai 1996). In line with this, linguistic anthropologists have turned their attention to the intertextual links among multiple, often distant contexts of communication through which texts, genres, registers, and languages themselves circulate (Shankar and Cavanaugh 2012).

Events of listening, too, are moments in such wider histories of communication and interaction. Much like speakers, listeners connect themselves and respond to others in other times and places through their practices of listening in the here and now of communicative interaction.

11. Besides requests for English lessons, the most common educational request I received was for workshops teaching people how to write applications for funding from granting agencies and consular offices.

12. As the evangelist himself points out, dystopian visions like this one are meant to induce fear (*pasol*) in their audience and, I might add, shame (*mayektok*). Both are understood to be potent emotions that drive people to act, and they play a large role in oratorical theory and practice in the region. As the evangelist once explained to me, orators sometimes must give their audiences "fire" (*kandap*), make them feel shame and fear so that they pay attention and act. He mentioned this after watching me try and fail several times to get people in Nian to adjust the way they were using the public water taps. (I was trying to help repair the village water system at the time.) I should stop giving people "cold water"—the standard metaphor for easy, gentle words—and start giving them fire, he suggested. He himself was known for his "fiery" speeches (see the earlier example), which several people complained to me about. Fiery talk cuts both ways; it may motivate people to act, but it can also backfire and turn audiences against the speaker or lead them to be so fearful or ashamed that they are completely unable to act and they withdraw from activities. On the role of fear and shame as important motives for action elsewhere in New Guinea, see Leroy 1979 and Schieffelin 1986.

13. The competition among villages that led to warfare in the past today manifests itself in a variety of forms: soccer matches and ceremonial dance competitions, the building of churches and the hosting of large events, and, as I discuss here, the education of children.

14. Politics in Melanesia has long been described as relatively egalitarian (Robbins 1994), a characterization that has been critiqued (e.g., Josephides 1985; Jolly 1987), and must certainly be carefully qualified if it is to be serviceable (as in Rio 2014). One important addendum to this characterization is that the egalitarianism found in the region is often "competitive" (Woodburn 1982; McDowell 1990), which means that people must

work to prove themselves the equals of others. Unlike societies where equality is an entitlement of all persons or all men, here equality is achieved, not ascribed.

15. By contrast, young women are educated in primary schools at about the same rate as young men. I was told this occurred because a well-educated young woman would have more options for marriage and her family could expect to receive more bridewealth when she married. There is also the possibility that a young woman would prove particularly bright and successful at school, becoming a family's best option for future employment.

16. People who work for the Lutheran church—pastors and evangelists—do not earn a wage, though they do receive monetary and non-monetary gifts from the communities they serve. Although teachers do get paid fortnightly, they generally depend on their own gardens and gifts of food for most of their meals. Paychecks are deposited in their bank accounts, and they do not have a way to get access to this money without traveling to cities where there are ATMs and bank branches. This is obviously an inconvenience. But teachers also note that not having ready access to their money keeps them from having to share it widely with family and friends. Especially for the growing number of people from the valley who work as teachers there, requests for money can quickly empty a person's bank account.

17. The institutional structure of the Lutheran church is not hidden away on an obscure organizational chart. It is regularly referenced in prayers and speeches, sermons and interviews. Here is how Sotine, a leader of the women's group in the Nian church, introduced a prayer during a women's church service.

> O God, in the name of Jesus Christ, our Lord, we say good morning to you. You give us this day, in the ELC (Evangelical Lutheran Church) *Ukata District*. All of us women are here. We can't hide. We are under your watch. Oh God . . . for us, the women who live in *Ukata District*, bad ways, bad spirits pull our thoughts toward them. These bad thoughts take hold of us. God father, hear us on this day that we have gathered, now we in the *ELC Teptep Circuit*, *Nokopo Parish*, we gather, the women of Nian village, we pay our respects in the place for doing that (i.e., church).

In the introduction to her prayer, Sotine in effect gives the "address" of herself and the other women there. They are in Nian village, which falls under Nokopo Parish, in the Teptep Circuit, in the Ukata District of the Evangelical Lutheran Church of Papua New Guinea. People are known to God by their place within the organizational chart of the institution. As participants in this institution, people participate in a wider social world through the institutional hierarchy, connected to God and to people elsewhere in Papua New Guinea and beyond.

18. The process I describe here has echoes in many small-scale anarchic and egalitarian societies around the world, where the pursuit of greater equality and empowerment through education, religion, and access to state resources has resulted in growing inequality (e.g., Sarmiento Barletti 2017; Buitron 2020; Stasch 2021).

19. The way global disparities are projected onto a more local scale is an instance of what Susan Gal and Judith Irvine (2019) term "fractal recursivity": the projection of a contrast in one domain or at one scale onto a different domain or scale.

EPILOGUE

1. The role of listening in ethnographic research was emphasized in the foundational models of ethnographic research provided by Malinowski and Boas, both of whom stressed the ethnographer's role as a collector and interpreter of texts. On Malinowski's emphasis on text collection (what he called a *corpus inscriptionum*), see Malinowski [1922] 1984, 22–24 and passim; Malinowski 1935. On Boas's concern with text and language more generally see Boas 1911; Darnell 1990; Bauman and Briggs 2003.

2. The communicative roles of ethnographer and ethnographic subject are, in practice, less distinguishable than this ideal suggests. Conversation analysts and interactional sociolinguists will rightly point out that interactions are in subtle ways jointly constructed, so the idea that listeners play no agentive role in shaping speech or that people do not alternate roles in interaction is misguided (Goodwin 1979). In a similar vein, Rabinow (1977) among many others has emphasized that ethnographic "findings" are jointly constructed in the interaction of ethnographer and subjects, vitiating any neat distinction between the roles they play. Roy Wagner (1981) has even gone so far as to make the case that ethnography involves the joint invention of culture, which is what the anthropological project is about in his view. As this suggests, the neat distinction of ethnographer and ethnographic subject, listener and speaker are unsatisfactory in numerous ways, but I maintain that something like the ideal type sketched here continues to remain a regulative ideal that guides most ethnographic practice.

3. For some of the ways ethnographers might listen, see Bitter 2022.

4. There are, of course, exceptions that probe this rule. John Hartigan's (2017) experiment in interviewing plants, as part of an effort to engage with them as ethnographic subjects, is one particularly thought-provoking example.

5. Of course, in the field the ethnographer acts as a speaker, and the interlocutor acts as a listener at times. In interviews for instance, the roles alternate—and in that sense, interviews like everything done in the field involves the shaping hand of the ethnographer (Bourdieu 1999). But quite often the ethnographies that result (including this one) disentangle this distributed agency (Enfield and Kockelman 2017), where again, the hand of the ethnographer shapes the now "doubly edited" account (Crapanzano 2013). This purified version of field encounter presents the ethnographer as "the transparent medium for the voices we encounter in the field" (Appadurai 1988, 16-17).

References

Abu-Lughod, Lila. 2005. *Dramas of Nationhood: The Politics of Television in Egypt.* Chicago: University of Chicago Press.

Adams, David Wallace. 1995. *Education for Extinction: American Indians and the Boarding School Experience, 1875–1928.* Lawrence: University of Kansas Press.

Agha, Asif. 2003. "The Social Life of Cultural Value." *Language & Communication* 23, no. 3: 231–73.

——, ed. 2005. Special Issue: "Discourse across Speech Events: Intertextuality and Interdiscursivity in Social Life." *Journal of Linguistic Anthropology* 15, no. 1.

——. 2007. *Language and Social Relations.* Cambridge: Cambridge University Press.

Akin, David, and Joel Robbins, eds. 1999. *Money and Modernity: State and Local Currencies in Melanesia.* Pittsburgh: University of Pittsburgh Press.

Althusser, Louis. 1971. "Ideology and Ideological State Apparatuses (Notes towards an Investigation)." In *Lenin and Philosophy and Other Essays*, translated by Ben Brewster, 127–86. New York: Monthly Review Press.

American Anthropological Association. 1947. "Statement on Human Rights." *American Anthropologist* 49, no. 4: 539–43.

Andersen, Barbara. 2013. "Tricks, Lies, and Mobile Phones: 'Phone Friend' Stories in Papua New Guinea." *Culture, Theory and Critique* 54, no. 3: 318–34.

Anderson, Benedict. 2006. *Imagined Communities: Reflections on the Origin and Spread of Nationalism.* Rev. ed. London: Verso.

Appadurai, Arjun. 1988. "Introduction: Place and Voice in Anthropological Theory." *Cultural Anthropology* 3, no. 1: 16–20.

——. 1996. *Modernity at Large: Cultural Dimensions of Globalization.* Minneapolis: University of Minnesota Press.

Arthurs, Jeffrey. 1994. "The Term Rhetor in Fifth- and Fourth-Century B.C.E. Greek Texts." *Rhetoric Society Quarterly* 23, nos. 3/4: 1–10.

Atkinson, Jane Monnig. 1984. "'Wrapped Words': Poetry and Politics among the Wana of Central Sulawesi, Indonesia." In *Dangerous Words: Language and Politics in the Pacific*, edited by Donald Lawrence Brenneis and Fred R. Myers, 33–68. New York: New York University Press.

Austin, John L. 1962. *How to Do Things with Words.* London: Oxford University Press.

Bainton, Nicholas A. 2004. *The Lihir Destiny: Cultural Responses to Mining in Melanesia.* Canberra: ANU E Press. https://library.oapen.org/handle/20.500.12657/33696.

Bakhtin, M. M. 1981a. "Discourse in the Novel." In *The Dialogic Imagination: Four Essays*, edited by Michael Holquist, 259–422. Austin: University of Texas Press.

——. 1981b. "Forms of Time and of the Chronotope in the Novel: Toward a Historical Poetics." In *The Dialogic Imagination: Four Essays*, edited by Michael Holquist, 84–258. Austin: University of Texas Press.

Bamford, Sandra. 2007. *Biology Unmoored: Melanesian Reflections on Life and Biotechnology.* Berkeley: University of California Press.

Barad, Karen. 2003. "Posthumanist Performativity: Toward an Understanding of How Matter Comes to Matter." *Signs* 28, no. 3: 801–31.

Barber, Benjamin R. 1984. *Strong Democracy: Participatory Politics for a New Age.* Berkeley: University of California Press.

Barker, John. 2004. "Between Heaven and Earth: Missionaries, Environmentalists, and the Maisin." In *Globalization and Culture Change in the Pacific Islands*, edited by Victoria S. Lockwood, 439–59. Upper Saddle River, NJ: Pearson Education.

Barth, Fredrik. 1975. *Ritual and Knowledge among the Baktaman of New Guinea.* New Haven: Yale University Press.

Barthes, Roland. 1972. *Mythologies.* New York: Hill and Wang.

Bashkow, Ira. 2000. "Confusion, Native Skepticism, and Recurring Questions about the Year 2000: 'Soft' Beliefs and Preparations for the Millennium in the Arapesh Region, Papua New Guinea." *Ethnohistory* 47, no. 1: 133–69.

——. 2006. *The Meaning of Whitemen: Race and Modernity in the Orokaiva Cultural World.* Chicago: University of Chicago Press.

Bassel, Leah. 2017. *The Politics of Listening: Possibilities and Challenges for Democratic Life.* London: Palgrave Macmillan.

Basso, Keith H. 1988. "'Speaking with Names': Language and Landscape among the Western Apache." *Cultural Anthropology* 3, no. 2: 99–130.

Bate, Bernard. 2009. *Tamil Oratory and the Dravidian Aesthetic: Democratic Practice in South India.* New York: Columbia University Press.

Battiste, Marie. 2013. *Decolonizing Education: Nourishing the Learning Spirit.* Saskatoon: Purich.

Bauman, Richard. 1984a. *Let Your Words Be Few: Symbolism of Speaking and Silence among Seventeenth-Century Quakers.* Cambridge: Cambridge University Press.

——. 1984b. *Verbal Art as Performance.* Rowley, MA: Newbury House.

——. 2004. *A World of Others' Words: Cross-Cultural Perspectives on Intertextuality.* Malden, MA: Blackwell.

Bauman, Richard, and Charles L. Briggs. 2003. *Voices of Modernity: Language Ideologies and the Politics of Inequality.* Cambridge: Cambridge University Press.

Beidelman, Thomas O. 1982. *Colonial Evangelism: A Socio-Historical Study of an East African Mission at the Grassroots.* Bloomington: Indiana University Press.

Bender, John, and David E. Wellbery. 1990. "Rhetoricality: On the Modernist Return of Rhetoric." In *The Ends of Rhetoric: History, Theory, Practice*, 3–39. Stanford: Stanford University Press.

Bendix, Regina, and Donald Brenneis, eds. 2005. Special Issue: "The Senses." *Ethnofoor* 18, no. 1.

Benedict, Ruth. 1946. *The Chrysanthemum and the Sword: Patterns of Japanese Culture.* Boston: Houghton Mifflin.

Berlin, Isaiah. 1964. "The Presidential Address: 'From Hope and Fear Set Free.'" *Proceedings of the Aristotelian Society* 64: 1–30.

Berman, Michael. 2020. "The Ear from Nowhere: Listening Techniques and the Politics of Negation in the Practice of Japanese Interfaith Chaplains." *Language & Communication* 71: 72–82.

Bessire, Lucas, and David Bond. 2014. "Ontological Anthropology and the Deferral of Critique." *American Ethnologist* 41, no. 3: 440–56.

Bewes, T. 2010. "Reading with the Grain: A New World in Literary Criticism." *Differences* 21, no. 3: 1–33.

Bhabha, Homi K. 1994. *The Location of Culture.* London: Routledge.

Bickford, Susan. 1996. *The Dissonance of Democracy: Listening, Conflict, and Citizenship.* Ithaca, NY: Cornell University Press.

Bitter, Joella. 2022. "Ten Ways to Listen." *Anthropology News.* February 17, 2022. https://www.anthropology-news.org/articles/ten-ways-to-listen/.

Blaser, Mario, Ravi De Costa, Deborah McGregor, and William D. Coleman. 2010. "Reconfiguring the Web of Life: Indigenous Peoples, Relationality, and Globalization." In *Indigenous Peoples and Autonomy: Insights for a Global Age*, 3–26. Vancouver: University of British Columbia Press.

Bloch, Maurice. 1975a. "Introduction." In *Political Language and Oratory in Traditional Society*, 1–28. London: Academic Press.

———, ed. 1975b. *Political Language and Oratory in Traditional Society*. London: Academic Press.

Boas, Franz. 1911. "Introduction." In *Handbook of American Indian Languages*, 1–83. Washington, DC: Government Printing Office.

Bohman, James. 1996. *Public Deliberation: Pluralism, Complexity, and Democracy*. Cambridge, MA: MIT Press.

———. 1998. "Survey Article: The Coming of Age of Deliberative Democracy." *Journal of Political Philosophy* 6, no. 4: 400–25.

Bourdieu, Pierre. 1991. *Language and Symbolic Power*. Cambridge, MA: Harvard University Press.

———. 1999. *The Weight of the World: Social Suffering in Contemporary Society*. Translated by Priscilla Parkhurst Ferguson et al. Stanford: Stanford University Press.

Bourdieu, Pierre, and Jean-Claude Passeron. 1990. *Reproduction in Education, Society and Culture*. Translated by Richard Nice. London: Sage.

Boyer, Dominic. 2008. "Thinking through the Anthropology of Experts." *Anthropology in Action* 15, no. 2: 38–46.

Breidlid, Anders. 2013. *Education, Indigenous Knowledges, and Development in the Global South: Contesting Knowledges for a Sustainable Future*. New York: Routledge.

Brenneis, Donald. 1984. "Grog and Gossip in Bhatgaon: Style and Substance in Fiji Indian Conversation." *American Ethnologist* 11, no. 3: 487–506.

Briggs, Charles L. 2005. "Communicability, Racial Discourse, and Disease." *Annual Review of Anthropology* 34, no. 1: 269–91.

———. 2013. "Contested Mobilities: On the Politics and Ethnopoetics of Circulation." *Journal of Folklore Research* 50, nos. 1–3: 285–99.

Briggs, Charles L., and Richard Bauman. 1992. "Genre, Intertextuality, and Social Power." *Journal of Linguistic Anthropology* 2, no. 2: 131–72.

Brison, Karen J. 1992. *Just Talk: Gossip, Meetings, and Power in a Papua New Guinea Village*. Berkeley: University of California Press.

Brown, Paula. 1963. "From Anarchy to Satrapy." *American Anthropologist* 65, no. 1: 1–15.

Brown, Penelope, and Stephen C. Levinson. 1987. *Politeness: Some Universals in Language Usage*. Cambridge: Cambridge University Press.

Brunton, Ron. 1980. "Misconstrued Order in Melanesian Religion." *Man*, New Series, 15, no. 1: 112–28.

Bubandt, Nils. 2014. *The Empty Seashell: Witchcraft and Doubt on an Indonesian Island*. Ithaca, NY: Cornell University Press.

Bucholtz, Mary, and Kira Hall. 2005. "Identity and Interaction: A Sociocultural Linguistic Approach." *Discourse Studies* 7, nos. 4–5: 585–614.

Buitron, Natalia. 2020. "Autonomy, Productiveness, and Community: The Rise of Inequality in an Amazonian Society." *Journal of the Royal Anthropological Institute* 26, no. 1: 48–66.

Buitron, Natalia, and Hans Steinmüller. 2020. "The Ends of Egalitarianism." *L'Homme* 236, no. 3: 5–44.

Burke, Kenneth. 1969. *A Rhetoric of Motives*. Berkeley: University of California Press.

Butler, Judith. 1990. *Gender Trouble: Feminism and the Subversion of Identity*. New York: Routledge.

——. 1997. *Excitable Speech: A Politics of the Performative*. New York: Routledge.

Butterwick, Shauna. 2012. "The Politics of Listening." In *Feminist Popular Education in Transnational Debates: Building Pedagogies of Possibility*, edited by Linzi Manicom and Shirley Walters, 59–73. New York: Palgrave Macmillan US.

Cadena, Marisol de la. 2010. "Indigenous Cosmopolitics in the Andes: Conceptual Reflections beyond 'Politics.'" *Cultural Anthropology* 25, no. 2: 334–70.

——. 2015. *Earth Beings: Ecologies of Practice across Andean Worlds*. Durham, NC: Duke University Press.

Calder, Gideon. 2011. "Democracy and Listening." In *Problems of Democracy: Language and Speaking*, edited by Mary-Ann Crumplin, 125–35. Freeland, Oxfordshire: Inter-Disciplinary Press.

Callon, Michel, Pierre Lascoumes, and Yannick Barthe. 2011. *Acting in an Uncertain World: An Essay on Technical Democracy*. Translated by Graham Burchell. Cambridge, MA: MIT Press.

Carr, E. Summerson. 2010. "Enactments of Expertise." *Annual Review of Anthropology* 39, no. 1: 17–32.

Cepek, Michael L. 2016. "There Might Be Blood: Oil, Humility, and the Cosmopolitics of a Cofán Petro-Being." *American Ethnologist* 43, no. 4: 623–35.

Chambers, Simone. 2003. "Deliberative Democratic Theory." *Annual Review of Political Science* 6, no. 1: 307–26.

Chowning, Ann. 1979. "Leadership in Melanesia." *Journal of Pacific History* 14, no. 2: 66–84.

Clastres, Pierre. 1987. *Society against the State: Essays in Political Anthropology*. Translated by Robert Hurley and Abe Stein. New York: Zone Books.

Cody, Francis. 2011. "Publics and Politics." *Annual Review of Anthropology* 40, no. 1: 37–52.

Cohen, David. 2004. "The Politics of Deliberation: Oratory and Democracy in Classical Athens." In *A Companion to Rhetoric and Rhetorical Criticism*, edited by Walter Jost and Wendy Olmstead, 22–37. Malden, MA: Blackwell.

Collins, Harry M., and Robert Evans. 2002. "The Third Wave of Science Studies: Studies of Expertise and Experience." *Social Studies of Science* 32, no. 2: 235–96.

Comaroff, Jean, and John L. Comaroff. 1991. *Of Revelation and Revolution: Vol. 1, Christianity, Colonialism, and Consciousness in South Africa*. Chicago: University of Chicago Press.

Conquergood, Dwight. 2002. "Performance Studies: Interventions and Radical Research." *TDR* 46, no. 2: 145–56.

Crapanzano, Vincent. 2013. *Tuhami: Portrait of a Moroccan*. Chicago: University of Chicago Press.

Crook, Tony. 1999. "Growing Knowledge in Bolivip, Papua New Guinea." *Oceania* 69, no. 4: 225–42.

Culler, Jonathan. 1982. *On Deconstruction: Theory and Criticism after Structuralism*. Ithaca, NY: Cornell University Press.

Dabek, Lisa, Peter Valentine, Jacque Blessington, and Karin R. Schwartz. 2021. *Tree Kangaroos: Science and Conservation*. London: Academic Press.

Danziger, Eve. 2013. "Conventional Wisdom: Imagination, Obedience and Intersubjectivity." *Language & Communication* 33, no. 3: 251–62.

Darnell, Regna. 1990. "Franz Boas, Edward Sapir, and the Americanist Text Tradition." *Historiographia Linguistica* 17, nos. 1–2: 129–44.

Dick, Hilary Parsons. 2010. "Imagined Lives and Modernist Chronotopes in Mexican Nonmigrant Discourse." *American Ethnologist* 37, no. 2: 275–90.

Dobrin, Lise M. 2012. "Ethnopoetic Analysis as a Resource for Endangered-Language Linguistics: The Social Production of an Arapesh Text." *Anthropological Linguistics* 54, no. 1: 1–32.

——. 2014. "Language Shift in an 'Importing Culture': The Cultural Logic of the Arapesh Roads." In *Endangered Languages: Beliefs and Ideologies in Language Documentation and Revitalization*, edited by Peter Austin and Julia Sallabank. Proceedings of the British Academy. https://academic.oup.com/british-academy-scholarship-online/book/325.

Dobson, Andrew. 2014. *Listening for Democracy: Recognition, Representation, Reconciliation*. Oxford: Oxford University Press.

Douglas, Bronwen. 2000. "Weak States and Other Nationalisms: Emerging Melanesian Paradigms?" State, Society and Governance in Melanesia (SSGM) Discussion Paper 00/3. Australian National University. https://openresearch-repository.anu.edu.au/handle/1885/41823.

Dreher, Tanja. 2009. "Listening across Difference: Media and Multiculturalism beyond the Politics of Voice." *Continuum* 23, no. 4: 445–58.

——. 2010. "Speaking up or Being Heard? Community Media Interventions and the Politics of Listening." *Media Culture & Society* 32, no. 1: 85–103.

Dreyfus, Hubert L., and Paul Rabinow. 1983. *Michel Foucault: Beyond Structuralism and Hermeneutics*. 2nd ed. Chicago: University of Chicago Press.

Dryzek, John S. 2000. *Deliberative Democracy and Beyond: Liberals, Critics, Contestations*. Oxford: Oxford University Press.

——. 2010. "Rhetoric in Democracy: A Systemic Appreciation." *Political Theory* 38, no. 3: 319–39.

Dunning, David. 2011. "The Dunning-Kruger Effect: On Being Ignorant of One's Own Ignorance." In *Advances in Experimental Social Psychology*, Vol. 44, edited by Mark Zanna and James Olson, 247–96. San Diego: Academic Press.

Duranti, Alessandro. 2015. "Opacity of Other Minds: Local Theories Revisited." In *The Anthropology of Intentions*, 175–86. Cambridge: Cambridge University Press.

Eisenlohr, Patrick. 2018. *Sounding Islam: Voice, Media, and Sonic Atmospheres in an Indian Ocean World*. Oakland: University of California Press.

Elliott, Philip. 1974. "Uses and Gratifications Research: A Critique and a Sociological Alternative." In *The Uses of Mass Communications: Current Perspectives on Gratifications Research*, edited by Jay G. Blumler and Elihu Katz, 249–68. Beverly Hills, CA: Sage.

Elliston, Deborah A. 1995. "Erotic Anthropology: 'Ritualized Homosexuality' in Melanesia and Beyond." *American Ethnologist* 22, no. 4: 848–67.

Enfield, N. J., and Paul Kockelman 2017. *Distributed Agency*. New York: Oxford University Press.

Englund, Harri, and James Leach. 2000. "Ethnography and the Meta-Narratives of Modernity." *Current Anthropology* 41, no. 2: 225–48.

Erlmann, Veit. 2004. "But What of the Ethnographic Ear? Anthropology, Sound, and the Senses." In *Hearing Cultures: Essays on Sound, Listening and Modernity*, edited by Veit Erlmann, 1–20. London: Routledge.

——. 2010. *Reason and Resonance: A History of Modern Aurality*. New York: Zone Books.

Errington, Frederick, and Deborah Gewertz. 1986. "The Confluence of Powers: Entropy and Importation among the Chambri." *Oceania* 57, no. 2: 99–113.

——. 1994. "From Darkness to Light in the George Brown Jubilee: The Invention of Nontradition and the Inscription of a National History in East New Britain." *American Ethnologist* 21, no. 1: 104–22.

——. 2004. *Yali's Question: Sugar, Culture, and History.* Chicago: University of Chicago Press.

Escobar, Arturo. 1995. *Encountering Development: The Making and Unmaking of the Third World.* Princeton: Princeton University Press.

Evans, Nicholas, and David Wilkins. 2000. "In the Mind's Ear: The Semantic Extensions of Perception Verbs in Australian Languages." *Language* 76, no. 3: 546–92.

Evans-Prichard, E. E. 1987. "The Nuer of the Southern Sudan." In *African Political Systems,* edited by Meyer Fortes and E. E. Evans-Pritchard, 272–96. New York: Routledge.

Fajans, Jane. 1997. *They Make Themselves: Work and Play among the Baining of Papua New Guinea.* Chicago: University of Chicago Press.

Fanon, Frantz. (1952) 2008. *Black Skin, White Masks.* Translated by Charles Lam Markmann. London: Pluto Press.

Faudree, Paja. 2012. "Music, Language, and Texts: Sound and Semiotic Ethnography." *Annual Review of Anthropology* 41, no. 1: 519–36.

Faulkner, Paul. 2007. "On Telling and Trusting." *Mind* 116, no. 464: 875–902.

Feld, Steve, and Donald Brenneis. 2004. "Doing Anthropology in Sound." *American Ethnologist* 31, no. 4: 461–74.

Felski, Rita. 2015. *The Limits of Critique.* Chicago: University of Chicago Press.

Ferguson, James. 1994. *The Anti-Politics Machine: "Development," Depoliticization, and Bureaucratic Power in Lesotho.* Minneapolis: University of Minnesota Press.

Fetterley, Judith. 1978. *The Resisting Reader: A Feminist Approach to American Fiction.* Bloomington: Indiana University Press.

Filer, Colin. 1990. "The Bougainville Rebellion, the Mining Industry and the Process of Social Disintegration in Papua New Guinea." *Canberra Anthropology* 13, no. 1: 1–39.

——. 2011. "New Land Grab in Papua New Guinea." *Pacific Studies* 34, nos. 2/3: 269–94.

Fisch, Harold. 1952. "The Puritans and the Reform of Prose-Style." *ELH* 19, no. 4: 229–48.

Fischer, Frank. 2000. *Citizens, Experts, and the Environment: The Politics of Local Knowledge.* Durham, NC: Duke University Press.

Fish, Stanley. 1980. *Is There a Text in this Class? The Authority of Interpretive Communities.* Cambridge, MA: Harvard University Press.

Fishkin, James S. 1997. *The Voice of the People: Public Opinion and Democracy.* New Haven: Yale University Press.

Fiske, John. 1987. *Television Culture.* London: Routledge.

Flanagan, James G. 1989. "Hierarchy in Simple 'Egalitarian' Societies." *Annual Review of Anthropology* 18, no. 1: 245–66.

Flores, Nelson, and Jonathan Rosa. 2015. "Undoing Appropriateness: Raciolinguistic Ideologies and Language Diversity in Education." *Harvard Educational Review* 85, no. 2: 149–71.

Foster, Robert J. 2002. *Materializing the Nation: Commodities, Consumption, and Media in Papua New Guinea.* Bloomington: Indiana University Press.

Foucault, Michel. 1972. *Archaeology of Knowledge.* Translated by A. M. Sheridan Smith. New York: Pantheon Books.

——. 1977. *Discipline and Punish: The Birth of the Prison.* New York: Vintage.

——. 1978. *The History of Sexuality: Vol. 1, An Introduction.* Translated by Robert Hurley. New York: Pantheon Books.

——. 1979. "Truth and Power." *Critique of Anthropology* 4, nos. 13–14: 131–37.

——. 1997. *The Politics of Truth.* Edited by Sylvère Lotringer and Lysa Hochroth. New York: Semiotext(e).

Gal, Susan. 1991. "Between Speech and Silence." In *Gender at the Crossroads of Knowledge: Feminist Anthropology in the Postmodern Era,* edited by Micaela di Leonardo, 175–203. Berkeley: University of California Press.

——. 2018. "Registers in Circulation: The Social Organization of Interdiscursivity." *Signs and Society* 6, no. 1: 1–24.

Gal, Susan, and Judith T. Irvine. 2019. *Signs of Difference: Language and Ideology in Social Life*. Cambridge: Cambridge University Press.

Garsten, Bryan. 2006. *Saving Persuasion: A Defense of Rhetoric and Judgment*. Cambridge, MA: Harvard University Press.

——. 2011. "The Rhetoric Revival in Political Theory." *Annual Review of Political Science* 14: 159–80.

Gell, Alfred. 1975. *Metamorphosis of the Cassowaries: Umeda Society, Language and Ritual*. London: Athlone Press.

Gewertz, Deborah B., and Frederick K. Errington. 1999. *Emerging Class in Papua New Guinea: The Telling of Difference*. Cambridge: Cambridge University Press.

Gibson, Thomas, and Kenneth Sillander, eds. 2011. *Anarchic Solidarity: Autonomy, Equality, and Fellowship in Southeast Asia*. New Haven: Yale University Southeast Asia Studies.

Giddens, Anthony. 1991. *Modernity and Self-Identity: Self and Society in the Late Modern Age*. Stanford: Stanford University Press.

Gitlin, Todd. 1978. "Media Sociology: The Dominant Paradigm." *Theory and Society* 6, no. 2: 205–53.

——. 1979. "Prime Time Ideology: The Hegemonic Process in Television Entertainment." *Social Problems* 26, no. 3: 251–66.

Glander, Timothy. 2000. *Origins of Mass Communications Research during the American Cold War: Educational Effects and Contemporary Implications*. New York: Routledge.

Goffman, Erving. 1959. *The Presentation of Self in Everyday Life*. New York: Doubleday.

——. 1976. "Replies and Responses." *Language in Society* 5, no. 3: 257–313.

——. 1979. "Footing." *Semiotica* 25, nos. 1–2: 1–30.

Goldman, Laurence. 1980. "Speech Categories and the Study of Disputes: A New Guinea Example." *Oceania* 50, no. 3: 209–27.

——. 1983. *Talk Never Dies: The Language of Huli Disputes*. London: Tavistock.

——. 2003. "'Hoo-Ha in Huli': Considerations on Commotion and Community in the Southern Highlands Province of Papua New Guinea." State, Society and Governance in Melanesia (SSGM) Program. Australian National University. https://doi.org/10.25911/5F2001D8A76AB.

Golub, Alex. 2014. *Leviathans at the Gold Mine: Creating Indigenous and Corporate Actors in Papua New Guinea*. Durham, NC: Duke University Press.

Goodman, Jane E., Matt Tomlinson, and Justin B. Richland. 2014. "Citational Practices: Knowledge, Personhood, and Subjectivity." *Annual Review of Anthropology* 43, no. 1: 449–63.

Goodwin, Charles. 1979. "The Interactive Construction of a Sentence in Natural Conversation." In *Everyday Language: Studies in Ethnomethodology*, edited by George Psathas, 97–121. New York: Irvington.

Goodwin, Charles, and Marjorie Harness Goodwin. 2005. "Participation." In *A Companion to Linguistic Anthropology*, edited by Alessandro Duranti, 222–44. Malden, MA: Blackwell.

Graeber, David. 2004. *Fragments of an Anarchist Anthropology*. Chicago: Prickly Paradigm Press.

——. 2010. "Are You an Anarchist? The Answer May Surprise You!" *Anarchist Library*. https://mirror.anarhija.net/theanarchistlibrary.org/mirror/d/dg/david-graeber-are-you-an-anarchist-the-answer-may-surprise-you.a4.pdf.

Graves, Lucas. 2016. *Deciding What's True: The Rise of Political Fact-Checking in American Journalism*. New York: Columbia University Press.

Green, Jeffrey Edward. 2010. *The Eyes of the People: Democracy in an Age of Spectatorship*. Oxford: Oxford University Press.

Habermas, Jürgen. (1962) 1989. *The Structural Transformation of the Public Sphere: An Inquiry into a Category of Bourgeois Society*. Translated by Thomas Burger. Cambridge, MA: MIT Press.

——. 1984. *The Theory of Communicative Action: Vol. 1, Reason and the Rationalization of Society*. Translated by Thomas McCarthy. Boston: Beacon Press.

——. 1996. *Between Facts and Norms: Contributions to a Discourse Theory of Law and Democracy*. Translated by William Rehg. Cambridge, MA: MIT Press.

Hacking, Ian. 1995. *Rewriting the Soul: Multiple Personality and the Sciences of Memory*. Princeton: Princeton University Press.

——. 1999. *The Social Construction of What?* Cambridge, MA: Harvard University Press.

——. 2002. *Historical Ontology*. Cambridge, MA: Harvard University Press.

Hall, Stuart. 1977. "Culture, the Media and the 'Ideological Effect.'" In *Mass Communication and Society*, edited by James Curran, Michael Gurevitch, and Janet Woollacott, 315–48. London: Edward Arnold.

——. 1980. "Encoding/Decoding." In *Culture, Media, Language: Working Papers in Cultural Studies, 1972–79*, edited by Stuart Hall, Dorothy Hobson, Andrew Lowe, and Paul Willis, 117–27. New York: Routledge.

——. 1986. "The Problem of Ideology—Marxism without Guarantees." *Journal of Communication Inquiry* 10, no. 2: 28–44.

Handman, Courtney. 2010. "Events of Translation: Intertextuality and Christian Ethnotheologies of Change among Guhu-Samane, Papua New Guinea." *American Anthropologist* 112, no. 4: 576–88.

——. 2014. *Critical Christianity: Translation and Denominational Conflict in Papua New Guinea*. Berkeley: University of California Press.

——. 2018. "The Language of Evangelism: Christian Cultures of Circulation beyond the Missionary Prologue." *Annual Review of Anthropology* 47, no. 1: 149–65.

Hanks, William. 2010. *Converting Words: Maya in the Age of the Cross*. Berkeley: University of California Press.

Hannerz, Ulf. 1989. "Notes on the Global Ecumene." *Public Culture* 1, no. 2: 66–75.

Hanson, Norwood Russell. 1958. *Patterns of Discovery: An Inquiry into the Conceptual Foundations of Science*. Cambridge: Cambridge University Press.

Haraway, Donna. 1988. "Situated Knowledges: The Science Question in Feminism and the Privilege of Partial Perspective." *Feminist Studies* 14, no. 3: 575–99.

Harding, Thomas G. 1967. *Voyagers of the Vitiaz Strait: A Study of a New Guinea Trade System*. Seattle: University of Washington Press.

Hardwig, John. 1991. "The Role of Trust in Knowledge." *Journal of Philosophy* 88, no. 12: 693–708.

Harkness, Nicholas. 2013. *Songs of Seoul: An Ethnography of Voice and Voicing in Christian South Korea*. Berkeley: University of California Press.

Harrison, Simon. 1989. "Magical and Material Polities in Melanesia." *Man*, New Series, 24, no. 1: 1–20.

——. 1990. *Stealing People's Names: History and Politics in a Sepik River Cosmology*. Cambridge: Cambridge University Press.

——. 1993a. *The Mask of War: Violence, Ritual, and the Self in Melanesia*. Manchester: Manchester University Press.

——. 1993b. "The Commerce of Cultures in Melanesia." *Man* 28, no. 1: 139–58.

Hartigan, John. 2017. *Care of the Species: Races of Corn and the Science of Plant Biodiversity*. Minneapolis: University of Minnesota Press.

Hastings, Adi, and Paul Manning. 2004. "Introduction: Acts of Alterity." *Language & Communication* 24, no. 4: 291–311.

Herdt, Gilbert H. 2003. *Secrecy & Cultural Reality: Utopian Ideologies of the New Guinea Men's House*. Ann Arbor: University of Michigan Press.

Herriman, Nicholas, and Monika Winarnita. 2016. "Seeking the State: Appropriating Bureaucratic Symbolism and Wealth in the Margins of Southeast Asia." *Oceania* 86, no. 2: 132–50.

Hetherington, Kregg. 2011. *Guerrilla Auditors: The Politics of Transparency in Neoliberal Paraguay*. Durham, NC: Duke University Press.

Hirschkind, Charles. 2001. "The Ethics of Listening: Cassette-Sermon Audition in Contemporary Egypt." *American Ethnologist* 28, no. 3: 623–49.

——. 2006. *The Ethical Soundscape: Cassette Sermons and Islamic Counterpublics*. New York: Columbia University Press.

Hirschman, Albert O. 1970. *Exit, Voice, and Loyalty: Responses to Decline in Firms, Organizations, and States*. Cambridge, MA: Harvard University Press.

Hoenigman, Darja. 2012. "A Battle of Languages: Spirit Possession and Changing Linguistic Ideologies in a Sepik Society, Papua New Guinea." *Australian Journal of Anthropology* 23, no. 3: 290–317.

Holbraad, Martin. 2012. *Truth in Motion: The Recursive Anthropology of Cuban Divination*. Chicago: University of Chicago Press.

Holbraad, Martin, and Morten Axel Pedersen. 2017. *The Ontological Turn: An Anthropological Exposition*. Cambridge: Cambridge University Press.

Hollan, Douglas W., and C. Jason Throop, eds. 2011. *The Anthropology of Empathy: Experiencing the Lives of Others in Pacific Societies*. New York: Berghahn.

hooks, bell. 1994. *Outlaw Culture: Resisting Representations*. New York: Routledge.

Horkheimer, Max, and Theodor W. Adorno. 2002. *Dialectic of Enlightenment: Philosophical Fragments*. Edited by Gunzelin Schmid Noerr. Translated by Edmund Jephcott. Redwood City, CA: Stanford University Press.

Hull, Matthew S. 2012. *Government of Paper: The Materiality of Bureaucracy in Urban Pakistan*. Berkeley: University of California Press.

Inoue, Miyako. 2006. *Vicarious Language: Gender and Linguistic Modernity in Japan*. Berkeley: University of California Press.

Irvine, Judith T. 1979. "Formality and Informality in Communicative Events." *American Anthropologist* 81, no. 4: 773–90.

——. 1996. "Shadow Conversations: The Indeterminacy of Participant Roles." In *Natural Histories of Discourse*, edited by Michael Silverstein and Greg Urban, 131–59. Chicago: University of Chicago Press.

——. 1998. "Ideologies of Honorific Language." In *Language Ideologies: Theories and Practice*, edited by Bambi B. Schieffelin, Kathryn A. Woolard, and Paul V. Kroskrity, 51–67. New York: Oxford University Press.

Iser, Wolfgang. 2000. *The Range of Interpretation*. New York: Columbia University Press.

Jackson, Jennifer. 2013. *Political Oratory and Cartooning: An Ethnography of Democratic Process in Madagascar*. Malden, MA: Wiley-Blackwell.

Jakobson, Roman. 1960. "Closing Statement: Linguistics and Poetics." In *Style in Language*, edited by Thomas A. Sebeok, 350–77. Cambridge, MA: MIT Press.

James, William. 1978. *Pragmatism and the Meaning of Truth*. Cambridge, MA: Harvard University Press.

Jasanoff, Sheila. 2009. *The Fifth Branch: Science Advisers as Policymakers*. Cambridge, MA: Harvard University Press.

Jebens, Holger. 2012. *After the Cult: Perceptions of Other and Self in West New Britain (Papua New Guinea)*. New York: Berghahn.

Johnson, James H. 1995. *Listening in Paris: A Cultural History*. Berkeley: University of California Press.

Jolly, Margaret. 1987. "The Chimera of Equality in Melanesia." *Mankind* 17, no. 2: 168–83.

Jones, Graham M. 2014. "Secrecy." *Annual Review of Anthropology* 43, no. 1: 53–69.

Jones, Richard F. 1930. "Science and English Prose Style in the Third Quarter of the Seventeenth Century." *PMLA* 45, no. 4: 977–1009.

Jorgensen, Dan. 1981. "Taro and Arrows: Order, Entropy, and Religion among the Telefolmin." PhD diss., University of British Columbia.

Jorgensen, Dan, and Ragnar Johnson. 1981. "Order or Disorder in Melanesian Religions?" *Man* 16, no. 1: 470–75.

Josephides, Lisette. 1985. *The Production of Inequality: Gender and Exchange among the Kewa*. New York: Tavistock.

———. 2001. "Straight Talk, Hidden Talk, and Modernity: Shifts in Discourse Strategy in Highland New Guinea." In *An Anthropology of Indirect Communication*, edited by Joy Hendry and C. W. Watson, 218–31. London: Routledge.

Juillerat, Bernard, Andrew Strathern, Ron Brunton, and Alfred Gell. 1980. "Order or Disorder in Melanesian Religions?" *Man* 15, no. 4: 732–37.

Katz, Elihu, Jay G. Blumler, and Michael Gurevitch. 1973. "Uses and Gratifications Research." *Public Opinion Quarterly* 37, no. 4: 509–23.

Katz, Elihu, Hadassah Haas, and Michael Gurevitch. 1973. "On the Use of the Mass Media for Important Things." *American Sociological Review* 38, no. 2: 164–81.

Keane, Webb. 2006. *Christian Moderns: Freedom and Fetish in the Mission Encounter*. Berkeley: University of California Press.

Keck, Verena. 2005. *Social Discord and Bodily Disorders: Healing among the Yupno of Papua New Guinea*. Durham, NC: Carolina Academic Press.

Keenan, Elinor Ochs. 1976. "The Universality of Conversational Postulates." *Language in Society* 5, no. 1: 67–80.

———. 1989. "Norm-Makers, Norm-Breakers: Uses of Speech by Men and Women in a Malagasy Community." In *Explorations in the Ethnography of Speaking*, edited by Richard Bauman and Joel Sherzer, 125–43. Cambridge: Cambridge University Press.

Kirsch, Stuart. 2006. *Reverse Anthropology: Indigenous Analysis of Social and Environmental Relations in New Guinea*. Stanford: Stanford University Press.

Kocher Schmid, Christin. 1991. *Of People and Plants: A Botanical Ethnography of Nokopo Village, Madang and Morobe Provinces, Papua New Guinea*. Basel: Wepf.

———. 1993. "Cultural Identity as a Coping Strategy towards Modern Political Structures, the Nayudos Case, Papua New Guinea." *Bijdragen Tot de Taal-, Land- En Volkenkunde* 149, no. 4: 781–801.

Kohn, Eduardo. 2013. *How Forests Think: Toward an Anthropology beyond the Human*. Berkeley: University of California Press.

———. 2015. "Anthropology of Ontologies." *Annual Review of Anthropology* 44, no. 1: 311–27.

Komter, Martha. 2019. *The Suspect's Statement: Talk and Text in the Criminal Process*. Cambridge: Cambridge University Press.

Koven, Michele. 2013. "Antiracist, Modern Selves and Racist, Unmodern Others: Chronotopes of Modernity in Luso-Descendants' Race Talk." *Language & Communication* 33, no. 4: 544–58.

Kramer, Elise. 2016. "Feminist Linguistics and Linguistic Feminisms." In *Mapping Feminist Anthropology in the Twenty-First Century*, edited by Ellen Lewin and Leni M. Silverstein, 65–83. New Brunswick, NJ: Rutgers University Press.

Kropotkin, Peter. 1902. *Mutual Aid: A Factor of Evolution*. New York: McClure Phillips.

Kroskrity, Paul V., ed. 2000. *Regimes of Language: Ideologies, Polities, and Identities*. Santa Fe: School of American Research Press.

Kuhn, Thomas S. 1970. *The Structure of Scientific Revolutions*. 2nd ed. Chicago: University of Chicago Press.

Kulick, Don. 1992. *Language Shift and Cultural Reproduction: Socialization, Self and Syncretism in a Papua New Guinean Village*. Cambridge: Cambridge University Press.

Kunreuther, Laura. 2014. *Voicing Subjects: Public Intimacy and Mediation in Kathmandu*. Berkeley: University of California Press.

Lacan, Jacques. 2002. *Ecrits: A Selection*. Translated by Bruce Fink. New York: Norton.

Lacey, Kate. 2013. *Listening Publics: The Politics and Experience of Listening in the Media Age*. Cambridge: Polity Press.

Langness, L. L. 1974. "Ritual, Power, and Male Dominance." *Ethos* 2, no. 3: 189–212.

Larkin, Brian. 1997. "Indian Films and Nigerian Lovers: Media and the Creation of Parallel Modernities." *Africa* 67, no. 3: 406–40.

Lasswell, Harold D. 1948. "The Structure and Function of Communication in Society." In *The Communication of Ideas*, edited by Lyman Bryson, 37–52. New York: Institute for Religious and Social Studies.

Latour, Bruno. 1987. *Science in Action: How to Follow Scientists and Engineers through Society*. Cambridge, MA: Harvard University Press.

——. 1993. *We Have Never Been Modern*. Cambridge, MA: Harvard University Press.

Lattas, Andrew. 1989. "Trickery and Sacrifice: Tambarans and the Appropriation of Female Reproductive Powers in Male Initiation Ceremonies in West New Britain." *Man*, New Series, 24, no. 3: 451–69.

Lawrence, Peter. 1964. *Road Belong Cargo: A Study of the Cargo Movement in the Southern Madang District, New Guinea*. Manchester: Manchester University Press.

——. 1965. "The Ngaing of the Rai Coast." In *Gods, Ghosts and Men: Some Religions of Australian New Guinea*, edited by Peter Lawrence and M. J. Meggitt, 198–223. Oxford: Oxford University Press.

——. 1984. *The Garia: An Ethnography of a Traditional Cosmic System in Papua New Guinea*. Manchester: Manchester University Press.

Lawy, Jenny R. 2017. "Theorizing Voice: Performativity, Politics and Listening." *Anthropological Theory* 17, no. 2: 192–215.

Leach, James. 2003. *Creative Land: Place and Procreation on the Rai Coast of Papua New Guinea*. New York: Berghahn.

——. 2011. "'Twenty Toea Has No Power Now': Property, Customary Tenure, and Pressure on Land Near the Ramu Nickel Project Area, Madang, Papua New Guinea." *Pacific Studies* 34. no. 2: 295–322.

Lederman, Rena. 1984. "Who Speaks Here? Formality and the Politics of Gender in Mendi, Highland Papua New Guinea." In *Dangerous Words: Language and Politics in the Pacific*, edited by Donald Lawrence Brenneis and Fred R. Myers, 85–107. New York: New York University Press.

——. 2015. "Big Man, Anthropology of." *International Encyclopedia of the Social & Behavioral Sciences* 2: 567–73.

Lee, Benjamin. 1997. *Talking Heads: Language, Metalanguage, and the Semiotics of Subjectivity*. Durham, NC: Duke University Press.

Lee, Benjamin, and Edward LiPuma. 2002. "Cultures of Circulation: The Imaginations of Modernity." *Public Culture* 14, no. 1: 191–213.

Lempert, Michael. 2022. "Free Speech, without Listening? On Democratic Technologies of Interaction." Unpublished manuscript, March 29, 2022.

Leroy, John D. 1979. "The Ceremonial Pig Kill of the South Kewa." *Oceania* 49, no. 3: 179–209.

Lévi-Strauss, Claude. 1966. *The Savage Mind*. Chicago: University of Chicago Press.

Levin, David Michael. 1989. *The Listening Self: Personal Growth, Social Change, and the Closure of Metaphysics*. New York: Routledge.

Lindstrom, Lamont. 1984. "Doctor, Lawyer, Wise Man, Priest: Big-Men and Knowledge in Melanesia." *Man*, New Series, 19, no. 2: 291–309.

——. 1990. *Knowledge and Power in a South Pacific Society*. Washington, DC: Smithsonian Institution Press.

LiPuma, Edward. 1998. "Modernity and Forms of Personhood in Melanesia." In *Bodies and Persons: Comparative Perspectives from Africa and Melanesia,* edited by Michael Lambek and Andrew Strathern, 53–79. Cambridge: Cambridge University Press.

Lo, Adrienne. 2021. "Whose Hearing Matters? Context and Regimes of Perception in Sociolinguistics." *International Journal of the Sociology of Language* 2021, nos. 267–68: 153–62.

Lo, Adrienne, and Joseph Park, eds. 2017. Special Issue, "Metapragmatics of Mobility." *Language in Society* 46, no. 1.

MacKinnon, Catharine A. 1983. "Feminism, Marxism, Method, and the State: Toward Feminist Jurisprudence." *Signs* 8, no. 4: 635–58.

Macnamara, Jim. 2020. "Listening for Healthy Democracy." In *The Handbook of Listening,* edited by Debra L. Worthington and Graham D. Bodie, 385–395. Hoboken, NJ: John Wiley & Sons.

Macpherson, C. B. 1962. *The Political Theory of Possessive Individualism: Hobbes to Locke*. New York: Oxford University Press.

Malbrancke, Anne-Sylvie. 2019. "Making the Baruya Great Again: From Glorified Great Men to Modern Suffering Subjects?" *Australian Journal of Anthropology* 30, no. 1: 68–83.

Malinowski, Bronislaw. (1922) 1984. *Argonauts of the Western Pacific: An Account of Native Enterprise and Adventure in the Archipelagoes of Melanesian New Guinea*. Prospect Heights, IL: Waveland Press.

——. 1935. *Coral Gardens and Their Magic: Vol. 2, The Language of Magic and Gardening*. London: Allen & Unwin.

Marker, Michael. 2006. "After the Makah Whale Hunt: Indigenous Knowledge and Limits to Multicultural Discourse." *Education and Urban Society* 41, no. 5: 482–505.

Marsilli-Vargas, Xochitl. 2014. "Listening Genres: The Emergence of Relevance Structures through the Reception of Sound." *Journal of Pragmatics* 69: 42–51.

Martin, Keir. 2013. *The Death of the Big Men and the Rise of the Big Shots: Custom and Conflict in East New Britain*. New York: Berghahn.

Masco, Joseph. 2010. "'Sensitive but Unclassified': Secrecy and the Counterterrorist State." *Public Culture* 22, no. 3: 433–63.

Mathur, Nayanika. 2016. *Paper Tiger: Law, Bureaucracy and the Developmental State in Himalayan India*. Delhi: Cambridge University Press.

Matoesian, Gregory M. 2001. *Law and the Language of Identity: Discourse in the William Kennedy Smith Rape Trial*. New York: Oxford University Press.

McDougall, Debra. 2016. *Engaging with Strangers: Love and Violence in the Rural Solomon Islands*. New York: Berghahn.

McDowell, Nancy. 1990. "Competitive Equality in Melanesia: An Exploratory Essay." *Journal of the Polynesian Society* 99, no. 2: 179–204.

McLeod, Christopher, dir. 2013. *Profit and Loss.* Berkeley, CA: Sacred Land Film Project. DVD.

Mead, Margaret. 1938. *The Mountain Arapesh: 1, An Importing Culture,* Vol. 36, pt. 3. Anthropological Papers of the American Museum of Natural History. New York: American Museum of Natural History.

Memmi, Albert. 1967. *The Colonizer and the Colonized.* Boston: Beacon Press.

Merlan, Francesca, and Alan Rumsey. 1991. *Ku Waru: Language and Segmentary Politics in the Western Nebilyer Valley, Papua New Guinea.* Cambridge: Cambridge University Press.

Mertz, Elizabeth. 2007. *The Language of Law School: Learning to "Think like a Lawyer."* New York: Oxford University Press.

Mezzenzana, Francesca. 2020. "Between Will and Thought: Individualism and Social Responsiveness in Amazonian Child Rearing." *American Anthropologist* 122, no. 3: 540–53.

Michel, Alexandra, and Stanton Wortham. 2007. "Listening beyond the Self: How Organizations Create Direct Involvement." *Learning Inquiry* 1, no. 2: 89–97.

Mitchell, Timothy. 2002. *Rule of Experts: Egypt, Techno-Politics, Modernity.* Berkeley: University of California Press.

Morley, David. 1980. *The Nationwide Audience: Structure and Decoding.* London: British Film Institute.

——. 1993. "Active Audience Theory: Pendulums and Pitfalls." *Journal of Communication* 43, no. 4: 13–19.

Munn, Nancy D. 1986. *The Fame of Gawa: A Symbolic Study of Value Transformation in a Massim (Papua New Guinea) Society.* Durham, NC: Duke University Press.

Myers, Fred. R. 1986. "Reflections on a Meeting: Structure, Language, and the Polity in a Small-Scale Society." *American Ethnologist* 13, no. 3: 430–47.

Nadasdy, Paul. 2021. "How Many Worlds Are There?" *American Ethnologist* 48, no. 4: 357–69.

Nakassis, Constantine V. 2013. "Citation and Citationality." *Signs and Society* 1, no. 1: 51–77.

Neufeld, Christine M. 2018. *Avid Ears: Medieval Gossips, Sound, and the Art of Listening.* New York: Routledge.

Ngugi wa Thiong'o. 1986. *Decolonising the Mind: The Politics of Language in African Literature.* London: Heinemann.

Nuckolls, Janis B. 2004. "Language and Nature in Sound Alignment." In *Hearing Cultures: Essays on Sound, Listening and Modernity,* edited by Veit Erlmann, 65–86. London: Routledge.

Ober, Josiah. 2009. *Mass and Elite in Democratic Athens: Rhetoric, Ideology, and the Power of the People.* Princeton: Princeton University Press.

Ochs, Elinor, Ruth Smith, and Carolyn Taylor. 1989. "Detective Stories at Dinnertime: Problem-Solving through Co-Narration." *Cultural Dynamics* 2, no. 2: 238–57.

Ong, Walter J. 1982. *Orality and Literacy: The Technologizing of the Word.* London: Routledge.

Oppermann, Thiago Cintra. 2015. "Fake It until You Make It: Searching for Mimesis in Buka Village Politics." *Oceania* 85, no. 2: 199–218.

Oring, Sheryl. 2016. "Listening Is a Democratic Act." *San Francisco Chronicle,* November 5. https://www.sfchronicle.com/opinion/article/Listening-is-a-democratic-act-10594805.php.

Paraide, Patricia. 2015. "Challenges with the Tuition Fee Free Education Policy Implementation in Papua New Guinea." *Contemporary PNG Studies* 23: 47–62.

Pennycook, Alastair. 2005. "The Modern Mission: The Language Effects of Christianity." *Journal of Language, Identity & Education* 4, no. 2: 137–55.

Peterson, Marina. 2021. *Atmospheric Noise: The Indefinite Urbanism of Los Angeles.* Durham, NC: Duke University Press.

Plato. 1892. "Gorgias." In *The Dialogues of Plato*, Vol. 2. Translated by B. Jowett, 1–119. London: Oxford University Press.

Pooley, Jefferson. 2008. "The New History of Mass Communication Research." In *The History of Media and Communication Research: Contested Memories*, edited by David Park and Jefferson Pooley, 43–70. New York: Peter Lang.

Potter, W. James. 2019. *Media Literacy.* 9th ed. Los Angeles: Sage.

Povinelli, Elizabeth A. 2011. *Economies of Abandonment: Social Belonging and Endurance in Late Liberalism.* Durham, NC: Duke University Press.

Power, Michael. 1999. *The Audit Society: Rituals of Verification.* Oxford: Oxford University Press.

Prakash, Gyan. 1992. "Postcolonial Criticism and Indian Historiography." *Social Text*, nos. 31/32: 8–19.

Proctor, Robert N. 2008. "Agnotology: A Missing Term to Describe the Cultural Production of Ignorance (and Its Study)." In *Agnotology: The Making and Unmaking of Ignorance*, edited by Robert N. Proctor and Londa Schiebinger, 1–33. Stanford: Stanford University Press.

Rabinow, Paul. 1977. *Reflections on Fieldwork in Morocco.* Berkeley: University of California Press.

Radway, Janice A. 1991. *Reading the Romance: Women, Patriarchy, and Popular Literature.* Chapel Hill: University of North Carolina Press.

Ratcliffe, Krista. 2005. *Rhetorical Listening: Identification, Gender, Whiteness.* Carbondale: Southern Illinois University Press.

Read, K. E. 1952. "Nama Cult of the Central Highlands, New Guinea." *Oceania* 23, no. 1: 1–25.

——. 1959. "Leadership and Consensus in a New Guinea Society." *American Anthropologist* 61, no. 3: 425–36.

Reed, Adam. 2006. *Papua New Guinea's Last Place: Experiences of Constraint in a Postcolonial Prison.* New York: Berghahn.

Rice, Tom. 2010. "Learning to Listen: Auscultation and the Transmission of Auditory Knowledge." *Journal of the Royal Anthropological Institute* 16, s1: S41–S61.

——. 2013. *Hearing and the Hospital: Sound, Listening, Knowledge and Experience.* Canon Pyon: Sean Kingston.

Rio, Knut. 2014. "Melanesian Egalitarianism: The Containment of Hierarchy." *Anthropological Theory* 14, no. 2: 169–90.

Robbins, Joel. 1994. "Equality as a Value: Ideology in Dumont, Melanesia and the West." *Social Analysis,* no. 36: 21–70.

——. 2001a. "God Is Nothing but Talk: Modernity, Language, and Prayer in a Papua New Guinea Society." *American Anthropologist* 103, no. 4: 901–12.

——. 2001b. "Ritual Communication and Linguistic Ideology: A Reading and Partial Reformulation of Rappaport's Theory of Ritual." *Current Anthropology* 42, no. 5: 591–614.

——. 2001c. "Secrecy and the Sense of an Ending: Narrative, Time, and Everyday Millenarianism in Papua New Guinea and in Christian Fundamentalism." *Comparative Studies in Society and History* 43, no. 3: 525–51.

——. 2004. *Becoming Sinners: Christianity and Moral Torment in a Papua New Guinea Society.* Berkeley: University of California Press.

Robbins, Joel, Bambi B. Schieffelin, and Aparecida Vilaça. 2014. "Evangelical Conversion and the Transformation of the Self in Amazonia and Melanesia: Christianity and the Revival of Anthropological Comparison." *Comparative Studies in Society and History* 56, no. 3: 559–90.

Romilly, Jacqueline de. 1975. *Magic and Rhetoric in Ancient Greece*. Cambridge, MA: Harvard University Press.

Rosaldo, Michelle. 1973. "I Have Nothing to Hide: The Language of Ilongot Oratory." *Language in Society* 2, no. 2: 193–223.

Roscoe, Paul. 2000. "New Guinea Leadership as Ethnographic Analogy: A Critical Review." *Journal of Archaeological Method and Theory* 7, no. 2: 79–126.

Rose, Nikolas. 1993. "Government, Authority and Expertise in Advanced Liberalism." *Economy and Society* 22, no. 3: 283–99.

———. 1999. *Governing the Soul: The Shaping of the Private Self*. 2nd ed. London: Free Association Books.

Rosenfeld, Sophia. 2011. "On Being Heard: A Case for Paying Attention to the Historical Ear." *American Historical Review* 116, no. 2: 316–34.

Rousseau, Jean-Jacques. 1987. "On the Social Contract." In *The Basic Political Writings*, translated by Donald A. Cress, 139–227. Indianapolis: Hackett.

Rumsey, Alan. 2013. "Intersubjectivity, Deception and the 'Opacity of Other Minds': Perspectives from Highland New Guinea and Beyond." *Language & Communication* 33, no. 3: 326–43.

Rumsey, Alan, and Joel Robbins, eds. 2008. Special Issue: "Anthropology and the Opacity of Other Minds." *Anthropological Quarterly* 81, no. 2.

Rutherford, Danilyn. 2003. *Raiding the Land of the Foreigners: The Limits of the Nation on an Indonesian Frontier*. Princeton: Princeton University Press.

Sahlins, Marshall D. 1963. "Poor Man, Rich Man, Big-Man, Chief: Political Types in Melanesia and Polynesia." *Comparative Studies in Society and History* 5, no. 3: 285–303.

———. 2012. "Alterity and Autochthony: Austronesian Cosmographies of the Marvelous, the 2008 Raymond Firth Lecture." *HAU* 2, no. 1: 131–60.

Said, Edward W. 1978. *Orientalism*. New York: Vintage Books.

Salisbury, Richard F. 1964. "Despotism and Australian Administration in the New Guinea Highlands." *American Anthropologist* 66, no. 4: 225–39.

Samuels, David W., Louise Meintjes, Ana Maria Ochoa, and Thomas Porcello. 2010. "Soundscapes: Toward a Sounded Anthropology." *Annual Review of Anthropology* 39, no. 1: 329–45.

Sanders, Lynn M. 1997. "Against Deliberation." *Political Theory* 25, no. 3: 347–76.

Sarmiento Barletti, Juan Pablo. 2017. "The Rise of the *Egalityrant* (Egalitarian Tyrant) in Peruvian Amazonia: Headpeople in the Time of the *Comunidad Nativa*." In *Creating Dialogues: Indigenous Perceptions and Changing Forms of Leadership in Amazonia*, edited by Hanne Veber and Pirjo Kristiina Virtanen, 107–26. Boulder: University Press of Colorado.

Schäfers, Marlene. 2017. "Voice." *Cambridge Encyclopedia of Anthropology*, edited by F. Stein, S. Lazar, M. Candea, H. Diemberger, J. Robbins, A. Sanchez, and R. Stasch. http://doi.org/10.29164/17voice.

Scheper-Hughes, Nancy. 1995. "The Primacy of the Ethical: Propositions for a Militant Anthropology." *Current Anthropology* 36, no. 3: 409–40.

Schieffelin, Bambi B. 1986. "Teasing and Shaming in Kahili Children's Interactions." In *Language Socialization across Cultures*, edited by Bambi B. Schieffelin and Elinor Ochs, 165–81. Cambridge: Cambridge University Press.

——. 1990. *The Give and Take of Everyday Life: Language Socialization of Kaluli Children*. Cambridge: Cambridge University Press.

——. 1995. "Creating Evidence: Making Sense of Written Words in Bosavi." *Pragmatics* 5, no. 2: 225–43.

Schieffelin, Bambi B., Kathryn A. Woolard, and Paul V. Kroskrity, eds. 1998. *Language Ideologies: Practice and Theory*. Oxford: Oxford University Press.

Schmidt, Leigh Eric. 2000. *Hearing Things: Religion, Illusion, and the American Enlightenment*. Cambridge, MA: Harvard University Press.

Schram, Ryan. 2018. *Harvests, Feasts, and Graves: Postcultural Consciousness in Contemporary Papua New Guinea*. Ithaca, NY: Cornell University Press.

Schwimmer, Erik. 1984. "Male Couples in New Guinea." In *Ritualized Homosexuality in Melanesia*, edited by Gilbert H. Herdt, 248–91. Berkeley: University of California Press.

Scott, James C. 2010. *The Art of Not Being Governed: An Anarchist History of Upland Southeast Asia*. New Haven: Yale University Press.

Sedgwick, Eve Kosofsky. 2003. "Paranoid Reading and Reparative Reading, Or, You're So Paranoid, You Probably Think This Essay Is about You." In *Touching Feeling: Affect, Pedagogy, Performativity*, 123–151. Durham, NC: Duke University Press.

Semali, Ladislaus M., and Joe L. Kincheloe, eds. 1999. *What Is Indigenous Knowledge? Voices from the Academy*. New York: Falmer.

Senft, Gunter. 2008. "The Case: The Trobriand Islanders vs H. P. Grice. Kilivila and the Gricean Maxims of Quality and Manner." *Anthropos* 103, no. 1: 139–47.

Shankar, Shalini, and Jillian R. Cavanaugh. 2012. "Language and Materiality in Global Capitalism." *Annual Review of Anthropology* 41, no. 1: 355–69.

Shapin, Steven. 1994. *A Social History of Truth: Civility and Science in Seventeenth-Century England*. Chicago: University of Chicago Press.

Shapin, Steven, and Simon Schaffer. 1985. *Leviathan and the Air-Pump: Hobbes, Boyle, and the Experimental Life*. Princeton: Princeton University Press.

Sherzer, Joel. 1990. *Verbal Arts in San Blas: Kuna Culture through Its Discourse*. Cambridge: Cambridge University Press.

Showalter, Elaine. 1979. "Towards a Feminist Poetics." In *Women Writing and Writing about Women*, edited by Mary Jacobus, 22–41. London: Croom Helm.

Sillitoe, Paul. 2010. "Trust in Development: Some Implications of Knowing in Indigenous Knowledge." *Journal of the Royal Anthropological Institute* 16, no. 1: 12–30.

Silverstein, Michael. 1976. "Shifters, Linguistic Categories, and Cultural Description." In *Meaning in Anthropology*, edited by Keith Basso and Henry Selby, 11–55. Albuquerque: University of New Mexico Press.

——. 1979. "Language Structure and Linguistic Ideology." In *The Elements: A Parasession on Linguistic Units and Levels*, edited by Paul R. Clyne, William F. Hanks, and Carol L. Hofbauer, 193–247. Chicago: Chicago Linguistic Society.

——. 1981. "Metaforces of Power in Traditional Oratory." Paper presented to the Department of Anthropology, Yale University, February.

——. 1996. "The Secret Life of Texts." In *Natural Histories of Discourse*, edited by Michael Silverstein and Greg Urban, 81–105. Chicago: University of Chicago Press.

——. 2003. *Talking Politics: The Substance of Style from Abe to "W."* Chicago: Prickly Paradigm Press.

——. 2005. "Axes of Evals." *Journal of Linguistic Anthropology* 15, no.1: 6–22.

Simpson, Audra. 2014. *Mohawk Interruptus: Political Life across the Borders of Settler States*. Durham, NC: Duke University Press.

Simpson, Christopher. 1994. *Science of Coercion: Communication Research and Psychological Warfare, 1945–1960*. New York: Oxford University Press.

Skafish, Peter William. 2011. "From Another Psyche: The Other Consciousness of a Speculative American Mystic (The Life and Work of Jane Roberts)." PhD diss, University of California, Berkeley.

Skouen, Tina, and Ryan Stark, eds. 2014. *Rhetoric and the Early Royal Society: A Sourcebook*. Leiden: Brill.

Slotta, James. 2014. "Revelations of the World: Transnationalism and the Politics of Perception in Papua New Guinea." *American Anthropologist* 116, no. 3: 626–42.

——. 2015. "The Perlocutionary Is Political: Listening as Self-Determination in a Papua New Guinean Polity." *Language in Society* 44, no. 4: 525–52.

——. 2017a. "Can the Subaltern Listen? Self-Determination and the Provisioning of Expertise in Papua New Guinea." *American Ethnologist* 44, no. 2: 328–40.

——. 2017b. Documenting Yopno Diversity: Dialect Variation in a Papuan Language. Endangered Languages Archive. http://hdl.handle.net/2196/00-0000-0000-0000-A926-6.

——. 2019. "The Annotated Donald Trump: Signs of Circulation in a Time of Bubbles." *Journal of Linguistic Anthropology* 29, no. 3: 397–416.

——. 2020. "Pragmatics." *International Encyclopedia of Linguistic Anthropology*. doi.org/10.1002/9781118786093.iela0323.

Smith, Linda Tuhiwai. 2012. *Decolonizing Methodologies: Research and Indigenous Peoples*. 2nd ed. London: Zed.

Smith, Mark M. 2001. *Listening to Nineteenth-Century America*. Chapel Hill: University of North Carolina Press.

Smithson, Michael. 1989. *Ignorance and Uncertainty: Emerging Paradigms*. New York: Springer-Verlag.

Spitulnik, Debra. 1996. "The Social Circulation of Media Discourse and the Mediation of Communities." *Journal of Linguistic Anthropology* 6, no. 2: 161–87.

Spivak, Gayatri. 1988. "Can the Subaltern Speak?" In *Marxism and the Interpretation of Culture*, edited by Cary Nelson and Larry Grossberg, 271–313. Chicago: University of Illinois Press.

Srinivasan, Amia. 2019. "Genealogy, Epistemology and Worldmaking." *Proceedings of the Aristotelian Society* 119, no. 2: 127–56.

Stasch, Rupert. 2008. "Knowing Minds Is a Matter of Authority: Political Dimensions of Opacity Statements in Korowai Moral Psychology." *Anthropological Quarterly* 81, no. 2: 443–53.

——. 2009. *Society of Others: Kinship and Mourning in a West Papuan Place*. Berkeley: University of California Press.

——. 2011a. "Ritual and Oratory Revisited: The Semiotics of Effective Action." *Annual Review of Anthropology* 40: 159–74.

——. 2011b. "Textual Iconicity and the Primitivist Cosmos: Chronotopes of Desire in Travel Writing about Korowai of West Papua." *Journal of Linguistic Anthropology* 21, no. 1: 1–21.

——. 2014. "Powers of Incomprehension: Linguistic Otherness, Translators, and Political Structure in New Guinea Tourism Encounters." *HAU* 4, no. 2: 73–94.

——. 2021. "Self-lowering as Power and Trap: Wawa, 'White', and Peripheral Embrace of State Formation in Indonesian Papua." *Oceania* 91, no. 2: 257–79.

Stoller, Paul. 1989. *The Taste of Ethnographic Things: The Senses in Anthropology*. Philadelphia: University of Pennsylvania Press.

Strathern, Andrew. 1966. "Despots and Directors in the New Guinea Highlands." *Man* 1, no. 3: 356–67.

——. 1973. "Kinship, Descent and Locality: Some New Guinea Examples." In *The Character of Kinship*, edited by Jack Goody, 21–33. Cambridge: Cambridge University Press.

——. 1975. "Veiled Speech in Mount Hagen." In *Political Language and Oratory in Traditional Society*, edited by Maurice Bloch, 185–203. London: Academic Press.

Strathern, Marilyn. 1972. *Women in Between: Female Roles in a Male World: Mount Hagen, Papua New Guinea*. London: Seminar Press.

——. 1987. "Introduction." In *Dealing with Inequality: Analysing Gender Relations in Melanesia and Beyond*, 1–32. Cambridge: Cambridge University Press.

——. 1988. *The Gender of the Gift: Problems with Women and Problems with Society in Melanesia*. Berkeley: University of California Press.

Street, Alice. 2014. *Biomedicine in an Unstable Place: Infrastructure and Personhood in a Papua New Guinean Hospital*. Durham, NC: Duke University Press.

Sweetser, Eve. 1990. *From Etymology to Pragmatics: Metaphorical and Cultural Aspects of Semantic Structure*. Cambridge: Cambridge University Press.

Tammisto, Tuomas. 2016. "Enacting the Absent State: State-Formation on the Oil-Palm Frontier of Pomio (Papua New Guinea)." *Paideuma* 62: 51–68.

Taylor, Charles. 2003. *Modern Social Imaginaries*. Durham, NC: Duke University Press.

Telban, Borut. 1997. "Being and 'Non-Being' in Ambonwari (Papua New Guinea) Ritual." *Oceania* 67, no. 4: 308–25.

Thaman, Konai Helu. 2003. "Decolonizing Pacific Studies: Indigenous Perspectives, Knowledge, and Wisdom in Higher Education." *Contemporary Pacific* 15, no. 1: 1–17.

Thill, Cate. 2009. "Courageous Listening, Responsibility for the Other and the Northern Territory Intervention." *Continuum* 23, no. 4: 537–48.

Tomlinson, Matt. 2004. "Perpetual Lament: Kava-Drinking, Christianity and Sensations of Historical Decline in Fiji." *Journal of the Royal Anthropological Institute* 10, no. 3: 653–73.

Tully, James. 2004. "Recognition and Dialogue: The Emergence of a New Field." *Critical Review of International Social and Political Philosophy* 7, no. 3: 84–106.

Turner, Stephen. 2003. *Liberal Democracy 3.0: Civil Society in an Age of Experts*. London: Sage.

Tuzin, Donald F. 1980. *The Voice of the Tambaran: Truth and Illusion in Ilahita Arapesh Religion*. Berkeley: University of California Press.

——. 1997. *The Cassowary's Revenge: The Life and Death of Masculinity in a New Guinea Society*. Chicago: University of Chicago Press.

Urban, Greg. 1991. *A Discourse-Centered Approach to Culture: Native South American Myths and Rituals*. Austin: University of Texas Press.

——. 2001. *Metaculture: How Culture Moves through the World*. Minneapolis: University of Minnesota Press.

Verdery, Katherine. 2014. *Secrets and Truths: Ethnography in the Archive of Romania's Secret Police*. Budapest: Central European University Press.

Vickers, Brian, and Nancy S. Struever. 1985. *Rhetoric and the Pursuit of Truth: Language Change in the Seventeenth and Eighteenth Centuries (Papers Read at a Clark Library Seminar, March 1980)*. Los Angeles: William Andrews Clark Memorial Library.

Villegas, Malia, Sabina Rak Neugebauer, and Kerry R. Venegas, eds. 2008. *Indigenous Knowledge and Education: Sites of Struggle, Strength, and Survivance*. Cambridge, MA: Harvard Educational Review.

Viswanathan, Gauri. 1989. *Masks of Conquest: Literary Studies and British Rule in India*. New York: Columbia University Press.

Viveiros de Castro, Eduardo. 2015a. *The Relative Native: Essays on Indigenous Conceptual Worlds*. Translated by Martin Holbraad, David Rodgers, and Julia Sauma. Chicago: HAU Books.

——. 2015b. *Cannibal Metaphysics*. Edited and translated by Peter Skafish. Minneapolis: Univocal Publishing.

Voloshinov, V. N. 1973. *Marxism and the Philosophy of Language*. Translated by Ladislav Matejka and I. R. Titunik. Cambridge, MA: Harvard University Press.

Wagner, Roy. 1977. "Analogic Kinship: A Daribi Example." *American Ethnologist* 4, no. 4: 623–42.

——. 1981. *The Invention of Culture*. 2nd ed. Chicago: University of Chicago Press.

——. 1984. "Ritual as Communication: Order, Meaning, and Secrecy in Melanesian Initiation Rites." *Annual Review of Anthropology* 13: 143–55.

Walton, Grant W. 2019. "Fee-Free Education, Decentralisation and the Politics of Scale in Papua New Guinea." *Journal of Education Policy* 34, no. 2: 174–94.

Ward, John O. 1988. "Magic and Rhetoric from Antiquity to the Renaissance: Some Ruminations." *Rhetorica: A Journal of the History of Rhetoric* 6, no. 1: 57–118.

Wardlow, Holly. 2006. *Wayward Women: Sexuality and Agency in a New Guinea Society*. Berkeley: University of California Press.

Warner, Michael. 1992. *The Letters of the Republic: Publication and the Public Sphere in Eighteenth-Century America*. Cambridge, MA: Harvard University Press.

——. 2002. "Publics and Counterpublics." *Public Culture* 14, no. 1: 49–90.

Wassmann, Jürg. 2016. *The Gently Bowing Person: An Ideal among the Yupno in Papua New Guinea*. Heidelberg: Universitätsverlag Winter.

Wassmann, Jürg, and Pierre R. Dasen. 1994. "'Hot' and 'Cold': Classification and Sorting among the Yupno of Papua New Guinea." *International Journal of Psychology* 29, no. 1: 19–38.

Watson-Gegeo, Karen Ann. 1986. "The Study of Language Use in Oceania." *Annual Review of Anthropology* 15: 149–62.

Watson-Gegeo, Karen Ann, and David Welchman Gegeo. 1992. "Schooling, Knowledge, and Power: Social Transformation in the Solomon Islands." *Anthropology & Education Quarterly* 23, no. 1: 10–29.

Webster, Anthony K. 2015. "The poetry of sound and the sound of poetry: Navajo poetry, phonological iconicity, and linguistic relativity." *Semiotica* 207: 279–301.

——. 2019. "(Ethno)poetics and Perspectivism: On the Hieroglyphic Beauty of Ambiguity." *Journal of Linguistic Anthropology* 29, no. 2: 168–74.

Weidman, A. 2014. "Anthropology and Voice." *Annual Review of Anthropology* 43: 37–51.

Weiner, Annette B. 1983. "From Words to Objects to Magic: Hard Words and the Boundaries of Social Interaction." *Man*, New Series, 18, no. 4: 690–709.

West, Paige. 2006. *Conservation Is Our Government Now: The Politics of Ecology in Papua New Guinea*. Durham, NC: Duke University Press.

Williams, Bernard. 2010. *Truth and Truthfulness: An Essay in Genealogy*. Princeton: Princeton University Press.

Williams, Raymond. 1977. *Marxism and Literature*. Oxford: Oxford University Press.

Wittgenstein, Ludwig. 1953. *Philosophical Investigations*. Translated by G. E. M. Anscombe. Oxford: Basil Blackwell.

Woodburn, James. 1982. "Egalitarian Societies." *Man* 17, no. 3: 431–51.

Wortham, Stanton, and Angela Reyes. 2015. *Discourse Analysis beyond the Speech Event*. London: Routledge.

Yanagisako, Sylvia, and Carol Delaney. 1995. "Naturalizing Power." In *Naturalizing Power: Essays in Feminist Cultural Analysis*, 1–22. New York: Routledge.

Young, Iris Marion. 2000. *Inclusion and Democracy*. Oxford: Oxford University Press.

Yunis, Harvey. 1996. *Taming Democracy: Models of Political Rhetoric in Classical Athens*. Ithaca, NY: Cornell University Press.

Žižek, Slavoj. 2008. *The Sublime Object of Ideology*. 2nd ed. London: Verso.

Index

Note: Page numbers in *italics* refer to illustrative matter.

ignorance, 65–71, 165n24
ignoring, as practice of listening, 22, 25, 26, 43, 46, 49, 52, 61, 97
Ilahita Arapesh, 163n6, 163n10
imaginaries, 130–31, 134–36, 139, 141–45, 150–52, 173n7. See also *las ples*
Independence Day celebrations, 30, 142
indirection, 108–10, 171n8, 171n11. *See also* deception
infrastructure, 45
Islamic tradition and listening, 19, 151, 152

James, William, 170n20
jobɨt. See curses
Jorgensen, Dan, 56, 75, 163n9, 164n11

kabary, 156n31
Kabwum, 86
Kâte language, 1, 123, 143. *See also* Lutheran missionaries
Kauso, 82–85, 168n9
kindergarten programs, 45, 126. *See also* education
knowledge production, 71–75, 83, 150. *See also* expertise
Kokwasu, 124–25, 140
kokwin aŋ, 160n15
Konu, 105–6
Korowai mythology, 61–62
Kulick, Don, 160n18, 171n5

Lacan, Jacques, 155n20
Lacey, Kate, 16, 153n7
laki (game), 140
land ownership, 29, 136, 145–46, 158n3, 159n6
las ples, 127–35, 141, 172n3, 173n4
Lasswell, Harold, 154n15
last place, as term. See *las ples*
Latour, Bruno, 102
Lawrence, Peter, 163n10, 165
leadership and power, 78–79, 97–98. *See also* authority; expertise
Lindstrom, Lamont, 162n5, 165n25
listening, 1–2; anarchy and, 13–15, 18, 24–27, 49–50, 99, 109–15; apophatic, 8; as a collective activity, 121–22; democratic, 15–17, 154n12; ethnography of, 14, 19, 151; evaluative, 22, 26, 38, 46–47, 70, 160n17; holding onto, 22, 26, 47-48, 49, 52, 162n30; in *las ples,* 131–35, 142–46; politics of, 6, 11–19, 156n25; powerful speech and passive, 5–11; rhetorical, 153n7; to the way others listen, 116–20; world-changing power of, 2–5. *See also* agency of the listener

listening publics, 153n7
literacy, 1
logical argumentation, 10
Luther, Martin, 128
Lutheran missionaries, 1, 3, 29–30, 123, 175n16. *See also* Christianity; churches; Kâte language
lying, 103–4, 168n11. *See also* deception; truth

Madagascar, 156n31
Malinowski, Bronislaw, 150, 175n1
Manambu, 167n2
Maŋnu, 114–15, 172n15
marriage, 31–32, 158n3
Marxist tradition, 155n17
mass communications, 154n15
Mead, Margaret, 163n10
men's houses, 1, 42, 53–55, 82, 162n5
men's roles, 31–32. *See also* gender differences
mibɨlɨ, 165n22
Minibao, 79, 80
mining-related development, 47
missionaries. *See* Lutheran missionaries
modernity, 11–12, 52, 126, 130, 163n7
money, 71–75, 76, 165n28, 175n16. *See also* bridewealth payments
Monji, 117–19, 145–46
murder, 28
mutual aid, 42–48
Muyan, 86–89, 99, 168n11

Nanda, 78–80, 104, 107–8, 116–20, 136, 172n15
nandak nandak amɨn, 82. *See also* expertise
Navajo, 14
netsa, 90–92
New Year's holiday, 27–28
NGOs (non-governmental organizations). *See* conservation NGOs
Nian village, Papua New Guinea, *27;* anarchy and, 27–32; church anniversary celebration in, 2–4, 24, 42, 158n1, 160n13
nickel-cobalt mining, 47
Nokopo Lutheran church, *2*
Nokopo Lutheran Primary School, *2,* 33, 95–96
not listening, as anarchic condition, 34–35. *See also* ignoring; listening
nurturance, 166n29

occult violence, 28–30, 35
oman amɨn, 34, 159n9